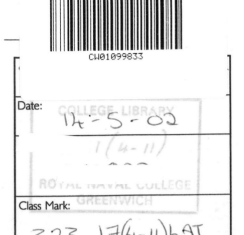

CONTEMPORARY NATIONALISM
IN EAST CENTRAL EUROPE

Also by Paul Latawski and from the same publishers

THE RECONSTRUCTION OF POLAND, 1914–23 (*editor*)

Contemporary Nationalism in East Central Europe

Edited by

Paul Latawski
Associate Professor of International Studies
New England College, Arundel, and
Honorary Visiting Fellow, School of Slavonic and
East European Studies, University of London

St. Martin's Press

First published in Great Britain 1995 by
MACMILLAN PRESS LTD
Houndmills, Basingstoke, Hampshire RG21 2XS
and London
Companies and representatives
throughout the world

A catalogue record for this book is available
from the British Library.

ISBN 0–333–60689–2

10	9	8	7	6	5	4	3	2	1
04	03	02	01	00	99	98	97	96	95

Printed and bound in Great Britain by
Antony Rowe Ltd
Chippenham, Wiltshire

First published in the United States of America 1995 by
Scholarly and Reference Division,
ST. MARTIN'S PRESS, INC.,
175 Fifth Avenue,
New York, N.Y. 10010

ISBN 0–312–12276–4

Library of Congress Cataloging-in-Publication Data
Contemporary nationalism in east central Europe /
edited by Paul Latawski.
p. cm.
Includes bibliographical references and index.
ISBN 0–312–12276–4
1. Europe, Eastern—Politics and government—1989–
2. Nationalism—Europe, Eastern.   I. Latawski, Paul C. (Paul
Chester), 1954–   .
DJK51.C68   1995
320.5'4'0947—dc20   94–16291
                                                                    CIP

Contents

Contents

List of Tables

Preface

Nationalism represents one of the serious challenges facing East Central Europe in the aftermath of communism. The tragedy of Bosnia indicates that it is far from being a spent force in regional politics. Bosnia, however, represents the worst imaginable case of nationality conflict in the region. Other parts of East Central Europe have defied sceptics and have demonstrated that perhaps hitherto dangerous nationalism is now benign. Thus evolves a highly complex and differentiated picture of post-communist nationalism in East Central Europe. This book attempts to offer a balanced look at nationalism in the region, placing contemporary problems in an historical perspective. In doing so it seeks to dispel some of the cliches and myths surrounding the phenomenon as it manifests itself in East Central Europe today.

The book owes its genesis to two conferences, which provided ideas and individuals interested in contributing to this collective effort. The New World Order Conference, held at New England College, Arundel, in May 1992, provided valuable inspiration and a core group of contributors interested in the problem of nationalism in East Central Europe. I am grateful to Mr Dudley H. Woodall, Director of the Arundel Campus, for his unstinting support in the organisation of the conference and in the preparation of this book. The success of the conference and the project it spawned owe much to the generosity of its sponsors: the governors of New England College, National Westminister Bank, Lloyds Bank, KRMG Peat Marwick, John Wiley and Son, and Thomas, Eggar, Verrall, Bowles. The British International History Group (BIHG) Annual Conference in Leeds in September 1992 provided more contributors, as well as another forum to consider the problem of nationalism. Thanks are due to Glyn Stone, the BIHG secretary, and to the conference committee for this further encouragement.

Additionally, I would like to thank Radio Free Europe/Radio Liberty Inc. for permission to use in Chapter 4 of this volume material from several of their articles on Bulgaria. Chapter 9 first appeared in the journal *Studies in East European Thought*, vol. 46, nos 1–2 (1994), pp. 69–89, and is reprinted by permission of Kluwer Academic Publishers.

Finally it remains for me to thank Clare Andrews of Macmillan for being helpful and patient throughout the project.

PAUL LATAWSKI

Eastbourne

Notes on the Contributors

Rebecca Ann Haynes recently completed her MA at the School of Slavonic and East European Studies, University of London. At present she is undertaking research on right-wing movements in East Central Europe.

John R. Lampe, Director of East European Studies at The Woodrow Wilson Center in Washington, DC, since 1987, is also Professor of History at the University of Maryland, College Park. He received his BA from Harvard University, his MA from the University of Minnesota, and PhD in 1971 from the University of Wisconsin. He was a Foreign Service Officer in Yugoslavia and Bulgaria from 1964 to 1967. He is the author of *The Bulgarian Economy in the Twentieth Century* (1986), coauthor of *Balkan Economic History, 1550–1950: From Imperial Borderlands to Developing Nations* (1982), which won the Vucinich Prize of the American Association for the Advancement of Slavic Studies, and *Yugoslav–American Economic relations since World War II* (1990).

Paul Latawski is Associate Professor of International Studies at New England College, Arundel, and an Honorary Visiting Fellow at the School of Slavonic and East European Studies, University of London. He has published widely on Polish and Czechoslovak history and politics and edited for Macmillan *The Reconstruction of Poland, 1914–23* (1992). He is currently writing a history of Poland since 1795.

Frances Millard is Principal Lecturer in Politics at the University of Portsmouth. She is coauthor of *Pressure Politics in Industrial Societies* (with Alan Ball, 1986); editor of *Social Welfare and the Market* (1989); and coauthor and editor of *The New Eastern Europe* (with Bob Deacon *et al.*, 1992). She has written widely on numerous aspects of Polish politics and social policy.

John Morison is Senior Lecturer in Russian and Eastern European History at the University of Leeds. He is President of the International Council for Soviet and East European Studies. He has recently edited for Macmillan *The Czech and Slovak Experience* and *Eastern Europe and the West* (1992).

Raymond Pearson is Reader in History, University of Ulster at Coleraine. His principal publications are *Revolution in Russia* (1973), *The Russian Moderates and the Crisis of Tsarism, 1914–1917* (1977), *National Minorities in Eastern Europe, 1848–1945* (1988) and *Russia and Eastern Europe, 1789–1985: A Bibliographic Guide* (1988). His *Companion to European Nationalism, 1789–1920* was published in 1993. He is currently working on *The Rise and Fall of the Soviet Empire*.

Duncan M. Perry is Deputy Director of the Analytic Research Department at the Radio Free Europe/Radio Liberty Research Institute in Munich. By training, he is a Balkan historian who received his PhD from the University of Michigan. Perry has written two books: *The Politics of Terror: The Macedonian Revolutionary Movements 1893–1903* and *Stefan Stambolov and the Emergence of Modern Bulgaria, 1870–1895*. He is also the author of many articles about the Balkans in the nineteenth and twentieth centuries.

Martyn Rady is Lecturer in Central European History at the School of Slavonic and East European Studies, University of London. He has published widely on Central and East European history and politics. His *Romania in Turmoil: A Contemporary History* was published in 1992.

Wojciech Roszkowski is ProRector and Professor, holding the Chair of Political Studies, at the Warsaw School of Economics. He is also a member of Institute of Political Studies, Polish Academy of Sciences. During 1988–9 he was Fellow at the Wilson Center in Washington, DC. His principal publications include *Ksztaltowanie się podstaw polskiej gospodarki państwowej w przemysle i bankowości w latach 1918–1924* (1982), *Gospodarcza rola wiekszej prywatnej własności ziemskiej w Polsce 1918–1939* (1986), *Najnowsza historia Polski 1918–1980 (1989)*, *Landowners in Poland 1918–1939* (1991) and *Historia Polski 1914–1991* (1992).

List of Abbreviations

AK	Armia Krajowa, Home Army
AL	Armia Ludowa, People's Army
BBC	British Broadcasting Corporation
BSP	Bulgarian Socialist Party
BTA	Bulgarian Telegraph Agency
CSCE	Conference on Security and Cooperation in Europe
EC	European Community
HDUR	Hungarian Democratic Union of Romania
HPSS	Hrvatska Pucka Seljacka Stranka, Croation People's Peasant Party
IMF	International Monetary Fund
IMRO	Internal Macedonian Revolutionary Organisation
IUMO	Iliden United Macedonian Organisation
KOR	Komitet Obrony Robotników, Workers' Defence Committee
KPN	Konfederacja Polski Niepodległej, Confederation for Independent Poland
MDF	Magyar Democratic Forum
MRF	Movement for Rights and Freedoms
NSF	National Salvation Front

NSZ	Narodowe Siły Zbrojne, National Armed Forces
NATO	North Atlantic Treaty Organisation
PZPR	Polska Zjednoczona Partia Robotnicza, Polish United Workers' Party
RdR	Ruch dla Rzeczpospolitej, Movement for the Republic
RFE	Radio Free Europe
RL	Radio Liberty
SDRP	Socjaldemokracja Rzeczpospolitej Polskiej, Social Democratic Party
SR	Situation Report
UDF	Union of Democratic Forces
UN	United Nations
ZChN	Zjednoczenie Chrześcijańsko-Narodowe, Christian National Union

1 The Problem of Definition: Nationalism, Nation and Nation-State in East Central Europe
Paul Latawski

INTRODUCTION

The historic demise of communism has heralded the revival of nationalism in East Central Europe.[1] Its reemergence as a powerful force comes at a time when strong intellectual currents in the West are arguing that nationalism, as a global phenomenon, has run its course. Prognosticators of future world orders, such as Francis Fukuyama and Paul Kennedy, illustrate this trend.[2] Fukuyama has stressed that 'it is important to recognise the transitional nature of the nationalist struggles now occuring in Eastern Europe . . .'[3] Although it may be argued that the long-term future of nationalism may be bleak in the face of an integrated world market and the global communications revolution, there are many observers that see its demise as premature. The British political commentator, Neal Ascherson, for example, sees the future as waving a flag: 'The West has been wrong about nationalism. It is not, as was supposed, an unpleasant remnant of the past. Instead, it is the future'.[4]

Whatever the future may hold for nationalism as a global phenomenon, there is no denying that it is very much part of East Central Europe's present and foreseeable future. Amid the daunting economic, ecological, political and social problems besetting the region after communism, nationalism stands alone as one of the most perplexing challenges to the construction of a new post-communist East Central European order.[5] Fundamental, however, to meeting the challenges presented by nationalism in East Central Europe (or anywhere else) is the need to come to grips with the problem of definition. As a phenomenon, nationalism and its related concepts – nation and nation-state – are subject to a wide variety of meanings.

1

NATIONALISM

What is nationalism? Should nationalism be considered in the singular or plural? Does East Central Europe harbour a distinctive nationalism? The answers to these questions have been as diverse as nationalism's interpretors; they have included historians and representatives of the social sciences who have offered a variety of approaches in describing nationalism. The lack of a consensus on the meaning of nationalism is well reflected by the definition proffered in Louis L. Snyder's *Encyclopedia of Nationalism*:

> Nationalism is a condition of mind, feeling or sentiment of a group of people living in a well-defined geographical area, speaking a common language, possessing a literature in which the aspirations of the nation have been expressed, and, in some cases, having a common religion. There are, of course, exceptions to every part of this definition.[6]

The ambiguity of the meaning of 'nationalism' is the product of the complexity of the phenomenon. The study of nationalism has produced a plethora of related terminology: nation, nation-state, nation-building, nationhood, national, nationality, national self-determination, national self-consciousness, nationality-state and nationalist. In recent times the waters have been muddied further by the emergence of a field related to nationalism: 'ethnicity'. It in turn has spawned its own language: ethnic group, ethnocentrism, ethnocide, ethnogenesis, ethnolinguistics, ethnomaniac, ethnonationalism, ethnopsychology and ethnosemantics.[7] Unfortunately the maelstrom of terminology more often than not serves to obfusticate as much as to illuminate nationalism's meaning.

The academic study of nationalism in the twentieth century really began in the wake of the First World War. The pioneering works of the American historians Carlton J. H. Hayes and Hans Kohn provided the foundation for subsequent study of the phenomenon. Hayes defined nationalism in four ways: (1) 'an actual historical process', (2) a 'theory, principle or ideal', (3) 'a particular political party' and (4) 'a condition of mind'.[8] Kohn, however, was more succinct in characterising it: 'Nationalism is first and foremost a state of mind, an act of consciousness, which since the French Revolution has become more and more common to mankind'.[9] Both Hayes and Kohn saw the 'age of nationalism' as a modern development, a somewhat contrived ideology that had deeper historical roots. Both men, moreover, were highly critical of nationalism. Hayes wrote that 'nationalism signifies a more or less purposeful effort to revive primitive tribalism on an enlarged and more artificial scale'.[10]

In Britain, Edward Hallett Carr's contribution to the study of nationalism was to launch a vigorous mid-century critique of nationalism. A committed internationalist, Carr saw nationalism as a corrosive force in the international order.[11] He also was highly critical of national self-determination, a principle that 'identified self-determination with nationalism, and treated the nation as the natural basis of the state'.[12] Perhaps his most significant contribution was to construct a model that described the evolution of nationalism as taking place in five stages and dividing Europe from west to east into four 'time zones', where some or all of the five stages unfold.[13] Carr represented an important shift toward the social sciences in the study of nationalism.[14]

The social-science view of nationalism produced not only new approaches to the study of nationalism, but less ambiguous definitions of the phenomenon. A few examples of these definitions suffice to illustrate this point. Elie Kedourie, a specialist in international politics, defined nationalism in this way:

> Nationalism is a doctrine invented in Europe at the beginning of the nineteenth century. It pretends to supply a criterion for the determination of the unit of population proper to enjoy a government exclusively its own, for the legitimate exercise of power in the state, and for the right organisation of a society of states. Briefly, the doctrine holds that humanity is naturally divided into nations, that nations are known by certain characteristics which can be ascertained, and that the only legitimate type of government is national self-government.[15]

Sociologists such as Ernest Gellner and Anthony D. Smith have also added important definitions. Gellner offers what must be one of the most succinct: 'Nationalism is primarily a political principle, which holds that the political and national unit should be congruent'.[16] Smith matched Gellner's view when he wrote that 'nationalism is first and foremost a political doctrine'.[17] In his more comprehensive elaboration of nationalism, Smith indicated its principal features as a political doctrine:

Fundamentally, nationalism fuses three ideals: collective self-determination of the people, the expression of national character and individuality, and finally the vertical division of the world into unique nations each contributing its special genius to the common fund of humanity. The doctrine leaves open the form of the self-determination as well as the content of the expression of national individuality. And that is what has endowed nationalism with its tantalising amorphousness, its doctrinal sketchiness and multifarious nature of the movements' activities and goals.[18]

Kedourie's contribution to the discourse on nationalism was to consider its metaphysical basis as an ideology. His analysis of nationalism is highly damning: 'The attempts to refashion so much of the world on national lines has not led to greater peace and stability. On the contrary, it has created new conflicts, exacerbated tensions, and brought catastrophe to numberless people innocent of all politics'.[19] Kedourie's harsh critique of nationalism is consistent with the bulk of the scholarly or journalistic treatment of the subject. Nationalism is rarely portrayed as being anything other than evil.[20]

Ernest Gellner, in contrast, develops a compelling theory of modernisation to explain the emergence of nationalism. He argues that the historic transition from agrarian to industrial society led to the rise of nationalism. Industrial society required a standard vernacular language, a 'high culture', mass education and a strong central state authority. All of these in Gellner's view were the ingredients necessary for nationalism's development and in transmitting national identity to the broad mass of the population. His theory clearly postulates a link between the rise of industrial society, the modern nation-state and nationalism. Moreover he views nationalism as a largely unitary and modern phenomenon.[21]

Anthony D. Smith, like Gellner, also approaches nationalism from a sociological perspective. While generally harbouring similar views to those of Gellner regarding the changes in society that shaped nationalism, Smith diverges significantly by seeing nationalism as having deeper roots. Its foundation lies, in Smith's view, in early modern ethnicism. He sees the relationship between this early ethnicism and the later nationalism as being one of 'continuity, but not identity'.[22]

Sociologists have not had all the running in contemporary discourses on nationalism. Historians such as Peter Alter and E. J.

Hobsbawm have also made significant contributions. Alter's definition of nationalism holds that it is both 'an ideology and a political movement which holds the nation and nation-state to be crucial indwelling values, and which manages to mobilize the political will of a people or a large section of a population'.[23] Hobsbawn, in contrast, defines nationalism in much the same way as Gellner and treats it as a product of modernity.[24]

Both these historians also speculate on nationalism's future. Neither believes that the future necessarily belongs to nationalism, given global economic and social integration. Hobsbawm seriously doubts the strength of nationalism and its continuance as a significant force in world affairs.[25] Alter takes a more cautious view, believing that nationalism and its by-product, the nation-state, will exist side-by-side with the forces of global integration: 'The choice for the present and immediate future cannot be a crude alternative between either unconditional affirmation of the nation-state in its traditional form and function, or swift replacement of it by supranational institutions'.[26]

In the course of this survey of definitions, nationalism has been variously described as a sentiment, a state of mind, a principle, an ideology, a doctrine, a theory of modernisation, an historical process and a catastrophe. Perhaps nationalism is all of these things. If a common thread of agreement can be found among nationalism's interpretors it can be found in the understanding of nationalism as a political doctrine.

Varieties of Nationalism

The idea that there should be varieties of nationalism is nothing new in the study of the phenomenon. Hayes and Kohn saw nationalism as a plural in their pioneering works half a century ago. Not all of nationalism's subsequent interpretors, however, have seen it as a pluralistic phenomenon. Academics such as Gellner and Hobsbawm tend toward a unitary understanding of the phenomenon. Nevertheless an important body of expert opinion, including such figures as Alter and Smith, see varieties of nationalism. Alter argues that 'it is more appropriate to speak of *nationalisms* in the plural than of *nationalism* in the singular'.[27] From this proposition he develops a typology of nationalisms that essentially sees two types: liberal, reformist, risorgimento nationalism and integral nationalism. The former is grounded in nineteenth-century liberalism, the latter in the narrow, exclusivist, right-wing European politics of the late nineteenth century. Alter treats each of these two types as broad categories that embrace further types of nationalisms. Under the 'broad church' of risorgimento nationalism he includes political, economic, cultural, linguistic and religious nationalisms.[28] He sees integral nationalism as a similarly wide category with fascist Italy and Nazi Germany representing its most extreme examples.

Smith addresses the issue of varieties of nationalism within the framework of a sophisticated model. 'Nationalism', for him, 'is most fruitfully conceptualised as a single category containing subvarieties, genus and species, a diversity within a unity'.[29] On a continuum, he sees the phenomenon ranging from 'ethnic' nationalism based on a cultural group to 'territorial' nationalism founded on the 'skeletal framework of the territorial state'. Between these two categories he places a third nationalism, a 'mixed' one that contains elements of both 'ethnic' and 'territorial' nationalisms.[30] Beneath this super-structure of broad categories, Smith elaborates numerous 'genus and species' to account for more variation.

More recently James G. Kellas, another contributor from the social sciences (politics), produced a typology of nationalisms that is less elaborate than Smith but nevertheless parallels his broad categories. Kellas distinguished between three types of nationalism: 'ethnic' (ethnonationalism), 'social' and 'official'. He defines these three variants in the following way: ethnic nationalism as being centred around a common descent or common ethnicity, which gives it an exclusive quality; social nationalism, 'based on a shared na-tional culture, but not on common descent'; and official nationalism, determined by citizenship and not ethnic or cultural factors.[31] Clearly Kellas overlaps Smith's 'ethnic' category while the 'social' model bears some resemblance to Smith's 'mixed' model. A rough cognate can also be found between Kellas' 'official' nationalism and Smith's 'territorial' nationalism.

The common elements in the typologies of nationalism described above are a useful starting point in addressing the question of the distinctiveness of nationalism in East Central Europe. If one accepts varieties of nationalism, which ones are most characteristic of the region?

Kohn, one of the earliest writers on nationalism, drew a sharp distinction between the characteristics of nationalism in the western and eastern halves of the continent. He stressed that:

The political and social changes confined to the West accentuated the deep differences existing between the two parts of Europe. The new ideas encountered in the different countries [produced] a great diversity of institutional and social conditions, bequeathed by the past, and were shaped and modified by them. Their different interpretations produced different types of nationalism – one based upon liberal middle-class concepts and pointing to a consummation in a democratic world society, the other based upon irrational and pre-enlightened concepts and tending towards exclusiveness.[32]

In more contemporary terms, Kohn's contrasting types of nationalism would be referred to by scholars as 'political', 'social' or 'territorial' nationalism in Western Europe versus 'ethnic' nationalism in Eastern Europe. Significantly, this dichotomy between nationalisms reflects the thinking of many Western scholars writing on East Central Europe as well as scholars from the region who have studied the phenomenon of nationalism.[33] This narrowly defined nationalism has often been buttressed in the twentieth century by 'economic nationalism', favouring autarchic economic policy and market protection. Economic nationalism is seen as being stronger in the region than in other parts of the world.[34] When taken together, the 'ethnic' and 'economic' nationalism of East Central Europe illustrate the tendency toward 'exclusiveness' in the region's nationalism, which both in degree and kind differentiate it from the western parts of Europe.

NATION AND NATION-STATE

What is a nation? How does a nation come into existence? What is a nation-state? These questions are natural colloraries to the idea of nationalism discussed in the previous section. The existence of nationalism is inextricably linked to the idea of the nation. Likewise, if nationalism, as Gellner postulates, 'is primarily a political principle, which holds that the political and national unit should be congruent',[35] then the 'nation-state' must have a central place in terms of the objectives of nationalism.

Defining 'nation' is a less complicated business than defining 'nationalism'. The existing definitions of nation are as general as those for nationalism but are more consistent with each other. *The*

8 *The Problem of Definition*

Oxford English Dictionary defines a nation as 'an extensive aggregate of persons, so closely associated with each other by common descent, language, or history, as to form a distinct race or people, usually organised as a separate political state and occupying a definite territory'.[36] Kellas, for example, closely mirrors this definition: 'A nation is a group of people who feel themselves to be a community bound together by ties of history, culture, and common ancestry'.[37]

As in the case of nationalism, nation can also be viewed in the plural. The typology of nations closely follows that of nationalisms. One can illustrate this point with Kellas' typologies. His 'ethnic', 'social' and 'official' nationalisms are paralleled by the existence of the 'ethnic nation', the 'social nation' and the 'official nation'.[38] In a similar vein, the differences in nationalism in Western and Eastern Europe find their counterparts in defining the 'nation'. In the western part of the continent the 'political', 'social' or 'territorial' nation predominates, while in the east it is the 'ethnic' or 'cultural' nation that holds sway.

Determining how a nation comes into existence is not as straightforward as defining a nation. Central to the origins of nations is their relationship to nationalism, which begs an important subsidiary question: which came first; the nation or nationalism? The authorities on the subject are divided on this matter. Gellner sees the nation as the product of nationalism. Smith, in contrast, sees the premodern *ethnie* (ethnic communities) as the ancestors of nations.[39] This debate often hinges on differing terms of reference and it is quite conceivable that the development of nation and nationalism parallel each other to the extent that they must be considered concomitant phenomena. Each shapes the other. Less controversial is how the consciousness of nationhood spreads or grows. Here the nation-building role of the intelligentsia is important, as from this social group comes the ideological foundation and 'organisational nuclei' vital for the growth of national consciousness.[40]

The relationship of nationalism to the nation-state is far less ambiguous than its links to the nation. With the most common definition of nationalism being a political ideology or doctrine, the natural goal of nationalism is easy to see: to marry the nation to the state. Defining what is the nation-state becomes less clear as an outcome, particularly if one accepts that there are varieties of nations. Despite these complications the expression nation-state has gained a global currency. Hugh Seton-Watson, in his *Nations and*

States, cast serious doubt on the validity of running together the concepts of nation and state in such an imprecise manner:

The belief that every state is a nation, or that all sovereign states are national states, has done much to obfuscate human understanding of political realities. A state is a legal and political organisation, with the power to require obedience and loyalty from its citizens. A nation is a community of people, whose members are bound together by a sense of solidarity, a common culture, a national consciousness.[41]

What Seton-Watson is highlighting in fact is that there are varieties of nation-states. The most simplistic (and commonly used) definition of nation-state equates the boundary of the nation and the state. Such a definition may suit the political/social/territorial nations of Western Europe (and other parts of the world) but not rest well with the ethnic nations of East Central Europe. It is a definition essentially grounded in political geography rather than a cultural identity.[42] In East Central Europe, however, nation-state really means a national state; it is a definition that assumes that the ethnic nation and the political boundaries of the state are one and the same.

Notes and References

1. East Central Europe is used in preference to Eastern Europe throughout this book. Following the geographical division of Europe set out by Oscar Halecki in his *Borderlands of Western Civilization: A History of East Central Europe* (New York: The Ronald Press Company, 1952, pp. 3–7), East Central Europe includes the following states: Albania, Bulgaria, former Czechoslovakia (the Czech Republic and Slovakia), Hungary, Poland, Romania, and former Yugoslavia (Bosnia-Hercegovina, Croatia, Macedonia, Montenegro, Serbia and Slovenia). The Baltic states (Estonia, Latvia and Lithuania) and Greece are also considered part of Halecki's scheme, but they are not discussed in this volume. The sub-regional term 'Balkans' refers to Albania, Bulgaria, Greece, Romania and the states of former Yugoslavia.
2. See Francis Fukuyama, *The End of History and the Last Man* (New York: the Free Press, 1992), pp. 266–75, and Paul Kennedy, *Preparing for the Twenty-First Century* (London: Harper Collins, 1993), pp. 122–34.
3. Fukuyama, p. 274.
4. Neal Ascherson, 'Why the Future Waves a Flag', *The Independent on Sunday*, 8 September 1991.
5. The literature highlighting the challenges includes Zbigniew Brzezinski, 'Post Communist Nationalism', *Foreign Affairs*, vol. LXVIII (Winter 1989/90), pp. 1–25; Jonathan Eyal, 'Eastern Europe: What About the Minorities', *The*

10   *The Problem of Definition*

World Today, December 1989; Misha Glenny, *The Rebirth of History: Eastern Europe in the Age of Democracy* (London: Penguin, 1990); Magarditsch Hatschikjan, 'Von der doppelten Mitgift der Altlasten – Zu einigen territorialen und nationalen Konfliktpotentialen in "Zwischeneuropa" ', Interne Studien, Nr. 27/1991, *Konrad Adenauer Stiftung*; Paul Lendvai, 'Eastern Europe I: Liberalism vs. Nationalism', *The World Today*, July 1990.

6. Louis L. Snyder, *Encyclopedia of Nationalism* (Chicago: St. James Press, 1990), p. 213.

7. For definitions of these terms see James G. Kellas, *The Politics of Nationalism and Ethnicity* (London: Macmillan, 1991), pp. 2–6; J. A. Simpson and E. S. C. Weiner (eds), *The Oxford English Dictionary*, vol. v (Oxford: Clarendon Press, 1989), pp. 423–6, and vol. x, pp. 231–5; Snyder, *Encyclopedia of Nationalism*.

8. Carlton J. H. Hayes, *Essays on Nationalism* (New York: Russell and Russell, 1926), pp. 5–6.

9. Hans Kohn, *The Idea of Nationalism: a Study in Its Origins and Background* (New York: Collier Books, 1944), pp. 10–11.

10. Carlton J. H. Hayes, *The Historical Evolution of Modern Nationalism* (New York: Macmillan, 1931), p. 12. In America the historian Boyd C. Shafer built upon the early work of Hayes and Kohn. Shafer concentrated on the myths associated with nationalism. See his *Nationalism: Myth and Reality* (New York: Harcourt, Brace and World, 1955) and *Faces of Nationalism: New Realities and Old Myths* (New York: Harcourt, Brace and Jovanovich, 1972).

11. Edward Hallett Carr, *Nationalism and After* (London: Macmillan, 1945), pp. 38–70.

12. See Edward Hallett Carr, *Conditions of Peace* (London: Macmillan, 1942), p. 38; see also pp. 37–66. A more comprehensive study of the concept of national self-determination can be found in Alfed Cobban, *The Nation State and National Self-Determination* (London: Collins, 1969).

13. See Carr, *Nationalism and After*, pp. 1–37. For a thought-provoking summary and analysis of Carr's stages and time zones, see Ernest Gellner, 'Nationalism Reconsidered and E. H. Carr', *Review of International Studies*, vol. xviii (October 1992), pp. 285–93.

14. Indeed, a study group chaired by Carr at the Royal Institute of International Affairs anticipated the future direction of research concerning nationalism in a report it produced in 1939:
'Nationalism cannot be properly appreciated if it is treated as an isolated political or psychological phenomenon. It must be regarded as a special case of the more general and permanent problem of group integration. Far-reaching questions of sociology and group psychology are involved, questions which admit of wide differences of opinion and to which scientific methods of study cannot be easily applied'. See *Nationalism: A Report by a Study Group of Members of the Royal Institute of International Affairs* (London: Oxford University Press, 1939), p. xiii.

15. Elie Kedourie, *Nationalism*, 3rd ed. (London: Hutchinson, 1969), p. 9.

16. Ernest Gellner, *Nations and Nationalism* (Oxford: Basil Blackwell, 1983), p. 1.

17. Anthony D. Smith, *Theories of Nationalism* (London: Duckworth, 1971), p. 19.

18. Smith, pp. 23–4.
19. Kedourie, p. 138.
20. Neal Ascherson stresses nationalism's 'Janus' like quality in his 'Why the Future Waves a Flag'.
21. See Gellner, *Nations and Nationalism*.
22. Anthony D. Smith, *The Ethnic Origins of Nations* (Oxford: Blackwell, 1986), p. 216.
23. Peter Alter, *Nationalism* (London: Edward Arnold, 1991), p. 8.
24. E. J. Hobsbawn, *Nations and Nationalism since 1780*, 2nd ed. (Cambridge: Cambridge University Press, 1992), pp. 9, 14.
25. Hobsbawm, pp. 191–2.
26. Alter, p. 124.
27. Alter, p. 5.
28. Alter, p. 33.
29. Smith, *Theories of Nationalism*, p. 193.
30. Smith, *Theories of Nationalism*, pp. 216–18.
31. Kellas, pp. 51–2.
32. Kohn, p. 457.
33. See Peter F. Sugar, 'External and Internal Roots of Eastern European Nationalism', in Peter F. Sugar and Ivo J. Lederer (eds), *Nationalism in Eastern Europe*, 2nd ed. (Seattle: University of Washington Press, 1973), pp. 3–54; Marek Waldenberg, *Kwestie narodowe w Europie Środkowo-Wschodniej* (Warszawa: PWN, 1992).
34. This was particularly true in the interwar years. See Jan Kofman, *Nacjonalizm gospodarczy: szansa czy bariera rozwoju* (Warszawa: PWN, 1992); H. Szlafer (ed.), *Essays on Economic Nationalism in East-Central Europe and South America 1918–1939*, (Genevé: Université de Genevé, 1990).
35. Ernest Gellner, *Nations and Nationalism*, p. 1.
36. *The Oxford English Dictionary*, vol. x, p. 231.
37. Kellas, p. 2.
38. Kellas, pp. 3–4.
39. Gellner, p. 55 and Smith, *The Ethnic Origins of Nations*, p. 154.
40. Józef Chlebowczyk, *On Small and Young Nations in Europe* (Wrocław: Ossolineum, 1980), p. 142 and chapter 6.
41. Hugh Seton-Watson, *Nations and States: An Enquiry into the Origins of Nations and the Politics of Nationalism* (London: Methuen, 1977), p. 1.
42. For a discussion of the idea of the nation-state, see Alfred Cobban, *The Nation State and National Self-Determination* (London: Collins, 1969), pp. 118–29.

2 Nationalism in East Central Europe: Old Wine in New Bottles?

Wojciech Roszkowski

East Central European cultures tend to use two basic terms to describe national phenomena: good 'patriotism', which is understood to be loyalty to one's own nationality, and bad 'nationalism', which is an abuse of national feelings.[1] West and East European perceptions of nationalism are not compatible. For the sake of the present study some categorisation of nationalisms is therefore necessary.

Nationalism in the broadest sense may be understood as a feeling of belonging to a nation. However definitions of the term 'nation' vary enormously.[2] Factors often used to define the 'nation' include language, literature, religion, common history, geographical proximity, political interest and social custom. Furthermore, what constitutes the nation and what propels nationalism has been subject to historical evolution. The determinants of national identity and nationalism have changed over time. Before the nineteenth century nationalism was mostly political; it was the prerogative of a dynasty, a political class or estate. The old Polish–Lithuanian Commonwealth and the old Kingdom of Hungary were East Central European manifestations of such a nationalism.[3]

Nationalism may be understood as a belief in the political system of a nation-state, as is especially the case in contemporary United States. The same meaning of the term can, with respect to proportions, be applied to the political nationalism of the old Polish–Lithuanian Commonwealth or the old Kingdom of Hungary. Let us call it a *political nationalism*. Nationalism may mean identification with a national state of a more or less definite ethnic nature, such as England or France. In the process of growth of such ethnic nation-states there were clearly many signs of ideological nationalism (for example the ideology of Joseph Gobineau, or the English battle-cry 'Rule Britannia'), but they were refined by success into a political nationalism.

The nineteenth century saw the emergence of a *romantic*, or

13

risorgimento, nationalism,[4] which was associated with liberal ideas
embodied in the proliferation of many movements modelled on
'Young Italy'. The climax of this process came with the Springtime
of Nations in the abortive revolutions of 1848. These movements
celebrated national identity and believed that nations should be free
to express themselves. In East Central Europe this kind of nationalism was a reaction against the absolutist supranational powers that
dominated the region. For many of the East Central European
peoples, *risorgimento* nationalism fostered the birth or renaissance
of national culture.[5] This kind of nationalism was a cry for freedom,
as is sometimes the case today. Lithuanians shouting 'Lietuva,
Lietuva' in front of Soviet tanks in Vilnius on 13 January 1991
meant 'we want to be free from oppression'! Of course there is no
guarantee that romantic nationalist feelings will not quickly change
into national chauvinism.

By the end of the nineteenth century frustrated romantic nationalism gave way to an integral model. Nationalism became an ideology
that made the nation more important than the individual. This form
of *ideological* or *integral nationalism* became a doctrine stressing
the idea of an ethnic, historic and cultural community whose interests were the top priority of political activity. For the integral nationalists the ultimate goal was to make the ethnic nation synonymous
with the totality of the state. Because of its exclusivity, the integral
nationalism in East Central Europe manifested itself in ugly ethnic
chauvinism characterised by an intensity of bad feelings about other
nations, be these oppressors, neighbours or scapegoats for national
misfortunes. This kind of nationalism usually feeds on humiliation
and fear.[6]

When an oppressed ethnic community takes the first steps toward
its own statehood, there often emerge various economic barriers to
its development. It is therefore no wonder that the national elites
follow a protectionist or nationalist economic policy. This *economic
nationalism* was clearly the case in interwar East Central Europe.[7]

It is extremely hard to locate the point at which 'decent' forms of
nationalism turn into national xenophobia, self-glorification, chauvinism and even aggression. Generally speaking the civilised forms
of nationalism grow on success, satisfaction and education, and then
usually change into *political nationalism*. On the other hand failures,
long-lasting oppression, poverty and ignorance stimulate *chauvinist
nationalism*.

THEM VERSUS US: THE HISTORICAL EVOLUTION OF NATIONALISM

When viewed from the outside, should nationalism in modern East Central Europe be treated as a negative phenomenon? It must be borne in mind that it was the inability of the oppressed peoples of East Central Europe to fulfil their aspirations that shaped the evolution of nationalism in the region. Under such conditions the peoples of the region lacked the opportunity to develop moderate political nationalism. Unlike peoples in Western Europe, they developed ideas of a nation in defiance of state power. Because East Central European nations have lacked separate states for most of the modern period, nationalism in the region has drawn on a variety of sources of inspiration: religion, language, history, race and – last but not least – dislike of the oppressor. Therefore a highly polarized nationalism that separates the good patriotism of 'us' from the bad nationalism of 'them' is characteristic of East Central Europe.

For the last two hundred years most of the region has been under the rule of one of four external powers – Russia, Germany, Austria and Turkey. Some of the region's nations had the misfortune of being divided between two or three of these powers. To make things even more complicated, Poland and Hungary have themselves been perceived by their neighbors as oppressors, because in the nineteenth century their position was altered from the niveau of 'political nations' to the level of oppressed nations dwelling on 'ideological nationalism'. The tensions that accumulated in the various nations due to their inability to realise political ambitions also affected ethnic communities living in many areas of East-Central Europe but not claiming any particular area for themselves – the Gypsies and the Jews. East European anti-Semitism grew on a fertile ground of national dissatisfaction, oppression, poverty and ignorance.

For the developing East Central European national cultures much depended on which of the external powers was the chief oppressor and which of the neighboring nationalities were allies or rivals in the struggle for independence, autonomy or simply survival. Some differences were also due to religious divisions, since the Roman Catholic and Protestant Churches considered education important – providing the region's first universities in Prague and Cracow in the fourteenth century – while the Orthodox and Muslims placed less emphasis on education. Also the Catholic, Protestant and Greek Orthodox priesthood sought to preserve national cultures, while Muslim and Russian Orthodox clergy more often simply represented the Turkish or Russian political power. Instruction in native languages was a Protestant invention, but it was soon taken up by most Catholic schools. Orthodox and Muslim schools were more conservative.

Until the Second World War nationalism in East Central Europe had a strong religious component. Estonians and Latvians were usually distinguished by Protestantism; Poles, Lithuanians, Croats and Slovaks by Roman Catholicism; Ukrainians by Greek Catholicism; Byelorussians, Romanians, Bulgarians, Montenegrians and Serbs by Orthodoxy; and Bosniaks by Islam. Religion helped to define who belonged and who did not, especially in the Polish–Byelorussian, Polish–Ukrainian, Serbo–Croat, Czech-Slovak and Bulgarian–Turkish borderlands. Everywhere it also distinguished other nationals from Jews.

INTERWAR NATIONALISM

The complexity of the nationality problem in interwar East Central Europe can be seen from the way in which territories emerged after the First World War. Poland was recreated from former German, Austrian and Russian territories. Thus western Poland had a German minority, while the easternmost territories were largely inhabited by Ukrainians and Byelorussians. Czechoslovakia included the Czech historic lands of Bohemia, Moravia and Silesia, which for a long time had belonged to Austria, as well as Slovakia and Subcarpathian Ruthenia, which had belonged to the Kingdom of Hungary. Therefore the Sudentenland had a large German population, while Slovakia was partly inhabited by Hungarians and Ruthenia by Ukrainians. Yugoslavia comprised the former states of Serbia and Montenegro, Slovenia and Dalmatia, which had belonged to Austria, as well as the Banat and Croatia, which had been part of the Kingdom of Hungary. Bosnia and Hercegovina had been under Austrian military occupation since 1878. Romania was enlarged by the addition of Transylvania from the Kingdom of Hungary, Bukovina from Austria and Bessarabia from Russia. Therefore there was a large Hungarian minority in Transylvania, and Ukrainian communities in Bukovina and Bessarabia. Hungary suffered the largest loss of territory, so its nationality structure within the 1920 frontiers was the most uniform.[8]

The frontier changes after the First World War exacerbated nationality problems in all but Hungary, Bulgaria and Albania, al-though in Hungary, too, the presence of German and Jewish minor-ities created some problems during the Second World War. At the same time there was question of Hungarians abroad, as nearly one third of all Magyar-speaking people lived outside Hungary, whose territory had been reduced by the 1920 Trianon Treaty. The minority problem was particularly grave in Czechoslovakia, where the German minority held a very strong economic position. Those ex-Habsburg Germans were not particularly attached to the Reich until the 1930s, when their nationalist feeling grew under the influ-ence of Nazism. In Slovakia, from the beginning the Magyar minor-ity was irredentist. In Western Poland the relatively small German minority was extremely powerful economically. It was also aggres-sively anti-Polish, as Germany had made it clear that it was willing to redraw the Polish–German frontier. German minorities in Hun-gary, Romania and Yugoslavia had no inclination to fight against the postwar status quo. Germans had lived in Hungary for a long time and were relatively prosperous in relation to their non-German neighbours. Hungarians, however, formed large minority groups in Romania, Czechoslovakia and Yugoslavia. They were also con-scious of their former position as the leading nationality in the border areas of Slovakia, Transylvania and the Banat and were unwilling to accept the new status quo.

A further cause of political difficulties in Poland, Yugoslavia and Czechoslovakia arose from tensions between the Slav nationalities. In Poland the pushing of the frontier eastward resulted in the inclu-sion within Poland of areas with large Byelorussian and Ukrainian communities, though most of the large estates were in Polish hands. In Czechoslovakia the trouble between Czechs and Slovaks was perhaps more latent than open. The Czechs, besides being more numerous, were economically and culturally more advanced, and more experienced in administration than the peasant Slovaks, who had suffered from the policy of Magyarisation. The relative back-wardness of Slovakia called for a redistribution of resources, which, according to the Slovaks, was carried out too slowly due to the Czech desire to dominate Czechoslovakia. The tension between Serbs, Croats and Slovenes was even more dangerous. The Serbs, who were more numerous and were the 'founder members' of the union, having provided it with a capital and the ruling dynasty, were less economically advanced than both the Croats, who had experienced some autonomy in the Habsburg Monarchy, and the Slovenes, who were economically the most prosperous. Along with each Yugoslav nationality's strong determination to achieve self-government, these discrepancies resulted in growing tension in Yugoslavia. There was also a conflict between Bulgaria and Serbia over Macedonia.

The distribution of populations among various religious denominations reinforced the differences and conflicts among the East Central European nationalities. There were several pronounced examples of this, such as the conflict between Roman Catholic Croats and Orthodox Serbs, between Greek Catholic Ukrainians and Roman Catholic Poles, and between Eastern Orthodox Bulgarians and Muslim Turks. The situation of the Jews was unique. As urban dwellers they were often perceived as a check to the natural advance of natives to towns, so their segregation was sometimes not only religious and political, but also economic.[9]

In the East Central European states that were created or reorganised after 1918, several aspects of economic nationalism have been recorded. One of these referred to land reform. The ruling nationalities wanted to consolidate power by ousting 'alien' landowners and dividing the land among native peasants. This 'national-revolutionary' pattern of land reform applied to Estonia, Latvia, Lithuania, Czechoslovakia, Romania and Yugoslavia, while in Poland, Hungary, Bulgaria and Albania land reforms were much less radical because, in the absence of 'alien' landowners, the demand for land could not be satisfied other than at the expense of natives. As a result of all these reforms the social and political role of the German, Austrian, Polish, Hungarian and Russian landowners was largely reduced everywhere except for the new Polish republic and Trianon in Hungary.[10]

The dissolution of large 'alien' estates created serious tensions between national governments and those of neighbouring countries whose nationals had lost their land, particularly in Germany's relations with the Baltic states, Poland's relations with Lithuania and Latvia, and Hungary's relations with Czechoslovakia, Romania and Yugoslavia. In most cases tensions had already existed because of territorial disputes, but expropriating large landowners aggravated these conflicts.

The redrawing of the map of East Central Europe after the First World War was only a reformulation of the old dilemmas and was by no means their solution. Given the instability of the Versailles system and the economic stagnation in interwar Europe, the multinational composition of most of the East Central European countries was one of the main sources of political conflicts in this part of Europe. New injustices were committed in an effort to compensate for earlier ones.

NATIONALISM UNDER COMMUNISM

The communist system imposed in the region by the Soviet Union after the Second World War was aimed at the Sovietisation of East Central Europe. If, as a result of forty-five years of communist rule, the East Central European countries came close to the Soviet pattern, it was due to the extraordinary rigidity of Soviet communism and the lack of serious challenges to its rule. Communism meant etatism of all aspects of social, economic and cultural life, the formation of a neo-feudal structure of power of the nomenklatura, secularisation, and a decline in civil virtues in the societies of the region.

The communist system in East Central Europe after the Second World War went through several stages. In 1956 the Stalinist era ended, which meant not only subjugation of the region and its Sovietisation, but also a 'permanent purge' in public life. In the post-Stalinist times the communists still had the ambition to create a new civilisation by means of coercion. The new stage included a contradiction: terror used to protect the system was justified, while terror among communists was abolished.[11] The climax of the post-Stalinist era came in the 1960s, with new attempts to revitalise the system. In Hungary this was by economic reform, Czechoslovakia promulgated the idea of 'socialism with human face', while in Romania and Poland attempts were made by the communist leadership to absorb nationalism.

The ultimate frontiers of satellite nationalism were set by the Kremlin, where similar dilemmas were faced. Although the quasi-nationalist ideology of Alexander Shelepin was weakened by his downfall in the mid-1960s, some of it was taken over by the ageing Brezhnevites. Facing economic stagnation and a declining proportion of Russians in Soviet society, the Kremlin advocated that the Russian nation should have a 'special role' in the union. The climax of official Russian chauvinism came during the Moscow Olympic Games in 1980.

By that time satellite nationalisms were important components of official ideologies everywhere in the bloc, but within carefully observed limits. Local nationalism was never allowed to challenge Russian or Soviet national interests. For instance, in the 1960s it was all right for the Polish communist strongman Mieczysław Moczar, the head of the 'partisan' hardliners, to advocate nationalist xenophobia and anti-Semitism, but when he once made a comment about Polish communists who came from Russia in military coats, he was rebuked in Moscow. In the case of Poland, which had had a particularly bad experience with the Russians and Soviets, communist nationalism was a monster of inconsistency and censorship was a particularly difficult task.[12]

Romania under Gheorghe Gheorghiu-Dej and Nicolae Ceauşescu was allowed to practice official nationalism and even had some liberty with regard to foreign policy, but only because the Romanian communists maintained very tight control over society. The Romanian case is probably the most characteristic of communist nationalism. In 1945 the Romanian Communist Party was based on Hungarians, Ukrainians and Jews. In the Stalinist years all 'aliens' were purged and a new generation of hardliners of 'pure Romanian blood' took over. The cost of Romanian communist nationalism – deteriorating relations with neighbouring Hungary – did not prevent the Soviet Union and many Western politicians from tolerating the excesses of the Romanian communist establishment.[13] In Albania Enver Hoxha's special brand of communist nationalism stimulated deviation from the Soviet orbit in the early 1960s.[14]

In Hungary the revolution of 1956 made the communist leadership very cautious about nationalism, but even here defending the Hungarian minority in Transylvania from persecution by Romanian communists was a nationalist policy.[15] Bulgaria went through a period of official nationalism in the mid-1980s, when the Zhivkov regime tried to mobilise Bulgarians against their Turkish fellow citizens in view of the deteriorating economic situation.[16] In Czechoslovakia only a moderate rebirth of nationalism was recorded before and during the 'Prague Spring' of 1968, especially in the Slovak section of the Communist Party.[17] Even in the Lithuanian Soviet Republic a limited return to national tradition was recorded in the early 1970s, during the last stages of the long-lasting rule of Antanas Sneckus, once a major oppressor of his nation.[18]

Only in Yugoslavia did the communists try to avoid similar policies, this because the Serbian, Croat and even Slovene nationalists were too volatile to handle. Until 1980, or as long as Josif Tito was alive, the federalist ideology of the Yugoslav communists sustained relative stability.[19] But even here the decline of the system encouraged the Serbian communist leader Slobodan Milošević to espouse Serbian nationalism in 1988. This policy not only failed it even accelerated the growth of Croatian and Slovene nationalism. As a result Yugoslavia is now involved in bloody civil war.

Apart from their chauvinist policies, the communist authorities created an atmosphere of a besieged fortress in which all foreigners were treated with mistrust. Despite official propaganda about 'the brotherhood of socialist nations', frontiers between neighbouring countries were strictly controlled. To explain the poor results of their economic policies, the authorities frequently spread rumours that market shortages were due to 'tourist shoppers', or that their country was especially handicapped by Comecon relations. The common practice of 'tourist' shopping as a result of the differences in price levels between the Comecon countries, caused hostilities even between friendly nations such as Poland and Hungary. Knowledge of the history and culture of neighbouring countries was restricted to an even lower level than that of the native heritage.

Although communism was initially an internationalist ideology, it gradually absorbed nationalist emotions. The crippled nationalism, or perhaps we should say chauvinism and xenophobia, that was expressed for instance during sporting events, seemed to the communists a low price to pay for the obedience of their societies.

Communism did not manage entirely to Sovietise East European societies. Exports of manpower and the self-government system of Yugoslavia, Hungary's economic reform, Romania's foreign policy, and private agriculture and the role of the Catholic Church in Poland were the best-known examples of deviation from Soviet orthodoxy. Communist terror tactics and censorship had for decades suppressed the positive values of East Central European national cultures. The moment this pressure was gone, the societies of the region began to grope for their roots, using nationalist emotions to compensate for the humiliation and fear they had experienced. Old grievances were brought to the surface and old hostilities were revived. Among the best-known examples of these were the Romanian pogroms of Hungarians in Transylvania, the Serbo–Albanian clashes in Kosovo, the Serbo–Croat war in Croatia, the Slovaks' resentment of the Czechs and Polish–Lithuanian mistrust. Mutual perceptions between Poles and Germans or Poles and Russians are not too good either.

On the other hand, having realised how the communists used nationalism to manipulate, some of the intellectual elites in East Central Europe have become more resistant to nationalist emotions than their fathers and grandfathers. For instance chauvinist nationalism now lives only on the outskirts of the post-'Solidarity' political movements in Poland. In Czecho-Slovakia the Civic Forum factions lack the prewar superiority complex that was displayed in relations with Slovaks and Poles. In Hungary the Free Democrats and the Young Democrats are also free from traditional nationalism, and even the Hungarian Democratic Forum can hardly be called a nationalist party. Even in Bulgaria most members of the Union of Democratic Forces have shown a critical attitude towards the anti-Turkish demonstrations inspired by the communists.

POST-COMMUNIST NATIONALISM

After the collapse of communism the level of political control of East European societies has been largely reduced. This has already led to the growth of nationalism. East Central European poverty will not be remedied in a short time, so this too is likely to cause problems. There also remain two other reasons of ideological or chauvinist nationalisms: ignorance or feelings of cultural failure, conscious efforts on the part of the nomenklatura to hold on to power by associating themselves with and promoting a nationalist agenda (nomenklatura nationalism).

The first kind of post-communist nationalism may seem the most widespread and dangerous. Nevertheless this is not the case. To date rather few manifestations of this kind of nationalism have been recorded, but one such is the alarming spread of the neo-Nazi skinhead movement in the former German Democratic Republic, now the eastern provinces of unified Germany. Elsewhere grassroot national xenophobia feeding on poverty and despair is still rather marginal.

The revival of ideological nationalism has found expression in a number of cases, such as the Hungarian writer István Csurka and the right wing of the Hungarian National Forum or the Polish National Community (Polska Wspólnota Narodowa), although the latter was started by a Communist Party member Bolesław Tejkowski. It remains to be seen, however, whether this potentially dangerous manifestation of nationalism will lead to conflict in the region.

More dangerous is nomenklatura nationalism, consciously spread by former communist officials in order to mobilise support among native majorities. The extreme cases of this phenomenon can be found in former Yugoslavia, where the relatively unchanged Communist Parties stayed in power and instigated ethnic hatred, which led to the outbreak of civil war and 'ethnic cleansing'. The dark angel of this kind of nationalism is Slobodan Milošević of Serbia. Less tragic in effect, but similar in origin, post-communist nationalism can also be seen, for instance, in Romania and Slovakia.

It is pointless to try to quench nationalist fires by outright rejection of nationalist values. After all, diversified national cultures enrich the human heritage. The guiding principle must be to do unto your neighbours what you would have them do unto you.

Can nationalism in East Central Europe be civilised and not destructive? Can the unhappy legacy be escaped and replaced with something that is accepting of diversity? The Czech and Slovak 'velvet divorce' is a beacon of hope against the horrors of the former Yugoslavia.

Notes and References

1. Dennis J. Dunn, 'Nationalism and Religion', in *Eastern Europe: Religion and Nationalism* (Washington, DC: The Wilson Center East European Program, Occasional Paper No 3, 1985), p. 33.
2. Peter Alter has recently suggested the following definition: 'The nation is a politically mobilized people' (*Nationalism*, London: Edward Arnold, 1989, p. 10). It may be too general, but otherwise very apt.
3. Andrzej Walicki, 'Three Traditions of Polish Patriotism', in Stanislaw Gomulka and Anthony Polonsky (eds), *Polish Paradoxes*, (London: Routledge, 1990), p. 22.
4. Alter, pp. 55–91.
5. See Alfred Bilmanis, *A History of Latvia* (Princeton: Princeton University Press, 1951), pp. 231–57; Evald Uustalu, *The History of Estonian People* (London: Boreas, 1950), pp. 122–46.
6. Marcin Kula has recently presented various roots of chauvinist nationalism, such as the desire to save a nation from decline, to compensate for humiliation at the hands of foreign oppressors, to overcome backwardness, and so forth. Marcin Kula, *Narodowe i rewolucyjne* (Warsaw: 'Więź', 1991), pp. 30–83.
7. Jan Kofman, 'Economic Nationalism in East-Central Europe in the Interwar Period', in Henryk Szlajfer (ed.), *Economic Nationalism in East-Central Europe and South America 1918–1939* (Geneve: Librairie Droz, 1990), pp. 133–250.
8. M. C. Kaser and E. A. Radice (eds), *The Economic History of Eastern Europe 1919–1975*, vol. 1, (Oxford: Clarendon Press, 1985), p. 24 ff.
9. See C. A. Macartney, *National States and National Minorities*, (Oxford:

Oxford University Press, 1934); Stephan M. Horak, *Eastern European National Minorities 1919–1980* (New York: Libraries Unlimited, 1985); Raymond Pearson, *National Minorities in Eastern Europe 1848–1945* (London: Macmillan, 1983).

10.   Wojciech Roszkowski, 'Land Reforms in East Central Europe after World War One', in *Eastern Europe and Latin America in the 20th Century* (forthcoming).

11.   'It is Not Hopeless if You Demand', interview with Miklos Harraszti', *Uncaptive Minds* no 1, (1988), p. 16.

12.   A comprehensive, although much exaggerated description of Polish communist nationalism may be found in Michael Checinski, *Poland, Nationalism, Anti-Semitism* (New York: Karz-Cohl, 1982). For instance, the term 'final solution', a reminder of the Nazi Holocaust, used for the communist anti-Semitic purge of 1968 is out of all proportions.

13.   Ghita Ionescu, *Communism in Rumania 1944–1962* (London: Oxford University Press, 1964); Stephen Fischer-Galati, *The New Rumania* (Cambridge, Mass: The MIT Press, 1967); Trond Gilberg, 'The Communist Party of Romania', in Stephen Fischer-Galati (ed.), *The Communist Parties of Eastern Europe* (New York: Columbia University Press, 1979), pp. 281–326; Vladimir Tismaneanu, 'Ceausescu's Socialism', *Problems of Communism*, vol. I (1985), pp. 5–62.

14.   J. F. Brown, *The New Eastern Europe. The Khrushchev Era and After* (New York: F. A. Praeger, 1966), pp. 192–202.

15.   Bennet Kovrig, *Communism in Hungary from Kun to Kadar* (Stanford: Hoover Institution Press, 1979).

16.   John D. Bell, *The Bulgarian Communist Party from Blagoev to Zhivkov* (Stanford: Hoover Institution Press, 1986).

17.   Carol Skalnik Leff, *National Conflict in Czechoslovakia. The Making and Remaking of the State 1918–1987* (Princeton: Princeton University Press, 1988).

18.   Romuald J. Misiunas and Rein Taagepera, *The Baltic States. Years of Dependence 1940–1980* (Berkeley University of California Press, 1983), p. 197.

19.   Pedro Ramet, *Nationalism and Federalism in Yugoslavia 1963–1983* (Bloomington: Indiana University Press, 1984).

3 Empire, War and the Nation-State in East Central Europe

Raymond Pearson

With European nationalism currently approaching its bicentenary, it bears emphasising from the outset that the nationalist upsurge of East Central Europe in the 1990s is not a novel *sui generis* phenomenon but only the latest – and emphatically not the last – phase in an ongoing historical process. Nationalist business may be unfinished; but the nationalist agenda is long-established. No balanced evaluation of contemporary nationalism in East Central Europe is possible without an appreciation of the cataclysmic impact of twentieth-century war upon the always complex, sometimes contradictory and often paradoxical relationship between empire and nation-state.

THE NATION-STATE AS DESTINY

Over the course of the nineteenth century, the pursuit of the sovereign nation-state became the central tenet of nationalism. Inspired by the seminal ideas of the French Revolution, early nationalists were fired by the concept of the nation as the only natural and therefore sole morally legitimate community. The exigencies of self-interest ensured that unanimity was never reached on the crucial question of a definition of 'natural', though nationalists were to quarrel over such classic identifiers as religion, race, language, culture and history in their attempts to come up with a mutually satisfactory formula. Consensus was much closer in perceiving nationalism as, to quote Ernest Gellner, 'primarily a principle which holds that the political and the national unit should be congruent'.[1] Early in the nineteenth century the philsopher Georg Hegel insisted that since world history 'takes account only of those nations which have formed themselves into states', then the career of nations prior to nation-statehood amounted to no more than 'prehistory'.[2] By 1870 the international jurist Johann Bluntschli was proclaiming uncompromisingly that 'every nation is called upon, and is thus entitled, to form a state. . . . The world should be split into as many states as humanity is divided into nations. Each nation a state. Each state a national entity'.[3] By the later nineteenth century the prime objective of nationalist 'self-determination' was to achieve the dream of the 'nation-state', what Max Weber called 'the nation's secular organisation of power', the ideal political construct in which 'nation' and 'state' were geopolitically identical.[4]

The attainment or – given the revivalist mythology favoured by nationalists – the regaining of the political paradise of nation-statehood was fraught with the most daunting practical difficulties. This most fundamental of nationalist principles presupposed incorporating all conationals within the territorial jurisdiction of the nation-state whilst simultaneously excluding all non-nationals. How this simplistic prescription might be applied to the pointillist ethnic canvas of twentieth-century East Central Europe has proved, to say the least, problematic. The formula could hardly have been more inapporpriate to the region, explicitly defying a demographic legacy of compact, mixed and diaspora settlement, which rendered the principle of nation-statehood ostensibly unrealisable.

At a more pragmatic level, fierce competition on the part of emergent national states that combined uncompromising insistence on nation-statehood with flagrant disregard for inherited ethnic settlement became endemic throughout East Central Europe. The Mazzini-style risorgimento nationalism of non-competitive universal emancipation and fulfillment was soon replaced by a more sinister 'integral nationalism' dedicated to exclusive 'destiny', the mystical right of the nation to pursue its ethnocentric *sacro egoismo* without regard for the sensibilities of others. The meretricious glamour of the concept of the nation-state proved virtually irresistible, prompting general and mutually damaging conflict.

At the most practical level of all, the very first obstacle in the path of realising the nation-state in Central and Eastern Europe was the self-interested opposition of the resident dynastic empires. Multilingual, multicultural and increasingly perceived as multinational, the avowedly supranational empires enjoyed (or suffered) very different states of political health. At one extreme the Ottoman Empire, the proverbial 'sick man of Europe', was succumbing fast before a great-power-regulated upsurge in Balkan nationalism, surrendering imperial territory to a succession of what purported to be new nation-states over the course of the nineteenth century. In contrast the

Russian Empire felt sufficiently vigorous and self-confident to greet the twentieth century with an ebullient preemptive campaign of cultural and political Russification against the non-Russian 60 per cent of the population within its extravagantly multiethnic jurisdiction.

In a median condition between the Ottoman and Romanov extremes, the Habsburg Empire, though without a unanimous diagnosis of terminal illness, was plainly not in the rudest political health: challenged by a rising tide of nationalism, the unitary Austrian Empire underwent a forced conversion to the dual monarchy of Austria–Hungary in 1867. After the *Ausgleich*, however, a stalemate between the forces of nationalism and empire prevailed, a fifty-year deadlock across Habsburg Europe that appeared incapable of being broken during peacetime.[5]

THE NATIONAL EXPERIENCE OF WAR

Victory or defeat in war has, of course, from time immemorial determined the peacetime geopolitical matrix, prompting many to perceive war as a major, if not the fundamental, factor in first state-formation and then nation-building in modern Europe.[6] With twentieth-century conflict moving inexorably towards 'total war', mobilising progressively larger proportions of society, it has become appreciated increasingly that the scope, intensity and especially the duration and frequency of war can be just as significant as its military outcome. Short wars (or the initial phase of longer wars) tend to reinforce the stability of a resident state as peacetime internal differences are set aside in a wartime solidarity against the common enemy. In contrast long wars – and especially wars more protracted than the participants have been led to expect – tend to strain even ethnically homogeneous states, often exacerbating social class cleavages. Ethnically heterogeneous multinational states are likely to suffer territorial fragmentation and eventual disintegration. Most pertinently of all for nationalism, incessant or regular war (whether won or lost) provides a continuous stimulus to internal solidarity, a collective *toujours en vedette* sentiment that may well foster both state-formation and an abiding sense of nationhood, favouring the development of a 'national state'.[7]

In shifting from the general to the particular, it is possible to discern in the period 1914–45 the incidence of all three categories of war. The First World War was universally expected to be short, prompting an initial defensive solidarity in all belligerent states. But when the six-month 'Mince-Pie War' unaccountably became a long war of attrition, the social and political repercussions on all the dynastic empires of Central and Eastern Europe were ultimately devastating. In contrast the Second World War was never expected to be anything but protracted, so the five-year conflict had (at least within Europe) fewer of the disintegrative political consequences now conventionally associated with a long war.

For East Central Europe, it is arguable that the even longer period 1912–45 was overshadowed by war to the point that the climate was of incessant warfare, whether actual or imminent. Most of Eastern Europe suffered longer periods of war than Western Europe: for example, for much of South Eastern Europe the two Balkan Wars introduced an extended experience of war lasting from 1912 to the Greek–Turkish debâcle of 1923; and for the Russian borderlands, war continued from 1914 to the end of the Civil War in late 1920. For so many of the people of the region the period was divisible into two periods of 'hot war', separated not by peace but by 'cold war', an interval dominated by the despairing realisation that the unexpectedly 'long war' of 1914–18 (extending for some from 1912 to 1923) had still not been long enough to decide the fundamental issues confronting Europe, which must accordingly be resolved by an early Second World War.

Within the overall wartime experience one can distinguish a range of complementary yet distinct features shared by the Balkan Wars, the First World War, the Russian Civil War and the Second World War, which acted as potent stimulants to nation-statehood across Central and Eastern Europe. An initial category is of subjective–psychological features promoting 'nation-states-of-mind'. Under this heading, twentieth-century war typically or commonly served as:

(1)   An *identity-reinforcer*, a bonding experience for 'proto-nations', crystallising an 'us-and-them' dichotomy and advancing the sense of a national 'community of fate'. This is in line with the so-called 'cohesion thesis', which contends that internal group solidarity is a sociational product of external armed conflict or its imminent threat.[8] The duration and intensity of the First and Second World Wars prompted an unprecedented scale of 'mobilisation' of the population, a state-sponsored *levée en masse* that increased the likelihood of a genuinely

national perception and experience of war. War acted as a national identity fixer, enhancing a sense of solidarity both in the exaltation of victory and especially in the collective trauma of defeat (like the Germans and Hungarians after the First World War).

(2)   An *ambition-raiser* for unsatisfied and/or recognised nations. 'First-wave' peoples such as Czechs, Poles and Ukrainians, for example, were effectively converted from autonomist to separatist nationalism by the First World War; 'second-wave' peoples such as Croats and Slovaks experienced their first tantalising and unforgettable taste of (perhaps pseudo) nation-statehood in the Second World War.

Another category of features may be described as objective–demographic phenomena promoting the political reality of nation-statehood. Under this heading too, twentieth-century war typically or commonly served as:

(1)   A *frontier-shifter*, furnishing pretexts for border adjustment either punitively imposed by external force (for example on Hungary after the First World War and Poland after the Second World War) or pursued by established states in the pursuit of territorial aggrandisement (for example Germany and Rumania in the First World War) irredentist or revanchist recovery (for instance Italy and Bulgaria in the First World War and Hungary in the Second World War) or indeed recovery *and* aggrandisement (Germany and the Soviet Union in the Second World War).

(2)   A *territorial homogeniser* promoting the ethnic 'purification' of claimed terrain through a variety of demographic processes. To employ the tasteless but striking metaphor favoured by the integral nationalists of the 1990s, ethnically heterogeneous 'dirty' territory had to be converted into ethnically homogeneous 'clean' settlement. To develop the now-conventional imagery, the phenomenon of 'ethnic cleansing' may be usefully (if imperfectly) sub-divided into 'self-cleansing' and 'scouring'.

'Self-cleansing', which suggests primarily individual, family or local initiative, included convenient *disaggregation* in mixed ethnic settlements and disengagement from joint community solidarity;

opportunistic *segregation* of ethnic communities into consolidated and concentrated settlement areas in the interests of self-protection (for example Hungarians in Slovakia and Transylvania in both World Wars); and expedient individual or family *relocation* (for instance the flight of Germans westward towards the end of the Second World War).

'Scouring', which necessarily involves the exercise of power by state authority in the interests of demographic engineering, included authority-promoted *transplantation* (for example Hungarian colonisation of reclaimed southern Slovakia after 1938 and northern Transylvania after 1940, Soviet deportation of Poles and Baltic peoples from their homelands to Siberia from 1939–40, and Nazi plantation of Baltic Germans in Poland from 1940); official *expulsion* of undesirable national groups (for example the forcible 'transfer' of Greeks from Turkey from 1920–3 and ejection of most Germans and many Hungarians from Czechoslovakia after 1945); and selective genocidal *liquidation* through the new technology of death of targeted minorities dehumanised by state propaganda to justify measures otherwise deemed 'inhumane' (most notoriously the 'holocausts' directed against Armenians by the Ottomans in the First World War and against Jews and Gypsies by the Nazis and *Ustasha* in the Second World War). War proved to be the supreme 'territorial homogeniser', sometimes accidentally or incidentally, but increasingly by design.

It is arguable that these four functions – catalogued here in broadly chronological order of historical occurrence – were not exclusive to the First and Second World Wars but were operative to some degree in nineteenth- as well as twentieth-century warefare. It may indeed be promptly conceded that frontier-shifting has always been both a reason for and a product of warfare. However the relative rarity as well as the short duration and limited scope of European wars over the century 1815–1914 undermines convincing comparisons with the 1914–45 period. Only the French Revolutionary-cum-Napoleonic quarter-century of virtually uninterrupted war from 1792–1815 may be perceived as comparable in nationalist impact with the thirty-year world war (parts one and two) between 1914 and 1945.

Although not unique to wartime, these functions were most widespread and uninhibited in war situations. And, as already suggested, they proved especially authoritative in wars that were prolonged, intense and involved an element of civil war as well as concerted resistance against a foreign foe or invader. The longer the war, the

more the combatants resembled each other and the dirtier the fight
(to break the stalemate and shorten the conflict by a decisive victory). For both established states and frustrated nationalities, the plea
of national security during a prolonged war supplied a mandate
legitimising the adoption of radical measures that would be morally
repugnant, financially prohibitive or politically unrealistic in peacetime. War emergency radicalised and accelerated peacetime policies
and both admitted and justified new extreme measures, from opportunistic frontier-shifting to merciless ethnic scouring.

EMPIRE, NATION-STATE AND THE FIRST WORLD WAR

The enduring impact of the two world wars on East Central Europe
may be gauged by comparing their divisive geopolitical legacies. In
the 'Versailles Europe' that was the composite geopolitical legacy of
the First World War and Paris Peace Settlement, nationalists were
divided by self-interest into two hostile camps.[9]

A beneficiary (or suprematist) view was adopted by majority
nationals (such as the Poles) and minority-but-dominant nationals
(such as the Czechs) in the new states, who argued that the dynastic
empires were just able to cope in peacetime but, unable to endure the
unprecedented extra strains imposed by the unexpectedly 'long war'
of 1914–18, collapsed under concerted nationalist upsurge in 1918.
By this interpretation the artificial concoctions of empire literally
'came unstuck' as the dynastic glue melted in the intense heat of
prolonged war. The First World War provided a welcome, eman-
cipatory *deus ex machina*, breaking the deadlock of peacetime
between the eventually irresistible force of nationalism and the
temporarily immovable object of empire. The First World War
served a unique historic purpose, dissolving resident dynastic empires, crystallising recently emerged nation-states and precipitating
new nation-states.

The opposition view advanced by the 'camp of the disadvant-
aged', composed of penalised states (such as Hungary, Germany
and, in a different sense, the Soviet Union) and unsatisfied minority
peoples (such as the Croats and Slovaks), was strikingly at odds with
this triumphalist chorus. No good could be expected from a postwar
settlement inspired by US President Woodrow Wilson, representing
an artificial political concoction opportunistically cobbled together
in brazen defiance of the principle of nation-statehood. That the

Versailles Settlement constituted a power-diktat of victors over vanquished, which blatantly breached its much-trumpeted principle of national self-determination, was irrefutable. The dynastic maxi-empires were replaced by 'successor states', which were either flagrantly larger or insultingly smaller than legitimate nation-states.

A nation attached to the winning side in the First World War was rewarded by expansion into a 'mini-empire' incorporating reluctant and apprehensive minorities. For example 29.2 per cent of the population of Romania was non-Romanian in 1930; 30.8 per cent of the population of Poland was non-Polish in 1921; and 35.9 per cent of the population of Czecho-Slovakia was neither Czech nor Slovak in 1930.[10]

A nation on the losing side in the First World War was punished by involuntary territorial shrinkage into a 'heartland state', leaving offensively substantial proportions of its conationals marooned as expatriates outside its reduced jurisdiction. For example, in 1930 30 per cent of Hungarians were resident outside Hungary, 16 per cent of Bulgarians outside Bulgaria and 11.5 per cent of Germans outside Germany.

Interwar East Central Europe was therefore irreconcilably divided by nationalist self-interest between the self-satisifed 'beneficiaries of Versailles', determined to retain the newly established (and therefore precarious) status quo, and the embittered 'victims of Versailles', dedicated to overturning the flawed, externally imposed geopolitical settlement of Versailles Europe.

EMPIRE, NATION-STATE AND THE SECOND WORLD WAR

In the 'Yalta Europe' that was the geopolitical legacy of the Second World War, nationalist opinion was self-interestedly united by general pessimism but divided by national circumstances and temperament into majority-catastrophist and minority-salvagist camps.

Endorsing the catastrophist view, all Versailles states and nations deprived of sovereignty either during or after the war regretted how independent Eastern Europe was first shamelessly partitioned (1939–41), then forcibly incorporated into the Nazi *Neuordnung* (1941–4), and finally occupied by Soviet military power (during 1945–5).

The tragic difference between the First and Second World Wars was that the First World War acted as the supreme solvent of empire, opening up opportunities for (if not automatically the establishment of) nation-states; the Second World War served as the enemy of the nation-state and patron of a new-style empire (with the Russian Civil War giving notice of the future role of the Second World War for most nation-states of East Central Europe by precipitating a refurbished empire over the ex-tsarist borderlands in the updated form of the Soviet Union).

For nationalists the First World War promoted a giant leap forward, the Russian Civil war and Second World War inflicted successive demoralising reversals of fortune. War was identified as the supreme agency of geopolitical shift, whether for good or ill. Therefore, regrettably, nationalists could applaud the First World War and bemoan the Second World War but – in a solidarity of misfortune – also felt constrained to resign themselves to waiting for a Third World War to effect any fundamental change in their political fortunes. If the First World War started the 'clock of history' for East Central Europe and the Second World War first stopped it and then set it back, only an apocalyptic Third World War could restart that clock of national history.

And yet, with the passage of time, a salvagist view emerged, an initially barely audible, minority judgement among nationalists who ventured to suggest that the Second World War was not an unmitigated disaster. If nation-statehood indeed constituted political paradise, the legacy of the Second World War for much of East Central Europe was not 'paradise lost' (necessitating nationalist commitment to a 'paradise regained') but rather 'paradise promised', for some quite sizeable crumbs of comfort could be gleaned from the general catastrophe.

Firstly, the Second World War selectively provided political opportunities unavailable in peacetime. 'Sub-nations' and –second-tier nations' failing to secure promotion after the First World War and frustrated by the peacetime establishment were offered another chance to stake a claim to nation-statehood during the Second World War. For instance, after the Bolshevik suppression of their first attempts at independence in 1920, Ukraine and Belorussia hoped for a degree of autonomy within the Nazi *Neuordnung* after 1941. Certain 'second-wave' nations were indeed favoured by the selective patronage of the *Neuordnung*, with Slovakia and Croatia permitted their first tastes of (pseudo) statehood (from 1939–44 and 1941–4 respectively). Despite their suppression over the last year of the Second World War, these chronologically ephemeral and politically disreputable states still constituted an ambition-raising experience that became indelibly imprinted on the collective memory (and further destabilised postwar Czechoslovakia and Yugoslavia).

Secondly, the Second World War effected (by the most conservative estimate) a halving of the minorities problem. Scouring through liquidation claimed, most notoriously, over 4.5 million East European Jews (or 61 per cent of the prewar total). Scouring also claimed almost 200 000 East European Gypsies (or 20 per cent of the prewar total). Even more significant for demographic 'simplification' or 'rationalisation' was the German exodus. A combination of self-cleansing (in the form of expedient relocation from 1934–44, which filtered almost one million Germans westward to 'Greater Germany') and scouring (in the shape of mass expulsion from 1945–7, wich siphoned nearly 9.5 million Germans westward to 'West Germany') effected a cumulative collapse in the diaspora of German minorities across the region. Almost 11 million Germans were physically displaced – to say nothing of those killed![11]

That the geopolitical losers in the traumatic ethnic-cleansing experience of the Second World War were generally national minorities may be judged from the fact that, in numerical terms, the total proportion of minorities in the region fell from about one quarter of the population of Versailles Europe to between one eighth and one fourteenth of the population of Yalta Europe (depending on whether Croats and Slovaks are regarded as minorities within, respectively, Yugoslavia and Czechoslovakia). By homogenising state territory at the expense of (especially) the German, Jewish and Gypsy diasporas, the Second World War reduced the overall incidence of national minorities in East Central Europe to a level that approached comparability with that in Western Europe.

Thirdly, the Second World War endorsed the retention of the right of prewar states to national jurisdiction. If national minorities were often losers, national majorities usually turned out winners. Notwithstanding frequently appalling wartime losses (particularly for the Poles and Serbs), nations with recognised pre-Second-World-War statehood still emerged as political victors. Although all the independent eastern states of Versailles Europe (bar Albania and Yugoslavia) were deliberately demoted to what amounted to colonial status in Yalta Europe, not one lost its right to territorial jurisdiction, whether as a 'people's democracy' in the newly reduced East Central Europe or as a 'union republic' within the expanded Soviet Union. The fundamental geopolitical matrix established after the First World

War was confirmed by the victors of the Second World War. In this rare – perhaps unique – respect, Yalta Europe 'restored' Versailles Europe after the alternative geopolitical dispositions of the wartime *Neuordnung*.

Thus, even while recriminations reverberated about whether the individual nations and states had been innocently crucified by malevolent and irresistible external *force majeure* or bore some collective responsibility for their common fate, it was acknowledged that three substantial items of political flotsam had been salvaged from the wartime sinking (or shipwreck) of independent East Central Europe.

WAR AND THE ZONING OF EAST CENTRAL EUROPE

The differential impact of the Second World War had the effect of deepening the division of the region earlier precipitated by the First World War into three distinct geopolitical 'zones'.

The largest zone was the expanded Soviet Union. Continuing the role of the Russian Civil War, the Second World War enabled the Soviet Union-in-Europe to advance territorially westward, on this occasion at the expense of all of Estonia, Latvia and Lithuania together with northern East Prussia and the most easterly properties of Poland, Czechoslovakia (Ruthenia) and Romania (Bessarabia/ Moldavia and northern Bukovina).[12] The Second World War thereby compounded the multinational complexion of the Soviet Union by transforming the 'lesser union' fringing Versailles Europe into a 'greater union' of unprecedented scale penetrating Yalta Europe.

The newest recruits (or conscripts) to the union were singled out for special treatment. The Romanians of the newly concocted Moldavian Union Republic were scoured after 1945 by the trans-plantation of up to 10 per cent of their indigenous population to other regions of the Soviet Union (in conjunction with a state-sponsored, large-scale influx of Russian, Ukrainian and Belorussian 'colonists') to reduce the Romanian demographic hegemony within Bessarabia/ Moldavia.

Even more targeted were ex-sovereign states swallowed whole by the Soviet territorial advance. During 1940–1 and post-1944, Esto-nia, Latvia and Lithuania were 'imperialised' by a Soviet programme of ethnic scouring that combined the deportation of indigenous nationalist cadres to central Asia with a mass, state-promoted influx of Russian 'colonists' into the Baltic 'people democracies'. The proportion of Lithuanians in Lithuania dipped by 4.6 per cent (from 83.9 per cent in 1923 to 79.3 per cent in 1959). The proportion of Latvians in Latvia fell 11.3 per cent (from 73.3 per cent in 1930 to 62.0 per cent in 1959). Most dramatically, the proportion of Estonians in Estonia, the second-closest to a nation-state among all the interwar successor states, dropped 13.6 per cent (from 88.2 per cent in 1934 to 74.6 per cent in 1959). The avowed objective of the 'reunification programme' – to employ the contemporary Soviet jargon – was to shift all three ex-sovereign states away from ethnic homogeneity and nation-statehood towards integration within the socialist, ostensibly supranational Soviet Union.

Yugoslavia all by itself comprised the second zone. Like the earlier Russian Civil War, the Yugoslav Civil War combined local resistance to foreign invasion, separatist attempts to secure new nation-states (under foreign patronage) and ferocious, almost internecine civil strife. Yugoslav casualties incurred in resisting German and Italian invaders were more than matched by casualties incurred in the war between the nations of Yugoslavia. The barbarous attempts of the *Ustasha* regime to scour Croatia of Serb, Gypsy and Jewish populations after 1941 provoked savage reprisals from 1945–6. During the 1939–47 period Yugoslavia lost some 286 000 Germans through both self-cleansing and scouring, together with 58 000 Jews and 40 000 Gypsies through genocidal scouring. And yet, in practice, the effect of the Second World War was not only to decimate three of the smallest national minorities but to debilitate the two most populous nations of Yugoslavia: the Serbs and Croats together dropped a critical 12 per cent from 77 per cent of the total state population in 1931 to only 65 per cent in 1953. Overall the demographic damage inflicted on the smallest minorities was echoed by the casualties sustained by the largest nations, to the advantage of the 'middling' minorities (most notably the Slovenes, Albanians and Turks). The Second World War thereby rendered the Yugoslavia of Yalta Europe less of a Balkan mini-empire than it had been in Versailles Europe but increased its demographic (and therefore political) instability.

The final zone consisted of 'classic' East Central Europe. The Second World War paradoxically both precipitated a Soviet super-empire (to which most previously recognised states of the region were subordinated) and, through differential demographic damage and great-power border adjustment, shifted all the mini-empires of the interwar period (except Yugoslavia) much closer to genuine nation-statehood. Just as the First World War had acted as the crucial solvent on the pre-1914 maxi-empires, so the Second World War acted as the critical solvent on the pre-1939 mini-empires.

Of the Allied-favoured mini-empires of Versailles Europe, all but Yugoslavia were transformed by the crucible of the Second World War. Romania was affected least but still became 16.2 per cent more Romanian (from 71.9 per cent Romanian in 1930 to 88.1 per cent in 1956). Czechoslovakia moved from 66.2 per cent Czech and Slovak in 1930 to 94.3 per cent Czech and Slovak by 1970, a 28.1 per cent increase that – ominously – rendered the Czech–Slovak dichotomy starker than ever before: postwar Bohemia and Moravia became sufficiently ethnically homogeneous to approximate a (possible) future Czech nation-state; though retaining some characteristics of a mini-empire, postwar Slovakia made considerable progress towards homogeneity (with non-Slovaks in Slovakia dropping from 32.9 per cent of the population in 1937 to only 13.4 per cent in 1950). The greatest shift was registered by Poland, which increased from only 68.9 per cent Polish in 1931 to 98.5 per cent by 1950 (according to official figures), or from only 61 per cent in 1931 to 92 per cent by 1950 (according to foreign calculations); by either set of statistics Poland increased its ethnic 'Polishness' by 29–31 per cent as a result of the Second World War. Even the Allied-penalised 'heartland states' of Versailles Europe made (necessarily modest) moves in the same direction: Hungary went from 92.1 per cent Hungarian in 1930 to 98.5 per cent Hungarian by 1970, a rise of 6.4 per cent; and Bulgaria edged up 0.8 per cent from 85.6 per cent Bulgarian in 1934 to 86.4 per cent Bulgarian in 1946. Not a single state of East Central Europe emerged from the Second World War without a demographically reduced internal minority problem.

The incidence of external minorities was also broadly reduced, albeit far less uniformly and authoritatively. Romania and Albania proved exceptions to the general rule: the loss of Bessarabia to the expanded Soviet Union in 1940–1 and from the end of the Second World War (to be reconstituted as the Moldavian Union Republic) substantially increased the proportion of ethnic Romanians outside 'Yalta Romania' in comparison with 'Versailles Romania'; and the exceptionally high birth rate and relatively low casualty rate characteristic of the Albanians in the Kosovo and western Macedonian regions of Yugoslavia increased the proportion of ethnic Albanians outside Albania during the Second World War. It is also true that expatriate Hungarian minorities in Yugoslavia, Rumania and Czecho-slovakia, and expatriate Turkish minorities in Yugoslavia and Bulgaria persisted at a disconcertingly high postwar level. But, as the German exodus highlighted, the overall trend in East Central Europe (excepting only Romania and Albania) was undeniably that the proportion of expatriate external minorities was in decline: although the national diasporas had not disappeared in Yalta Europe, they were reduced in comparison with the levels in Versailles Europe.

All available statistics are open to dispute in detail, whether on technical and therefore politically innocent grounds or (more often) on administrative and therefore politically sinister grounds. But although the scale of demographic change is impossible to pin down precisely, the direction of overall shift is irrefutable. According to both crucial demographic criteria, East Central Europe was moving towards state homogenisation. The significant reduction of both internal and external minorities meant that, although their jurisdiction was collectively (and in most cases individually) smaller than before and no longer in practice sovereign, the states of East Central Europe survived the Second World War to shift closer to demographic nation-statehood than ever before.

WAR AS PROMOTER OF THE NATION-STATE

To conclude, twentieth-century war has proved more ambivalent in geopolitical impact than at first appears. Authoritative rumours of the imminent demise of empire current at the start of the twentieth century turned out to be greatly exaggerated: multinational or multiethnic political entities proved remarkably resilient, with the process of war apparently changing only the geopolitical number and size of empires. Both world wars, effectively successive stages in a semicontinuous war experience, simultaneously strained statehood whilst enhancing nationhood. The First World War was less of a victory and the Second World War was less of a defeat for nationalism than commonly preached (especially by indigenous nationalist historians of East Central Europe).

Within the broad context of a strategically partitioned Europe, the Second World War bequeathed not only a militarily zoned Central Europe but a geopolitically zoned Eastern Europe. For Yugoslavia and the expanded Soviet Union, the Second World War inflicted almost unimaginable damage to both personnel and matériel whilst reinforcing their geopolitical predicaments as mismatched but twin imperial dinosaurs in a postwar era of galloping global decolonisation.

Within a half-continent over which first dynastic maxi-empire, then nationalist mini-empire and finally socialist super-empire prevailed, twentieth-century war perversely propelled 'prehistoric' East Central Europe further up the long winding road towards the 'historic' achievement of demographic nation-statehood. Although nationalist business remained tantalisingly uncompleted, the keenly anticipated destination (or destiny) of nation-statehood at last came into sight: with their long-term prospects cumulatively promoted by both the First and Second World Wars, the ex-independent states of East Central Europe were converted into genuine candidate nation-states, effectively nation-states-in-waiting within an over-arching Soviet 'last empire' living on borrowed time.

Notes and References

1. Gellner's pithy definition constitutes the arresting first sentence of his *Nations and Nationalism* (Oxford: Blackwell, 1983), p. 1.
2. Georg Wilhelm Friedrich Hegel, *Lectures on the Philosophy of World History: Introduction* (Cambridge: Cambridge University Press, 1975), pp. 96, 134.
3. Johann Caspar Bluntschli, 'Die nationale Staatenbildung und der moderne deutsche Staat', quoted in Peter Alter, *Nationalism* (London: Edward Arnold, 1989), p. 95.
4. Max Weber also quoted in Alter, *Nationalism*, p. 92.
5. For the geopolitical partition of pre-First World War Eastern Europe, see Martin Gilbert, *Recent History Atlas: 1860 to 1960* (London: Weidenfeld and Nicolson, 1977), maps 1, 5, 6, 7, 8, 13, 22.
6. For example, Frederick Hertz, *Nationality in History and Politics* (New York: Humanities Press Inc, 1944), pp. 217–23.
7. Anthony D. Smith, 'War and Ethnicity: the role of warfare in the formation, self-images and cohesion of ethnic communities', *Ethnic and Racial Studies*, vol. 4, no 4 (October 1981), pp. 390–1.
8. A classic exposition of the 'cohesion thesis' is G. Simnel, *Conflict, and the Web of Group-Affiliation* (London: Macmillan, 1964).
9. See Gilbert, *Recent History Atlas*, for the impact on the geopolitical cartography and demography of Eastern Europe of the First World War (maps 32, 34, 36, 37, 38), Russian Civil War (maps 37, 39, 40, 45) and Versailles Settlement (maps 42, 43, 45, 46, 57, 61).
10. Unless otherwise indicated, all census statistics are cited from Stephan M. Horak (ed.), *Eastern European National Minorities, 1919/1980: a handbook* (Littleton, Co: Libraries Unlimited, 1985), *passim*, or Raymond Pearson,

National Minorities in Eastern Europe, 1848–1945 (London: Macmillan, 1983), chapter 6.

11.   For statistics on the demographic impact of the Second World War see Eugene M. Kulischer, *Europe on the Move: War and Population Changes, 1914–1947* (New York: Columbia University Press, 1948), and Joseph B. Schechtman, *European Population Transfers, 1939–1945* (Ithaca, NY: Cornell University Press, 1946).

12.   For changes in geopolitical cartography effected by the Second World War, see Gilbert, *Recent History Atlas*, maps 53, 56, 58, 59, 60, 64, 72, 81, 86, 88, 89, 93, 94.

4 Bulgarian Nationalism: Permutations on the Past[1]
Duncan M. Perry

INTRODUCTION

Nationalism in the nineteenth-century Balkans stimulated periodic patriotic resistance to, and insurrections against, Ottoman rule. In their turn, Serbia, Greece, Romania and Bulgaria each broke away from the Ottoman centre, achieving at least autonomy. Once this happened the nationalism that motivated state building was transformed into an ideology that promoted ethnic and religious differentiation among peoples, separating majority and minority populations and giving majority peoples the central role in society. It also became a significant factor behind aggressive irredentist behaviour.

Bulgaria, a land that is largely ethnically homogeneous, confronts two sub-species of nationalism: xenophobic and irredentist (territorial) nationalism. The distinction between the two is clear, but in practice the feelings motivating them are often merged in the popular mind. The former results from a complex set of factors, in large part evolved from long-held resentments stemming from the 500-year heritage of Ottoman rule. The latter has been born of Bulgaria's short history as a state and its yearning for, and failure to gain and hold, title to lands claimed by Bulgarians, notably Macedonia.

Nascent Bulgarian nationalism served to stimulate the creation of a national identity. The first of three stages in the development of Bulgarian nationalism came to an end with the creation of the principality in 1879; a direct outcome of the Russo–Turkish War of 1877–8, which was concluded by bilateral treaty at San Stefano in 1878. This agreement ceded to Bulgaria much of the Ottoman central Balkans. Three months later, at the Berlin Congress, the great powers both legitimised Bulgaria, by making it a principality under the Ottoman sultan, and circumscribed it, reducing it to a rump state north of the Balkan Mountains. Here began the second and longest phase of Bulgarian nationalism, an era in which national sentiments were primarily territorially directed. Bulgarians remained largely preoccupied with irredentist considerations throughout the period

41

that ended with the Second World War – and made some gains, notably Eastern Rumelia in 1885 and southern Dobruja in 1940. But it also suffered the humiliation of having occupied Macedonia three times, only to relinquish it each time.

The year 1944 marked the onset of the third phase of Bulgarian nationalism, one wherein the state manipulated territorial nationalism for purposes of national unity and foreign policy gains, and from time to time also stimulated xenophobic concerns, usually in the form of minority assimilation programmes, for the same reasons – and to deflect attention from failed government policies.

THE DEVELOPMENT OF BULGARIAN NATIONALISM

The lands of what is modern Bulgaria, settled by Slavs in the sixth and seventh centuries and invaded by Turkic Bulgars in the seventh, became a loosely organised medieval kingdom in the ninth century. At this point Bulgars disappeared, having been assimilated by the sedentary Slavs, leaving only their name.

Bulgaria had its share of rulers who prosecuted wars to expand holdings and secure borderlands. Perhaps the best known were Khan Krum (803–14), Tsar Simeon (893–927), Tsar Samuel (986–1014) and the Aseniads (1180s–1280s). Following this era of conquest, Bulgaria slipped into obscurity as it was taken over by the Byzantine Empire in the eleventh and twelfth centuries. Invaded by the Ottomans in the fourteenth century, it was they who remained Bulgaria's suzerains, at least titularly, into the twentieth century.

Ottoman rulers employed what was called the 'millet' system to classify their subjects, using religious affiliation, not ethnic or national identities. For ethnic Bulgarians and ethnic Turks, as well as other Muslims in Bulgaria, religion was historically the single most important point of differentiation and remains so today. Religion helped to shape the national consciousness. A Bulgarian national consciousness, however vague, seems to have existed at least among a few before the nineteenth century.

The year 1762 is cited as a watershed in Bulgarian history for it was then that a Bulgarian monk resident on Mount Athos, Father Paisii of Hildendar (1722–98?), 'lit the flame of passionate nationalism'[2] by completing his *Slavianobulgska istoriia* (History of the Bulgarian Slavs). Paisii, driven by a fervent Bulgarian national consciousness, extolled Bulgaria's past glories and railed at those Bulgarians who had become hellenised. His history, while suffering many flaws from a scholarly point of view, seems to have had major impact over time. Initially circulated by apostles and through manuscript versions of the work, it was not actually published until 1844.

With the advent of the 'national revival' (roughly 1830–70), Bulgaria's metaphorical awakening to a glorious medieval history, and to a culture and experience shared among brethren throughout Ottoman Bulgaria, Thrace and Macedonia, after some 500 years under the sultan, gradually gave flight to a national consciousness, then nationalism. This was manifested in such developments as the founding of schools where lessons were taught in Bulgarian, the first in 1835, and the subsequent opening of reading rooms in many towns. These were a unique Bulgarian cultural institution where people gathered to read and discuss current affairs.

The seeds of nationalism were broadcast by the new class of merchants and traders that Bulgaria spawned. They gradually supplanted Greeks and Jews, who traditionally controlled economic activities. Guilds formed and it was these organisations that fostered Bulgarian culture and education. From their efforts sprang an intelligentsia, many of whose members were educated abroad in such places as Belgrade, Odessa, Paris and Constantinople. With the rise of this small, educated class, change – linguistic, cultural, economic and political – began. Soon revolutionary leaders emerged, first and foremost the expatriates Georgi Stoikov Rakovski (1824–67) and Liuben Karavelov (1834–79).

It was the intelligentsia – teachers, students, priests and others – who guided the peasantry toward a national consciousness based on cultural and linguistic similarities as well as on shared history. And the task was made easier by virtue of the fact that most Bulgarian peasants lived in isolated villages wherein they had preserved their language and heritage. They were thus a resource waiting to be tapped, an army waiting to be trained and mobilised by those with nationalist agendas.

The national revival helped to inform the Bulgarian Slavs of what they were, and perhaps more importantly, what they were not. It served to differentiate ethnic Bulgarians from ethnic Turks, the remnants and reminders of the Ottoman domination that had delivered, according to popular thought, only darkness and injustice. Of course this new way of seeing one's self also set apart Christians from Muslims.

The nascent Bulgarian nationalist movement first directed its fer-

vour against the Greek Orthodox patriarchate, the more accessible of
the two forces stifling the growth of national identity – the second
being the Ottoman Empire.[3] Given that the lives of Bulgarian peasants were strongly tied to their faith and that it was the Church that
served to provide a potent common denominator among Bulgarian
Christians, nationalist actions were first channeled toward replacing
the Greek church with a Bulgarian one. The patriarchate had controlled Bulgarians' religious life since the 1760s and Greek Orthodox
clergy were often less than sympathetic to their Slav parishioners, to
whom they often ministered in Greek. With Russian help, Bulgarian
intellectuals pressed the Ottoman sultan to establish a separate
Bulgarian-rite church, the Exarchate, in 1870. L. S. Stavrianos rightly
calls this 'the first great victory of Bulgarian nationalism'.[4] It was
certainly a driving force in the Bulgarian principality's creation eight
years later, for the Exarchate quickly achieved ecclesiastical dominance over at least 80 per cent of the population and gave a common
weave to Bulgarian national consciousness. The Bulgarian Exarchate
Church quickly became a key to facilitating a Bulgarian identity and
promoting education in what were to become Bulgarian lands and in
Ottoman Macedonia. Through it, many Slavs found their Bulgarian
identity and turned their attention to agitating for separation from
the Muslim and theocratic Ottoman Empire.

Life in the Ottoman Balkans was insecure in the eighteenth and
nineteenth centuries as central authority broke down and local bar-
ons, war lords and bandits competed to fill the vacuum. Bulgarian
nationalists brought matters to a head in April 1876 by instigating an
uprising, inspired by the then ongoing revolt in Bosnia–Herzegovina.
It was intended to provoke the great powers into liberating Bulgaria
from Turkey and indirectly it succeeded. Thanks to bloody outrages
committed by Turkish irregulars and the associated international
attention the attacks attracted, following the revolt Russia had a
pretext to declare war on Turkey. This was launched by Tsar Alexander II (r. 1855–81) after an international conference in Constantinople in 1877 had failed to yield Ottoman reforms.

The treaty that ended the Russo–Turkish War (1877–8) was signed
in the village of San Stefano on 3 March 1878. It was a bilateral
agreement that created an autonomous Bulgaria, nominally under
Ottoman suzerainty. The new Bulgarian state, arguably a manifestation of growing Bulgarian national sentiment, embraced not only
Bulgaria, but also Thrace and Macedonia. Within three months this
treaty was nullified and replaced by another signed by all the great

powers in Berlin. 'Great Bulgaria', as San Stefano Bulgaria was called, was an enterprise that Greece and Serbia, backed by Austria–Hungary and Great Britain, found unacceptable. It made Bulgaria the dominant power in the Balkans and gave Russia, Bulgaria's patron, much potential influence over peninsular affairs, including the possibility of controlling access to the Black Sea.

When Bulgaria achieved autonomy within the Ottoman Empire in 1878 it gained a large measure of freedom, and with it a series of problems concerning ethnic and religious minorities. On the one hand the constitution promulgated in 1879 did not recognise any legal status for non-Orthodox, non-Slav Bulgarians.[5] Instead it conferred citizenship on all Bulgarians and thus no special rights were developed for ethnic and religious minorities. Ethnic Turks, defined by culture, language and confession, lost the privileged position they had held under Ottoman theocratic administration. Orthodox Christian Bulgarian Slavs, the numerically superior population, took up the controls of state. Following the Ottoman defeat in 1878, those ethnic Turks who chose not to emigrate were tolerated, 'but their rights were grudgingly given, inconsistently applied, and often arbitrarily withdrawn'.[6] 'Until 1945', wrote J. F. Brown, 'ethnic Turks and Bulgarians lived in one country but two separate worlds'.[7]

The Berlin Treaty's reversal of the Treaty of San Stefano and the concomitant destruction of Great Bulgaria was, and still is, Bulgaria's greatest irredentist sore. It was one that Bulgarians sought to cure by reincorporating the lost territories – and they partially succeeded. Bulgaria united with a large segment of Thrace, called Eastern Rumelia, in 1885, then weathered the abdication of its first prince, Alexander of Battenberg (r. 1879–86) as a consequence of Russian interference in Bulgaria's internal affairs in 1886, without losing territory. In 1887 Stefan Stambolov, nineteenth-century Bulgaria's most important political figure, saw to the selection of another prince, Ferdinand of Sax-Coburg-Gotha (r. 1887–1918), over Russian objections. Symbolically then, 1878 marked the transition from state-building nationalism to a preoccupation with irredentist nationalism, a stage that was to last until 1944.

The union of Bulgaria with Eastern Rumelia was an important milestone of Bulgarian territorial nationalism. It was prompted in large measure by Bulgarian nationalists in Eastern Rumelia seeking, in effect, to reinstate the Treaty of San Stefano, at least insofar as Thrace was concerned. Their efforts were rewarded by reluctant great-power approval of the union.

The Bulgarian principality was to gain full independence in 1908 when Prince Ferdinand, backed by Austria–Hungary, declared himself tsar. In the Balkan Wars of 1912–13 Bulgaria at first allied with other Balkan states against the Ottomans in a war meant in part to liberate Macedonia. When it became clear that Bulgaria would not acquire title to the territories it sought, Ferdinand audaciously declared war on his former allies. Turkey joined the fray against Bulgaria, which was beaten ignominiously, forfeiting much of the Macedonian prize it so earnestly sought. Bulgaria joined the central powers during the First World War, largely to regain, but it backed the losing side.

Instability and unrest followed Bulgaria's defeat and agrarian Prime Minister Alexander Stamboliiski, who sought to reform the economic and political scene, was brutally assassinated in 1923 by members of the Internal Macedonian Revolutionary Organisation (IMRO), in part because of his advocacy of rapprochement with the new Yugoslav state, which possessed about 40 per cent of geographic Macedonia. Conditions continued to deteriorate, and in 1934 King Boris III (r. 1918–43) established a dictatorship in the wake of a successful military campaign launched against IMRO, whose factions justified political in fighting with the holy banner of Macedonia and threatened political stability.

In the Second World War Bulgaria, again allied with Germany, reoccupied Macedonia, and once more was among the defeated. With the aid of the Soviet army, communists took over the country in 1944 and remained in power until 1990. During that period both irredentist nationalism and xenophobic nationalism were at play. The government used the Macedonian question as a bargaining chip in its affairs with Yugoslavia and xenophobic nationalism as a weapon in its arsenal against Turkey, as well as a mask for its policy failures.

THE BULGARIAN NATIONAL IDENTITY

Bulgaria's national image has been shaped by its history. Militarily it lost not only the Balkan Wars (it was victorious in the first but lost the decisive second), but also the First and Second World Wars, having won only the Serbo–Bulgarian War of 1885, an important and heroic effort. In recent times Bulgaria has reputedly been a haven for terrorists, a conduit for drugs and weapons, a manufacturer of arms for Third World dictators, and allegedly the sponsor of several well-publicised murder attempts, at least one of which was fatal, that of BBC commentator Georgi Markov in 1978.

Bulgaria's history has frequently been unstable and violent: witness the coup that ousted Prince Alexander in 1886 and the assassinations of Stefan Stambolov in 1895, Dimitur Petkov in 1907 – both former prime ministers – and Alexander Stamboliiski in 1923, a serving prime minister. The interwar years of instability, aggravated by warring rival Macedonian organisations, did the country no credit, nor did the authoritarian regime of Boris III. The purges, arbitrary rule, labour camps, assimilation campaigns, and more, of the communist years served further to tarnish its name.

But this is not to say that Bulgaria has not produced heroes, nearly all of whom were active before the communist era, mostly during the period of the revival, during liberation, or in the years immediately thereafter. Most of them died at the hands of the Turks in the national struggle – Vasil Levski, the best known of the charismatic revolutionary leaders, was hanged in 1873; Hristo Botev, another important revolutionary figure, died alongside most of his band in a skirmish with Ottoman forces in 1876; and Gotse Delchev, an early leader of IMRO (who is claimed both by Bulgarians and Macedonians) was killed in a clash with Turks in 1903. Each was felled in defence of the nation. Myths have grown up around these and other heroes, making them larger than life *figures*. They became part of the nation-building process and were integral to the affirmation of Bulgarianness. The fact that most died in battle as part of the struggle for Bulgarian (or Macedonian) liberation, and usually at the hands of the Turks, further enhanced their status.

The signing of the Treaty of San Stefano on 3 March 1878 and its reversal at Berlin served to inflict a wound in the hearts of many Bulgarians that festers to this day, as they claim Macedonia to be western Bulgaria and Macedonians as Bulgarians who speak an amusing and strange dialect. That this issue is not dead can be seen by the fact that 3 March was officially made the Bulgarian national holiday in 1989, and it remains so today. Moreover, although Bulgaria was the first state to recognise the sovereignty of the Republic of Macedonia in 1992, like the communists after 1956 it refused to acknowledge that the Slavs of this nascent country possessed a distinct nationality called Macedonian.

The two uprisings that occupy pride of place in the nationalist histories of Bulgaria are the April uprising of 1876 and the Ilinden–Preobrazhenski uprising of 1903. The first led to Russian intervention and liberation. The second was a calculated act to foment revolt in Ottoman Macedonia before the IMRO collapsed. The glorification of such failures even today stimulates animosities between Bulgarians and Turks, while Ilinden also remains a symbol of unredeemed Macedonia.

The xenophobic features of Bulgarian nationalism cloaks ethnic and religious discrimination in patriotic wrappings, placing homogeneity and the fatherland above all – and the fatherland is defined as the *heimat* of the majority, which seeks to ensure that all non-members conform, assimilate, leave or die out. It denies and denigrates the rights of others, to paraphrase William Echikson.[8] This brand of nationalism in Bulgaria is grounded in a national inferiority complex, which has it that the era of Ottoman dominion was a blot on Bulgarian history, a period during which time stood still and the people were oppressed and forced to remain unenlightened.[9] Thus they were unable to undergo the transformations experienced by Western Europe, notably an industrial revolution, or so goes the logic. Such pronouncements seem to be both an excuse for Bulgarian national failures and traits, and a rallying cry to explain all that is evil in the land and heritage.

COMMUNIST BULGARIA: TURKISH ASSIMILATION AND EMIGRATION

The communist credo was that all citizens of Bulgaria were Bulgarians; the concept of ethnic or religious minorities was not recognised constitutionally (for statistics of national minorities see Table 4.1). When introduced, communism appealed to many ethnic Turks (Bulgaria's second largest population group after ethnic Bulgarians), but they quickly discovered that xenophobic nationalism was masquerading as international communism. The communist recruitment effort and associated ideology was meant to enforce a homogenisation process where minority identities were submerged in Bulgarianness. Some 150 000 Turks therefore left Bulgaria instead of subscribing.

Growing xenophobia led to the withdrawal of those attributes of the society that enabled Turks to maintain a separate identity. The observance of Islam was discouraged and nearly all mosques were closed following the communist takeover. In the realm of education, Turkish-language schools disappeared during the 1970s, as did Turkish language courses in non-Turkish schools. Turkish literature was

Table 4.1   Ethnic composition of Bulgaria

Ethnic group	1992 Census[1] (number)	(%)	1987 Estimates[2] (number)	(%)
Bulgarians	7 271 608	85.8	7 643 519	85.3
Turks	822 253	9.7	761 664	8.5
Roma (Gypsies)	287 732	3.4	232 979	2.6
Other	91 131	1.1	322 587	3.6
Total[3]	8 472 724	100.0	8 960 749	100.0

Notes:

1. In 1992 Bulgaria conducted a national census intended to show accurately the ethnic and religious composition of the citizenry. The results are hotly disputed because of alleged irregularities in the census-taking process, which in turn makes the information suspect. Such problems notwithstanding, Bulgarians constitute the large majority, while ethnic Turks make up the largest minority population. The 'Other' category includes Bulgarian Muslims (also called Pomaks), Tatars, Vlachs, Gagauzi and Macedonians. The 1992 data is derived from *Standart*, 27 April 1993.
2. Census statistics between 1965 and 1992 provided no information about national minorities. The 1985 census indicated that there were 8 948 649 inhabitants of Bulgaria. The figures provided here reflect estimates computed by the Central Intelligence Agency; see *The World Factbook 1987*, p. 35, cited in Richard F. Staar, *Communist Regimes in Eastern Europe*, 5th ed. (Stanford: Hoover Institution Press, 1988), p. 54.
3. Comparing official census statistics between 1985 and 1992 indicates a population decline of 475 925 or 0.053 per cent. This decline results from a combination of factors, including a declining birth rate among ethnic Bulgarians and the emigration of ethnic Turks to Turkey, along with the economic emigration of Bulgarians to the West.

eliminated from the national school curriculum. The Turcological faculty of Sofia University was closed in 1974, and in 1985 the last newspaper in Turkish stopped publishing. In short, over time a concerted effort was made, using state security agencies where necessary, to transform the Muslim population of Bulgaria into 'Bulgarians'. The official position was that there were no Turks in Bulgaria, only Bulgarians whose forebears converted to Islam under pressure – the state was simply redressing the error.[10] Communist officials failed to take account of the fact that national consciousness is not an empirically provable phenomenon, but rather something based on feelings, which in turn are a result of communicated and accumulated experiences. They could not be mandated out of existence, as was to be proved later.

When large-scale collectivisation got underway in the early 1950s, many Turks were reluctant to participate – they possessed excellent lands, especially in the southern Dobruja. The Bulgarian government pressed them to emigrate, thereby relinquishing their land. The government announced that as many as 250 000 ethnic Turks wanted to move to Turkey, but the Turkish authorities, unable to accommodate the anticipated influx of refugees, closed their borders and threatened to bring the matter before the United Nations. After a bilateral accommodation, in all about 150 000 were accepted by Turkey in 1950–1.[11] In the face of sustained adverse world opinion, the Bulgarian government gradually moved away from this policy and granted ethnic Turks cultural autonomy. Later, however, in the 1970s, it initiated assimilation campaigns aimed at purifying Bulgaria – Turks, Pomaks and Gypsies became targets.

The issue of Turkish emigration receded until 1984, although there were signs of a policy change in 1982 and 1983, when another campaign to eradicate cultural differences between ethnic Bulgarians and ethnic Turks was launched. This programme was decidedly unsuccessful, so the Bulgarian government issued a decree in December 1984 stating that all Muslims were required to change their Turkish and Arabic-sounding names to Bulgarian-sounding names. Speaking Turkish in public was forbidden, wearing Turkish-style clothing was outlawed.

During the first year of this campaign, which was not repealed until December 1989 and about which the government officially said little, a number of Muslims, perhaps as many as 100, died from beatings and attacks by police – others were imprisoned, internally exiled or harassed for failing to change their names. Between 1985 and 1988 Turks organised various protests and petition drives against the government's action.[12] The strategy was simple. In using violence and the threat of violence and by denying basic human rights to Turks and other targeted groups, the government hoped to coerce conformity. The opposite was achieved however. Of course, officially, those who changed their names to Slavic-sounding ones did so 'voluntarily'. Ethnic Turks gradually came to identify more closely with Islam and Turkey, and less with a Bulgarian ethnos.

In the early months of 1985 the government labelled the reports about forced name-changes 'disinformation' intended to damage Bulgarian–Turkish relations. The Bulgarian authorities went on the offensive and the minister of internal affairs, Dimitûr Stoianov, claimed that

> all of our fellow-countrymen who reverted to their Bulgarian names are Bulgarians. They are the bone of the bone and flesh of the flesh of the Bulgarian nation. Although the Bulgarian national consciousness of some of them may still be blurred, they are the same Bulgarian flesh and blood; they are children of the Bulgarian nation; they were forcibly torn away and now they are coming back home. There are no Turks in Bulgaria. The issue is closed.[13]

Assimilation activities persisted.

OPPOSITION TO COMMUNIST ASSIMILATION POLICY

The Independent Association for the Defence of Human Rights was founded in 1988 to defend Muslim rights. Membership grew rapidly. Three other groups were founded in the first half of 1989, each with the objective of pressing for an end to human-rights abuses in Bulgaria, especially those perpetrated against Turks, and to fight the assimilation programme of the government.[14]

By late summer/early autumn 1989 some non-Muslim citizens were quietly subverting the government campaign, which by then included circulating petitions in workplaces for worker endorsement of government actions. Few workers actually signed. Many people, especially among the intelligentsia, regarded the assimilation programme as a national embarrassment, if not a national tragedy, though few protested. Other people roundly favoured it as a way to rid the state of a major source of tension and/or a means by which to earn a profit from Turkish misfortunes. The majority of the Bulgarian population stood passively by, with many afraid of state retribution in the event of protest and thus de facto supporting the assimilation.

In May 1989 Muslim protests intensified against Bulgarian government policy, stimulated by the efforts of the Independent Association for the Defence of Human Rights. Turkish demonstrations and hunger strikes followed. Reports were heard of police beating

demonstrators, then deporting some to Turkey. Officially such demonstrators were called extremists and were accused of causing
'riots'.[15] Between three and thirty people were killed that May as an
unpublicised martial law was imposed in regions where Turks re-
sided in eastern Bulgaria. Turkish radio and television were jammed.
By the end of the month as many as 350 ethnic Turks had been
expelled from Bulgaria and sent to Vienna. On 29 May 1989 Todor
Zhivkov, Bulgaria's chief of state, made a dramatic nationwide
television broadcast in which he looked to Ankara to accept all
Bulgarian Muslims wishing to depart for Turkey. It was one of the
clearest expressions of xenophobic nationalism yet. In effect he
encouraged all ethnic Turks to leave Bulgaria for Turkey. Bulgaria's
Turkish outpouring commenced in earnest on 2 June.

Between May and December more than 350 000 Turks left Bulgaria, leaving behind most of their belongings and holdings. The
government evidently failed to take account of potential economic
ramifications, or did not feel these were as important as achieving
national purification. The result was that the economy was severely
damaged, losing 1.5 – 2.5 billion leva, or \$1.3 – 2.1 billion (at
the then official exchange rate), largely because of labour-related
problems.[16]

In the meantime ethnic Bulgarians were finding their voices. On
18 July 1989 a petition bearing the signatures of 121 people was
presented to the National Assembly. It read in part that those signing
were concerned deeply about events in Bulgaria and blamed the
government for using violence

> against the ethnic identity of Bulgarian citizens who, regardless of
> their origin, feel themselves to be Turkish. These are people who,
> together with us Bulgarians, took part in constructing socialist
> Bulgaria and, under their original names, spread its fame through-
> out the world.[17]

It stated further:

> the policy of violence against ethnic consciousness, as well as the
> fanning of animosity and hostility between the masses and parts of
> the intelligentsia, is contrary to our national character, humiliating
> for our national dignity, and disruptive of our tradition of toler-
> ance. Such a policy discredits us before the world and degrades
> us in our own eyes.

The petition also advocated reconciliation, dialogue, peace and co-operation. It was an important statement because it was signed by nationally prominent figures.

This was followed on 1 August 1989 by a strong condemnation of the government issued by the Independent Discussion Club for *Glasnost* and *Perestroika*, a newly founded group of dissidents. The signatories noted:

As we have been denied the opportunity of discussing publicly the burning issues facing our country, our alarm as citizens obliges us to publish a declaration which lays the blame squarely on the government for the massive Turkish exodus and the resultant crisis. This crisis, which has economic, political, moral, and ideological dimensions, is the direct result of the abrupt change in policy toward citizens with Turkish ethnic consciousness that was made in 1984 and 1985.[18]

The authors pointed out that Bulgaria had become isolated internationally as *glasnost* and *perestroika*, so vocally endorsed by the government, were being ignored in practice. They argued against xenophobic nationalism, saying that all people should have the right to choose their own names and that the state should protect minority cultures, languages and faiths. They submitted that national cooperation and dialogue were the key to Bulgaria's salvation. Interestingly, the nationalist anti-Muslims were neither mobilised nor organised, perhaps because the government saw no need to involve them on the logic that protest could be controlled and, if need be, extinguished, using tested methods.

Meanwhile, partially overwhelmed by the numbers and demands of so many immigrants and partially motivated by the wish to draw attention to events, the government of Turkey was forced to close its border with Bulgaria on 22 August 1989. Sofia indignantly complained as Zhivkov accomplished what even his neighbouring dictator, Nicolae Ceauşescu, never dared attempt in Transylvania against Romania's Hungarians.

For its part, Turkey has taken and continues to take a serious interest in Bulgaria's Muslims, especially its Turks. Thus like Bulgarian nationalists, Turkish nationalists have been guilty of escalating the tensions. Comments such as the following have no doubt inflamed the xenophobes:

Turkey is a country which always had and still has the right and
duty to speak on behalf of the Turks in Bulgaria, to protect their
rights and freedoms. This is the case since the Berlin Treaty of
1878, i.e., from the very beginning of the Bulgarian State. No
Turkish government can give up these rights and neglect these
duties. The Turks in Bulgaria were never left solely to Bulgaria's
one-sided discretion; they never became solely an internal affair
of Bulgaria.[19]

Such statements, in view of the increasing importance of Turkey in
the Mediterranean and Black Sea regions today, seem all the more
ominous to Bulgarian xenophobes, who fear that a more powerful
Turkey may somehow overwhelm its much smaller neighbour.

Why did the assimilation process occur? The government sought
to Bulgarise minorities in order to defuse separatist movements and
minority-rights organisations.[20] Moreover, the disparity between birth
rates among ethnic Bulgarians and ethnic Turks inspired fear among
Bulgarian nationalists. Turks were proliferating, Bulgarians were
not. Even some members of the intelligentsia saw in this a sort of
Ottoman-cum-Turkish revanchism mounted by means of demographic
insurgency, which, if unchecked, could gradually lead to the Muslim
population someday outnumbering that of the Orthodox Slavs. Furthermore ethnic Turks, especially in regions where they predom-
inate, are viewed by Bulgarian nationalists as threats to security
because of supposed allegiances to Turkey.[21] Such attitudes have led
to Muslim alienation from non-Muslim Bulgaria, further encourag-
ing ethnic Turks to identify with predominantly Muslim Turkey. By
reducing the number of Turks the authorities appear to have sought
a purification of Bulgaria. The assimilation efforts came at a time
when the economy was on a strong downturn and as communism
began to show wear.

Greed also had a role in this process. Many Bulgarians profited
from the Turkish departures, capitalising on Turkish misfortune.
Then too, revenge seemed to have been part of the script. Turks had
behaved defiantly toward the government and these were their just
desserts, argued the nationalist politicos. Moreover there was a dose
of retribution directed at Turkey, since a heavy refugee influx, it was
expected, would overextend Ankara, which in turn would be forced
to go back on a promise to accept all of those Turks from Bulgaria
who sought to emigrate.[22] Thus another factor was to discredit the
Turkish government, leaving Bulgaria's Turks without a spiritual

homeland and causing them to settle their affairs with the government in Sofia. But even if the Turkish government accepted all who wished to emigrate, that too would be a victory for Bulgarian nationalists and for Zhivkov, since it would reduce the number of Turks in the land and provide a purification of Bulgaria.

MUSLIMS AND BULGARIAN NATIONALISM AFTER COMMUNISM

With the fall of communism, efforts to address national questions have been made. In October 1990 the first Islamic Institute, a kind of junior college that teaches Muslim culture, was founded in Sofia. A Muslim high school was opened soon afterwards in Shumen, a centre of ethnic Turks in northeastern Bulgaria. Then reaction set in, and in November 1990 the so-called Razgrad Bulgarian Republic was set up by Bulgarian nationalists with a decided anti-Turkish bent as a protest against the restoration of rights to ethnic Turks. It was centred in the city of Razgrad, located in a region heavily populated by Muslim Turks. State President Zhelyu Zhelev, speaking on national television at the time, was highly critical of the Razgrad Republic; local politicians would have nothing to do with such 'anti-constitutional' groups.[23]

The first Turkish-language newspaper to be reestablished began appearing in February 1991, and the government of Dimitûr Popov, Bulgaria's first post-communist, politically unaffiliated prime minister, promised full rights to the ethnic Turks. Intellectuals and others supported the restoration to ethnic Turks of those human and civil rights provided for in Article 45 of the constitution. Many non-Muslims living in predominantly Turkish regions opposed such measures.

Of the 300 000 to 375 000 ethnic Turks who fled to Turkey in 1989, about half have returned. When they left, many of their belongings and much of their real estate were sold at low prices to non-Muslims or were simply forfeited to the state. Now the government is seeking to provide restitution. Xenophobes see the return of Turkish names and property to ethnic Turks, as well as the acquisition of cultural autonomy by them, as a threat to Bulgarian culture and security. They continue to fear the influx of Turkish money, laundered through Bulgarian Turks, and the gradual acquisition of the Bulgarian economy by Turkish interests. Moreover the high birth rate among ethnic Turks continues to encourage a fear among non-Muslims of a gradual Turkification or Islamisation of parts of Bulgaria.[24] Such alleged tendencies, in their view, throw open the possibility of invasion by the Turkish army and the creation of a Cyprus-like situation, that is, the creation of a Turkish republic within Bulgaria; a most unlikely eventuality.

Further angering the anti-Turkish element was the Ministry of Education's decision in January 1991 to sanction the teaching of the Turkish language in public schools. In fact, because of nationalist obstruction, the programme was postponed. Turks protested and perhaps as many as 20 000 school children in Turkish regions struck in February 1991, demanding the right to have Turkish taught in their schools. Most political parties supported the idea, but in those areas heavily populated by ethnic Turks, non-Muslim parents and children loudly protested. Strikes and counterstrikes continued. Finally, in March 1991 the government announced that the study of Turkish would be instituted that year on an experimental basis in selected regions, and in 1991–2 it would become an optional subject in Bulgarian schools.[25] The move satisfied neither Turks nor nationalists.

Bulgarian xenophobes present themselves and Bulgaria as Europe's last bulwark against Islam. They trumpet the dangers of the advance of Islam and Muslim fundamentalism into Europe. Such behaviour is having a severely negative impact on Bulgarian–Turkish relations, which were on the mend, and could result in the loss of the increasing material assistance provided by Ankara. At the same time such talk finds receptive listeners in other Orthodox lands, including Serbia, Russia, Romania and Greece.

As 1992 drew to a close political events surrounding the toppling of the first democratic government, elected in 1991, created great tension. Integral to the downfall of this Union of Democratic Forces (UDF) cabinet was the unlikely, if temporary, partnership of the Movement for Rights and Freedoms (MRF), a predominantly Turkish and Muslim party that represents ethnic Turks, and the Bulgarian Socialist Party (BSP), heirs of the Bulgarian Communist Party.

The MRF gained official recognition on 4 January 1990, despite constitutional injunctions against the formation of ethnic or religious parties. Its roots go back to 1984–5 and the onset of the Muslim assimilation campaign initiated by the government. Members were active in advocating Turkish autonomy and even separation from

Bulgaria, something its leader, Ahmed Dogan, explained in retro-
spect by saying that 'secessionist tendancies accrue to any organisation which seeks to guarantee the survival of an ethnic community'.[26]
Dedicated to the introduction of human rights for all, the MRF
claims to be opposed to both nationalism and Islamic fundamentalism.

In the June 1990 elections the MRF won twenty-three parliamentary seats, and it became the third largest parliamentary bloc as well
as the most visible and articulate organisation representing Muslim
interests in Bulgaria. In the parliamentary elections of 1991 the MRF
increased its number of seats in the legislature to twenty four, a fact
that made possible the constitution of Bulgaria's first elected non-
communist government. But after that government took office, relations gradually soured as the MRF leadership fell out with the UDF
government, headed by Filip Dimitrov. Dogan and his colleagues
said that the cabinet was not sufficiently mindful of Turkish issues.
Moreover, as the lynchpin in the three-party Sûbranie, the MRF
evidently made a conscious decision to assert itself and thereby gain
greater influence. The decision worked, for the MRF has had a
significant say in the constitution of the government of reconciliation, headed by Liuben Berov, that was created in 1993, and there is
one MRF member in the cabinet, albeit an ethnic Bulgarian. However, given the volatility of interethnic relations and the everpresent
possibility of conflict, one needs to recognise that while these changes
signal progress, they may also trigger strife. The acquisition of
greater MRF power and increasing demands for concessions, along
with the perception among many Bulgarians of significant backing
from Ankara, could touch off a nationalist backlash.

MACEDONIA IRREDENTA

Bulgaria's other major national question is that of Macedonia.
Bulgaro–Macedonian nationalist groups fell into disarray following
the failed Ilinden–Preobrazhenski uprising of 1903. The IMRO returned as a force in Bulgarian politics only after the First World War,
when rival organisations vied for power. Stifled in 1934 by the
military, Macedonian nationalism did not reemerge until the onset of
democratisation in Bulgaria. Then, freedom of expression gave rise
to the regeneration of Macedonian nationalist groups, including the
IMRO incarnate, and the century-old issues of: what are the borders

of Macedonia? To whom does Macedonia belong? Who lives there? With what nationality do they identify?[27]

The name 'Macedonia' has been used over time to designate various regions of the central Balkan peninsula. Owing to historical, political and ethnic considerations it has never been possible to achieve unanimity over the precise boundaries of Macedonia, parts of which are now in Bulgaria, Greece and the Republic of Macedonia.[28] In the former Yugoslav state, the Slavs of Macedonia constituted a nationality sharing the cultural characteristics of, but remaining different from, Bulgarians and Serbians.[29] Prior to this, however, Macedonian Slavs inhabiting Bulgarian, Greek and Serbian territory experienced significant pressure to assimilate with the majority populations of their respective regions.

There was a tendency among Macedonians within the boundaries of the republic to be aggressive in the affirmation of their newly recognised nationality, a fact that Greece, possessing 51 per cent of geographic Macedonia, viewed with alarm. It feared that Macedonians would foster and pursue irredentist aims in Greek territory where there had been a sizable Slav population before the Second World War. As many as 100 000 emigrated after the war and during the Greek civil war, the majority settling in the Yugoslav Federal Republic of Macedonia.[30]

Yugoslavia's recognition of Macedonian nationality was meant to diminish, if not invalidate, the legitimacy of any Bulgarian claim on Yugoslav territory or people. It was also a means of defusing a sensitive political problem, for the Serbs had managed to alienate the Slavs of Macedonia before and during the Second World War by means of their attempt to Serbianise the population. For postwar Bulgaria the creation a Macedonian nationality was a reasonable compromise, for as a defeated power it could not lay claim to Macedonia. But it could hope that the population of Macedonia, if made identifiably separate from the Serbs, and given its Serbian antipathies, might move toward Bulgaria in time as the two lands shared significant cultural, linguistic and historical ties. Bulgaria maintained this line after Tito fell from Stalin's grace, because the alternative was that Macedonia might be reincorporated into Serbia.

A long-standing theme in Balkan affairs was federalism among neighbouring states in the interest of peace and security. Bulgarian nationalists, immediately following the Second World War, were horrified when communist leaders in Yugoslavia and Bulgaria talked about a federation that would unite their two countries in the spirit of international communist proletarianism. A friendship pact was signed in 1947 that was intended to end territorial disputes, notably over Macedonia. However the new arrangement was never to be, as the 1948 Tito–Stalin split gave Bulgaria the excuse to withdraw. Bulgarian leaders were never comfortable with the idea and they were again free rhetorically to espouse internationalism while pursing narrow nationalist goals.

A few years later, and under some pressure from the Soviet Union to promote communist solidarity, the Bulgarian government formally conceded that there was such a thing as a 'Macedonian' nationality. In the 1956 Bulgarian census, 187 729 Macedonians were listed as living in Bulgarian or Pirin Macedonia. In 1965, however, this number shrank to 8750. By 1968 Bulgaria had readopted the idea that Macedonians were Bulgarians. In the 1975 census there were no Macedonians listed.[31] Communist internationalism again gave way to more narrow nationalist–irredentist perspectives.

Since the fall of Zhivkov, nationalists in Bulgaria are once again stirring the pot of irredentist aspirations and historical grievances. On 2 August 1990, the eighty-seventh anniversary of the Ilinden uprising, they accused former Bulgarian communist governments of having turned a blind eye to the 'truth' about Macedonia in deference to political expediency. They argued that after the Second World War communist leaders had officially recognised the existence of a separate Macedonian nationality in Yugoslavia, and thus sacrificed national interests to ensure international communist unity. For their part, certain Yugoslav Macedonians argued for the recognition of Macedonian minorities in Bulgaria and the union of all Macedonians in one Macedonian state.

Since the beginning of reform in Bulgaria, nationalist groups have been founded that support various positions on the Macedonian question. Among the largest is the Ilinden United Macedonian Organisation (IUMO), established in November 1989. Although unrecognised by the authorities, the IUMO's fundamental goals are official affirmation of a Macedonian minority in Bulgaria, and the right to use the Macedonian language and to foster Macedonian culture.[32]

The district court found the IUMO petition for recognition to be in violation of Article 52 of the Bulgarian Constitution, which stipulates that organisations are forbidden whose activities are directed 'against the sovereign, territorial integrity of the country and the unity of the nation'.[33] The official reactions to the IUMO are a measure of the gravity with which the authorities view the question of recognising a separate Macedonian nationality. To do so would erode claims to Macedonia on national lines, strengthen the position of those seeking an autonomous or independent Macedonia, and potentially threaten the territorial integrity of Bulgaria, with the possibility, however remote, of Pirin Macedonia seceding and uniting with the Republic of Macedonia.

On the opposite side is a Bulgarian nationalist organisation critical of the Bulgarian government's historical stand on Macedonia – the Club for Radical Reform of the BSP in the Blagoevgrad Region. This group's members believe that the BSP 'bears moral and political responsibility for the politically short-sighted and criminal underestimation of the ethnic issue in public activities'. Club leaders strongly criticised the government's acquiescence in the establishment of a Macedonian nationality in Yugoslavia after the Second World War. A spokesman called this 'an outrageous crime'.[34]

The All-Bulgarian Union also protested the encroachment on Bulgarian cultural integrity, on the rights of people to national self-determination and self-awareness, as a form of assimilating the Bulgarians in Vardar Macedonia. The Union declared itself prepared to lead a 'struggle against pan-Serbian chauvinism and Macedonianism until the ultimate triumph of truth'.[35] That is, members were ready to seek means to advance Bulgarianness in the Republic of Macedonia that would serve to eliminate the Macedonian nationality and presumably sway the inhabitants of Macedonia into the Bulgarian sphere. How such objectives would be reached was not made plain.

The IMRO-Union of Macedonian Societies in Bulgaria was founded officially in December 1990. It leaders believe that the Slavs of the Republic of Macedonia and Greek Macedonia, like their brothers and sisters in Bulgarian Macedonia, are Bulgarians. The organisation's mission is thus to create the 'moral unity of the Bulgarian people'.[36]

Violence resulting from nationalist sentiment on all sides of the Macedonian question, remains a possibility. At present Macedonians are focusing on internal matters and the wars of Yugoslav succession; where Macedonian irredentism has surfaced, it has been directed at Greece. For their part Bulgarians are preoccupied with economic, political and broad foreign-policy concerns rather than with the Macedonian question. Still, as witnessed by Greece's obstruction of international recognition of Macedonia because of grievances about the name of the new country and the state symbols it chose, historical and territorial issues in the Balkans can easily surface, becoming tinder for an inflamed nationalism that could engulf Macedonia and Bulgaria.

CONCLUSION

National consciousness, a feeling bred of a sense of historical, cultural and linguistic kinship and identity, defines affinity group membership. At the same time it often delineates the circles to which one does not belong. Nationalism, the bonding agent that ties together like-minded people possessing the same national consciousness, is often a negative force for change, in that it can be socially corrosive and stimulate violence and interethnic animosities among peoples. In the Balkans and elsewhere it leads to ethnocentrism, particularly in times of economic stress, and it can pit one nationally conscious group against others, promoting prejudice and enmity among rival groups. The events in former Yugoslavia add poignancy to these words and demonstrate that nationalism unleashed can be vicious, brutal and politically destabilising. There, people are reenacting nineteenth-century feuds in the interest of creating monoethnic states.

Contentious interethnic problems point to stark differences in Bulgarian society, which has not succeeded in integrating, let alone reconciling, the needs and values of majority and minority. With the advent of democratisation, of course, freer rein is given to prejudice, because freer expression is permissible.

Bulgarian nationalism, at first the expression of patriotic strivings, resulted in three key achievements: the founding of the Exarchate, the creation of a Bulgarian principality, and the union of Bulgaria with Eastern Rumelia. Once accomplished this nationalism was channelled along xenophobic and irredentist lines, with the strands becoming intermingled, bringing both cohesive and destructive force to bear on national problems. Measuring the animosity harboured by contemporary Bulgarians of non-Muslim background toward Muslim 'Turks' and vice versa is difficult. Certainly there is a mutual lack of trust, and for some non-Muslims a lingering bitterness fed by historical factors rooted in nationalistic notions concerning the 'Ottoman yoke' syndrome. Still, despite historic hostility between Muslims and Christians, the roots of which are sunk deep in Bulgaria's Ottoman heritage, a civil balance has so far been maintained.

Today, given the recent periods of forced assimilation and the virulence of contemporary xenophobic nationalism among ethnic Bulgarians, ethnic Turks, who at one time were integrated into Bulgarian society, have begun to look to Turkey.

In the meantime contemporary political parties in Bulgaria are employing nationalist ideology to further their own objectives. All parties are guilty of this abuse, but the BSP is particularly adept at using the national issue to electoral advantage. Cases of former communist nomenklatura seeking to obstruct reform through demonstrations, such as those in February 1991 protesting the teaching of Turkish, are well documented. In the end, such manifestations serve to discredit Bulgaria's efforts to be accepted among and aided by more developed democratic nations, by creating internal stress that could present a backward and discriminatory image abroad at a time when the country needs substantial assistance.

Likewise, irredentist nationalism plays against the interests of Bulgaria. More than 100 years have elapsed since the Treaty of San Stefano, but still there are Bulgarians who harbour claims to the lost territory, part of which lies in Greece and part in the Republic of Macedonia. That Bulgaria still does not recognise Macedonian nationality is both backward looking and a measure of the importance of history to Balkan peoples. Should Macedonia break up as a result of the strife in former Yugoslavia, a Balkan land grab will surely result and Bulgarian irredentism, now simmering, will boil over.

Bulgaria, a land bridge between the predominantly Islamic Middle East and non-Islamic Europe, at times has been schizophrenic. During the communist era, when nationalism was officially prohibited, a surrogate version was adroitly employed by state head Todor Zhivkov to stimulate national pride and Bulgarian exclusiveness – witness his Muslim assimilation programmes – while keeping alive irredentist longings for Macedonia without expressing territorial claims. During his administration the Yugoslav Republic of Macedonia was generally recognised as a political entity whose majority population was Bulgarian, despite their claims to a Macedonian identity.

Bulgaria's struggle for international acceptance as a modern and democratic state is tied up with its struggle for national dignity, and the way has been arduous. With neither a democratic image nor a democratic tradition in the Western sense, contemporary nationalism is doing little to improve the country's image. Nevertheless it appears that the government, with strong support from the intelligentsia, is seeking to promote interethnic understanding. The problem is that the rural population in predominantly Turkish regions is not comforted by intellectual expressions of brotherhood and solidarity. It is accustomed to the 'them and us' mentality promoted by the previous regime and exacerbated by the perceived threat of an influx of Turkish money, which would be used to buy up properties belonging to ethnic Bulgarians, thus ultimately causing their departure from homes and land and converting a Bulgarian birthright into Turkish territory.

No grass-roots dialogue has been undertaken and the nationalists seem disinclined to negotiate. In their view the 'Turkish threat' can only be eliminated through Turkish emigration or assimilation. Thus the efforts of those among the Bulgarian population attempting to achieve a reconciliation are likely to prove futile, since such rudimentary matters as property, language and culture – the nationalists' paraphernalia – are at stake. Pragmatists in Bulgaria plead that stability, peace and cooperation are necessary for Bulgaria to progress. Racial and ethnic tension, they warn, would result in chaos, violence and international loss of face, for anti-Muslim elements are undermining the work of such leaders as Zhelev, who is seeking to persuade the world that Bulgaria is an emerging European democracy. But even Zhelev has so far been unwilling to recognise Macedonian nationality, an indication that Bulgarians have yet to put their past behind them.

Notes and References

1. Several passages in this chapter have appeared previously in the *RFE/RL Research Report*. Thanks to Kjell Engelbrekt and J. F. Brown, both of the RFE/RL Research Institute, for their valuable suggestions concerning this chapter. Thanks too, to Elizabeth Hudson for her careful reading of the manuscript. See Stefan Troebst, 'Nationalismus vs. Demokratie: Der Fall Bulgarien', in Margareta Mommsen, *Nationalismus in Osteuropa* (Munich: Beck, 1992), pp. 167–85 for a succinct and provocative study of Bulgaria's democratisation and the role of nationalism.
2. Marin V. Pundeff, 'Bulgarian Nationalism', in Peter F. Sugar and Ivo J. Lederer (eds), *Nationalism in Eastern Europe* (Seattle: University of Washington Press, 1969), p. 93.
3. Michael B. Petrovich, 'Religion and Ethnicity in Eastern Europe', in Peter Sugar (ed.), *Ethnic Diversity and Conflict in Eastern Europe* (Santa Barbara: ABC-Clio, 1980), p. 391.
4. L. S. Stavrianos, *The Balkans Since 1453* (New York: Holt, Rinehart and Winston, 1953), p. 371.

5. 'Tûrnovska konstitutsiya ot 1879', *Bûlgarski konstitutsii i konstitutsionni proekti* (Sofia: Petûr Beron, 1990), pp. 24–5.
6. J. F. Brown, *Nationalism, Democracy and Security in the Balkans* (Aldershot: Dartmouth Publishing and Rand, 1992), p. 118.
7. John Feffer, *Shock Waves, Eastern Europe After the Revolutions* (Boston: South End Press, 1992), p. 228.
8. William Echikson, *Lighting the Night* (New York: William Morrow, 1990), p. 258.
9. See Machiel Kiel, *Art and Society of Bulgaria in the Turkish Period* (Maastrict: Van Gorcum, 1985).
10. See Hristo Hristov (ed.), *Stranitsi iz Bûlgarskata Istoriya*, (Sofia: Nauka i Izkustvo, 1989) for examples of history turned into a propaganda vehicle to serve state interests. See also Stephen Ashley, 'The National Assimilation Policy Seems to be Faltering', *RFE Bulgarian Situation Report*, SR/4, 22 May 1989, p. 7 and Amnesty International, *Bulgaria: Imprisonment of Ethnic Turks* (Lasa: Amal International, 1956), pp. 4–5.
11. Nissan Oren, *Revolution Administered* (Baltimore: Johns Hopkins University Press, 1973), p. 122.
12. Amnesty International, *Bulgaria: Imprisonment of Ethnic Turks* (London: Amnesty International, 1986), pp. 12–14. See also Hugh Poulton, *The Balkans: Minorities and States in Conflict* (London: Minority Rights Group, 1991), chapters 9–12.
13. Quoted in G. S. Nikolaev, 'Forced Assimilation of the Turks', *Borba*, 9 March 1985, p. 192.
14. These groups are the Democratic League for the Defence of Human Rights, the Independent Association for the Defence of Human Rights, and the Muslim Initiative Group. Membership was small – 135 for the first, forty for the second, and thirty for the third.
15. Bulgarian Telegraph Agency (BTA), 23 May 1989; Stephen Ashley, 'Protests by Ethnic Turks Escalate', *RFE Bulgarian Situation Report*, SR/6, 3 July 1989, p. 3.
16. See Rada Nikolaev, 'Counting the Costs of the Turkish Exodus: The Shortage of Labor', *RFE Bulgarian Situation Report*, SR/9, 5 October 1989, p. 10.
17. See Kjell Engelbrekt, 'Intellectuals Stand Up for Ethnic Turks', *RFE Bulgarian Situation Report*, SR/8, 1 September 1989, pp. 10–12.
18. See Stephen Ashley, 'Discussion Club Criticizes the Government for Creating a National Crisis', *RFE Bulgarian Situation Report*, SR/8, 1 September 1989, pp. 15–18 for the text of the document.
19. Bilâl N. Şimşir (ed.), *The Turks of Bulgaria in International Fora: Documents*, vol. I (Ankara: Turkish Historical Society Printing House, 1990), p. 3.
20. *Nova Svetlina*, 5 April 1990.
21. Ivan Ilchev and Duncan M. Perry, 'Bulgarian Ethnic Groups: Politics and Prospects', *RFE/RL Research Report*, vol. II, no. 12, pp. 35–41.
22. Ashley, 'Protests', p. 11.
23. *Duma*, 3 March 1990; BTA, 23 November 1990.
24. Stephen Ashley, 'Ethnic Unrest during January', *Report on Eastern Europe*, vol. I, no. 6 (1990) 9 February.
25. Radio Sofia, 15 February 1991, 3:00 p.m.; AP, 15 February 1991.
26. *Duma*, 5 November 1990.

27. See 'Makedoniya – Stipchivata Yabûlka na Razdora', *Obshetstvo i Pravo*, no. 10 (1990), for example.

28. See H. R. Wilkinson, *Maps and Politics: A Review of the Ethnographic Cartography of Macedonia* (Liverpool: University of Liverpool, 1951); Petûr Koledarov, *Imeto Makedoniya v istoricheskata geografiya* (Sofia: Nauka i izkustvo, 1985); and Ilija Petruševski (ed.), *Makedonija na stari mapi* (Skopje: Detska radost and Makedonija revija, 1992).

29. See Victor A. Friedman, 'Macedonian Language and Nationalism during the Nineteenth and Early Twentieth Centuries', *Balkanistica*, vol. II (1975), pp. 83–98; Horace G. Lunt, 'Some Sociolinguistic Aspects of Macedonian and Bulgarian', in Benjamin A. Stolz *et. al* (eds), *Language and Literary Theory* (Ann Arbor: Department of Slavic Languages and Literatures, 1984), pp. 83–132; Blazhe Koneski, *Kon Makedonskata prerodba: Makedonskite uchebnitsi od 19 vek* (Skopje: Institut za Natsionalna Istorija, 1959).

30. Evangelos Kofos, 'Greece and the Balkans in the 70's and 80's', in Hellenic Foundation for Defense and Foreign Policy, *Yearbook 1990* (Athens: ELIAMEP, 1991), p. 203. See Elizabeth Barker, *Macedonia: Its Place in Balkan Power Politics* (London: Royal Institute of International Affairs, 1950), pp. 78–129; Stephen E. Palmer and Robert R. King, *Yugoslav Communism and the Macedonian Question* (New Haven: Archon Books, 1971).

31. Patrick Moore, 'Bulgaria', in Teresa Rakowska-Harmstone (ed.), *Communism in Eastern Europe*, 2nd ed. (Bloomington: Indiana University Press, 1984), p. 209. For an exposition of opposing views, See Tsola Dragoicheva, *Takava e Istinata* (Sofia: Partizdat, 1981); Dragan Tašovski, *Za Makedonskata Nacija* (Skopje: Naša Kniga, 1975); Vangja Časule (ed.), *From Recognition to Repudiation* (Skopje: Kultura, 1972).

32. *Duma*, 19 June 1990.

33. *Dûrzhaven Vestnik*, 10 April 1990.

34. BTA, 31 July 1990.

35. BTA, 2 August 1990.

36. *Trud*, 31 July 1991.

5 The Road to Separation: Nationalism in Czechoslovakia
John Morison

The Czechs and Slovaks have a common ancestry in the myriad Slavonic tribes that occupied their territories in the sixth century as part of the great migration of Slavs into Eastern, Central and South Eastern Europe. They also have a common political ancestor in the Great Moravian Empire, which in the ninth century occupied a territory significantly larger than modern Czechoslovakia. The claims of some contemporary Slovak patriots that this was the first Slovak state seem to be wide of the mark. Archaeological evidence suggests that its capital was in Moravia, perhaps at Mikulcice. Moreover the terms 'Czech' and 'Slovak' were meaningless in those days of predominantly tribal identity.

THE SLOVAKS UNDER HUNGARIAN DOMINION

The Moravian Empire collapsed at the beginning of the tenth century, squeezed between the Germans to the west and the invading Magyar horde from the east. As a consequence the Slovaks were to remain under Hungarian dominion until the collapse of the Austro–Hungarian Empire at the conclusion of the First World War. There was no identifiable Slovak historical state. The nobility of that geographical area, of whatever ethnic origin, communicated with each other in Latin. The peasantry was tied to the land, united by poverty rather than by nationality. There was no common Slovak literary language until the modern period, and regional differences in the spoken language were considerable. Genuine signs of a developing Slovak national consciousness did not come until the late eighteenth century. The development of a literary language was crucial to this process. Early efforts focused on Czech. Many Czech Protestants had found refuge in Slovakia after the crushing of independent Bohemia at the Battle of the White Mountain in 1620. Czech thus became the means of literary expression of the small Slovak Protestant-educated group, and when the Catholic clergy found it necessary to develop a standard literary language in the late eighteenth century, Anton Bernolák, a priest, chose the western Slovak dialect as the basis for his grammatical system as it was close to Czech. If Bernolák's work had taken root, a genuinely unified Czechoslovak language might have developed. However the peoples to the east found this western dialect difficult to understand, and the Protestants held fast to their biblical Czech.

Confronted by pressure from a Magyar nationalism that was becoming increasingly aggressive as the nineteenth century progressed, the diminutive band of Slovak nationalists debated whether to throw in their lot with the Czechs or to strike out on their own. In the end, Ludovit Štúr and other scholars in his group made a decisive move in 1843 when they adopted the central Slovak dialect as the basis for a Slovak literary language, which, as a consequence, would be distinct from Czech. Štúr thereby hoped to persuade the Hungarian authorities that the Slovaks were a distinct nation deserving separate rights, but he only succeeded in inciting increased Magyar aggression, thereby laying the foundation of a separate Slovak national identity. Despite contrary voices raised in spirited debate, Štúr's line became increasingly accepted as Slovak intellectuals decided to write in a language that would be understood by the common people. Štúr saw this as a vital part of the process of building a self-conscious, independent Slovak 'tribe' within the Slav 'nation'. 'Slav life is divided like a linden tree into many branches, the nation is one, but one in diversity'.[1] Štúr was thus far from supporting a separatist nationalism, but his work was an essential step on the path leading in that direction.

The 1848 revolutions were an important stage in the development of Slovak nationalism. At the beginning of the eighteenth century Slovaks had joined willingly in Raköczi's revolt against Habsburg rule, but in 1848 Štúr and other leaders made national demands in their rebellion against the Hungarians. However the number of Slovak volunteers was small, peasants showed themselves still to be peasants rather than Slovak nationalists, and not a few Slovaks supported the Hungarians.

The Habsburgs rewarded the Slovaks for their support against the Hungarian rebels by effectively delivering them into the hands of the Hungarians. If the Slovaks had hoped for individual status within a federal system, the *Ausgleich* of 1867 declared them to be part of the indivisible and unitary Hungarian nation. Magyarisation proceeded apace. The *Matica Slovenská*, a cultural centre intended by Slovak intellectuals to promote the spread of Slovak cultural consciousness, was closed down in 1875. Slovak secondary schools were shut and Slovak students wishing to use their own language were forced to flee abroad in order to promulgate the Slovak idea in freedom. This aggressive Magyarisation was to be counterproductive in the long run since the persecution provoked opposition and stimulated national consciousness through resentment. However it was not solely because of Hungarian high-handedness that Slovak nationalists were pursuing an uphill struggle. Their society was still largely peasant in composition, and urban society and industry were underdeveloped. Thus the preconditions for mass nationalist movement were not present: illiterate or semiliterate peasants in the Slovak valleys and mountains were generally as unresponsive as peasants anywhere to such appeals.

THE CZECH NATIONAL REVIVAL

The conditions for development of nationalism in the Czech lands were much more favourable than in Slovakia. Firstly, they had a genuine tradition of independent statehood to which they could appeal. The kingdom of Bohemia, with its mixed Czech and German population, had been one of the great states of medieval Europe. A Czech literary language had flourished. Jan Hus was no nationalist, but the Czech reformation was to demonstrate national features. Even if Bohemia was far from being a modern nation state, it did contain national elements that could inspire and be magnified by nineteenth-century Czech patriots.

Secondly, the turning of Bohemia and Moravia into the industrial powerhouse of the Habsburg Empire led to significant population movements in their racially mixed societies. Even in medieval Bohemia the towns had been dominated by Germans. This tendency had been strengthened after the defeat of the Protestant nobility at the Battle of the White Mountain in 1620. The demands of new industry for labour led to an influx of Czechs into the towns. The struggle of these migrants for opportunities for upward mobility or even survival in this new industrial society led to considerable tension between the communities and to an increased national awareness and a demand for national rights by ordinary Czechs.[2] Czech intellectual nationalists could thus find support in society at large. A minority intellectual movement could be transformed into a mass nationalist movement of the modern variety.

The Czech 'national revival' had begun in the late eighteenth century as a part of a general European movement stemming from the Enlightenment and the ideas of the French Revolution. The enlightened Habsburg Emperor Joseph II had forwarded the cause of the rights of man in Bohemia by giving more rights and educational opportunities to the Czech peasantry. His tolerance had allowed a group of nobility and scholars to start a revival in the use of the old Czech language and to stimulate an interest in Bohemian history. Josef Dobrovský's work in reviving the Czech language was of particular importance, despite his personal pessimism about its future and his personal use of German most of the time.

The second stage in this revival was to be expressed in cultural terms by a fraternity of scholars who were now openly aiming to create a Czech nation, or, if one accepts their premises, to revive it. Through study of popular Czech speech in villages, linguists hoped to produce a sophisticated and modern literary language, purged of Germanisms. Josef Jungmann, one of the leading Czech spirits in this campaign, produced a five volume Czech–German dictionary and a *History of Czech Literature*. If Jungmann helped to weld an instrument of expression for the Czechs, František Palacký guided them to a discovery of their national soul. His great *History of the Czech Nation in Bohemia and Moravia*, written in Czech, was as significant a landmark in the development of Czech nationalism as Karamzin's *History of the Russian State*, written in Russian, was in the parallel Russian movement. In this work Palacký interpreted Czech history as being dominated by the struggle between Slavdom and Germandom, two distinct national types. The sensitive, peace-loving and religious Slavs were contrasted with the predatory and militaristic Germans.

> Czech history is based chiefly on a conflict with Germandom, that is on the acceptance and rejection of German custom and laws by the Czechs . . . a struggle not only on the borders but in the interior of Bohemia, not only against foreigners but among native inhabitants, not only with sword and shield but with spirit and word, laws and customs, openly and covertly, with enlightened zeal and blind passion, leading not only to victory or rejection but also to reconciliation.[3]

Czech national consciousness found its expression and was fostered in a wide range of literary, cultural and artistic organisations, activities and achievements. The Austrians were more tolerant than their Hungarian counterparts and allowed the establishment of a Czech National Theatre in 1881 and of a Czech university in Prague in 1882. Music was very important in this process, and Bedrich Smetana above all others embodied this new national spirit in his patriotic operas, such as *The Brandenburgers in Bohemia*, which celebrated the expulsion of Germanic occupiers, and *The Bartered Bride*, which was received as a celebration of Czech folk music even if the direct quotations are very few indeed.

The June uprising of 1848 in Prague injected a strong political element into Czech national revival. Students supported by workers held out for six days against overwhelming Austrian military force. The involvement of the lower orders in this quixotic venture was indicative of the much wider social base available for this development in Prague than was present in the Slovak capital. The rapid development of industry with flourishing Czech native middle and working classes provided the essential base for a genuine nationalist movement. Even if peasant petitions flooded into the National Council in Prague in 1848–9, the sources of support for the patriotic movement were predominantly urban. Slovakia, in contrast, remained an overwhelmingly rural society, with a consequent delay in the development of a mass national consciousness.[4]

THE DEVELOPMENT OF THE CZECHOSLOVAK IDEA

The politicisation of the Czech national movement and the widening of its social base led to a protracted debate about the relationship of the incipient Czech nation with its neighbours. It was a debate that was joined by the Slovaks, albeit from a different perspective. In the first half of the nineteenth century, cultural pan-Slavism was to become a popular concept with both Czech and Slovak intellectuals. The Slovak Kollár preached the idea of Slav reciprocity in a cultural rather than a political unity. The Czech Reiger bravely reminded his Russian audience at Moscow University on 19 May 1867 that ancient Greek civilisation had flourished on the basis of diversity. The Slavs should follow this example by developing in harmonious diversity. If all the Slav bells were fused into one enormous bell, the latter would produce a mighty sound, but one that would be less agreeable than that of a number of smaller bells ringing in harmony. However his Russian hosts had already made their position clear by their firm repression of the Polish revolt of 1863. For them, the sound from a Slav bell should be made by a Russian clapper with Russian hands on the bell-ropes directing operations. Many Czechs were to retain a sentimental affection for their big brother to the east, but the journalist Karel Havlíček spoke for many in his scepticism, pointing to the bitter divisions between Russians and Poles. He characterised the Russians' attitude towards the other Slavs as being imperialist in nature. 'We Czechs are of Czech nationality and want to remain so; we do not want to become Germanised or Magyarised, but neither do we want to become Russians; therefore, let us remain cool to the Russians and their overtures to us'.[5]

The Czechs were becoming increasingly assertive in claiming national rights, but were not necessarily hostile to their Habsburg masters. Czech nationalism fed off anti-German sentiment, but nevertheless many Czechs saw their future as lying within the Habsburg empire. Palacký, in 1849, proposed a plan for a federal, multinational empire in which power would have been shared between eight national units and the central government in Vienna. This proposal was rejected, as were his subsequent variations on the same theme. The proclamation of dualism in the *Ausgleich* of 1867 was a cruel blow to Palacký and his sympathisers in the National or Old Czech Party, who retreated into passive opposition. The more belligerent Young Czech Party began a more aggressive tactic in parliament in the 1890s to extract a series of concessions in the area of Czech national rights. Nonetheless they and other Czech parties that emerged in the first decade of the twentieth century were still operating under the protective Habsburg umbrella and were not seeking to destroy it, since it at least provided a shield against German expansionism.

The Slovaks, in contrast, could not hope to achieve national rights by parliamentary means after 1867. Their Hungarian rulers were uncompromising in their determination to impose a unitary Magyar state. These tactics were successful in the short run in smothering the development of the Slovak national movement. There was no realistic possibility of carrying on a successful struggle for concessions from within the Hungarian half of the Habsburg Empire. While some of the older generation of Slovak nationalists might hope for salvation from Russia, many of the younger breed, generally forced to find education abroad, more sensibly began to build links with the Czechs. Their objective was either to establish a third Slav section to the Empire, or to achieve some form of political union with the Czechs in an independent state, an idea promoted by the shortlived journal *HLAS* between 1898 and 1904.

The views of the Hlasists found a sympathetic echo in the intellectual and political evolution of a small group of Czech activists towards a realisation that an independent Czechoslovak state was not only desirable but also possible. This tendency only became a potent force during the First World War as the Habsburg Empire began to disintegrate. Its organising genius was Thomas G. Masaryk, aided by Edvard Beneš and Milan Štefánik. Increasing domestic support for the Czechoslovak idea amongst both Czechs and Slovaks underpinned a determined diplomatic campaign to sway opinion and influence governments in Britain, France and the United States. The Czechs and Slovaks in union presented the image of a national unit sufficiently large to be viable and, after President Woodrow Wilson had adopted the principle of national self-determination, their campaign achieved a notable victory at the peace negotiations when the Czechoslovak republic was proclaimed in 1919.

THE NEW CZECHOSLOVAK STATE

Masaryk and his associates had created a state, but they had not achieved a unified nation. In fact their diplomatic success had won them a multinational state (see Table 5.1). Over three million Germans, three quarters of a million Hungarians, 80 000 Poles and many gypsies had been included against their will, and many of the two million Ruthenes had confidently expected autonomy within the new state.[6] Slovak autonomists based their expectations on the Pittsburgh Declaration, which had been drafted in Masaryk's presence on 30 May 1918 and which promised Slovaks their own parliament, administration and law courts. The seven million Czechs, the dominant ethnic group, preferred to remember the Martin Declaration of 30 October 1918, which defined the Slovaks as a linguistic and cultural–historical part of a united Czechoslovak nation. This was much more in line with Masaryk's own thinking. He certainly considered the Slovaks to be a branch of the Czech nation, their language to be a dialect of Czech. The Czechs' cultural superiority gave them the right to leadership. Their numerical superiority was to give them dominance in a unitary democracy.

Table 5.1   Ethnic composition of Czechoslovakia (per cent)

Ethnic group	1930	1950	1970	1987
Czecho-Slovaks	66.9	–	–	–
Czechs	70.0 (est.)	68.0	65.0	62.9
Slovaks	20.0 (est.)	26.3	29.3	31.8
Magyars	4.7	3.0	4.0	3.8
Poles	0.5	0.6	0.5	0.5
Germans	22.3	1.3	0.6	0.3
Ukrainians/ Ruthenians	5.7	0.6	0.4	0.4
Others	–	0.3	0.2	0.3

Sources: The statistics for 1930 are as quoted in Hugh Seton Watson, *Eastern Europe Between the Wars 1918–1941*, 3rd ed. (New York: Harper and Row, 1962), p. 414. The census of 1930 offered no breakdown of numbers of Czechs and Slovaks and the percentages given are based on figures offered by Seton-Watson. The percentages for 1950, 1970 and 1987 are taken from Sharon L. Wolchik, *Czechoslovakia in Transition: Politics, Economics and Society* (London: Pinter, 1991), p. 186.

The new state would have been wise to have looked to the federal structure of the Habsburg empire for inspiration. Instead the 1920 constitution was strictly centralist in tone. The official ideology was that there was a single Czechoslovak nation, with a single Czechoslovak language, and the constitution provided for a single government located in Prague. Although this may have initially seemed sensible to many Slovaks as a guarantee against a resurgence of Hungarian dominion over them, it was to be a solution that the majority of Slovaks were consistently to reject.

From 1925 onwards the belligerently autonomist Slovak People's Party of Monsignor Andrej Hlinka was to win significantly more votes than any other party in Slovakia. Its clear statement that the Slovaks were a separate nation with their own language struck a sympathetic chord with deep-rooted Slovak resentment of the insidious dominance of Prague. Strongly Catholic Slovaks felt ill at ease with the Protestant inheritance, which was more apparent in

Bohemia, and could only be suspicious of President Masaryk's conversion from Catholicism to Protestantism and certain anticlerical measures. Competition from the more advanced Czech industry inhibited industrial development in Slovakia. The numerical inadequacy of educated Slovaks made necessary an inflow into Slovakia of Czech administrators, teachers and specialists whose presence soon became resented and less necessary, as a new generation of Slovaks acquired the skills needed to take over from them. Ironically, Prague's relative enlightenment in promoting Slovak secondary and higher education bred a numerous class of literate Slovaks, proud of their national inheritance and forming the leading edge of what had now become a deep-rooted and widespread Slovak nationalism. In contrast, Czech dominance in the first Czechoslovak republic meant that they did not have to stress their own nationalism, a force that was less strong in Czech politics.

The Czechoslovak constitution picked out the 'Czechoslovak nation' as the state-forming one. The remaining nations within the state were categorised as being in a subordinate role as 'nationalities'.[7] Slovak nationalists joined their Czech counterparts in vigorously defending this affirmation of their superior status over Germans, Poles, Hungarians, Ruthenes and gypsies. Although the Czechoslovak state may have been more generous than some others in its treatment of its minorities, its record was far from perfect. Language and laws were seen as discriminatory, and Konrad Henlein had a fertile soil of resentment in which to nurture his pro-Nazi movement among the Sudeten Germans, with fatal consequences for the Czechoslovak republic (although Hitler's drive eastwards would no doubt have taken place anyway, with or without a pretext).

THE IMPACT OF THE SECOND WORLD WAR

Despite the powerful advocacy of Masaryk, the concept of a Czechoslovak nation had taken only partial root in interwar Czechoslovakia. It was under severe challenge from both Slovak and German nationalism, not to mention the nationalist movements among other minorities. The German occupation during the Second World War gave a powerful boost to Slovak nationalism. Whereas the Czechs and Moravians were put under an exploitative and brutal protectorate, the Slovaks successfully petitioned Hitler for an independent state. Whilst it is true that the alternatives could well have been reincorporation with Hungary, and that considerable Nazi pressure was brought to bear on Slovak autonomist politicians, there is also no doubt that many Slovak nationalists saw in a positive light the establishment of a clerical fascist Slovak state under the presidency of the priest Josef Tiso. For the first time Slovaks could claim to have an independent state, even if its existence was dependent on obedient collaboration with Hitler and its freedom of action was severely circumscribed. With help of German capital inflows, Slovak industry developed and Slovakia's viability as a potential independent nation state was demonstrated. But in order to survive, Tiso passed from nationalist politician to active collaborator and proved unable to restrain the aggressively pro-German fascist, Vojtech Tuka, his foreign minister. As a result the regime cooperated actively in the deportation of over two thirds of Slovakia's Jews to extermination camps abroad, Many Slovaks willingly took over their property and businesses and actively profited from their misfortune.

Slovakia's wartime experience thus considerably advanced its national cause but at the same time left it tainted with collaborationism and with participation in the holocaust. It had no chance of survival after the war. Already in August 1944 a coalition of communists and other opponents of Tiso had staged the unsuccessful 'Slovak national uprising', an event that was later to be lauded by official communist ideologists, after earlier doubts, as an act of moral rehabilitation. An objective of the uprising was significantly proclaimed to be the return of Slovaks to a reunited Czechoslovak state, on a basis of equality. Beneš, the president of the Czechoslovak government-in-exile, was certainly determined to reestablish a unitary state. He consequently responded to Slovak aspirations by conceding not a federation but the status of a nominally autonomous province that was de facto controlled from Prague.

THE COMMUNIST TAKEOVER

The renewal of the Czechoslovak state after the war seemed to mark a significant stage in the development of a Czechoslovak nation. The cause of Slovak nationalism had ostensibly been set back by its collaboration with the Nazis. The forced deportation of over two million Germans, and the more gentle removal of more, had left only 165 000 in Czechoslovakia. The transfer of a segment of territory to the Soviet Union sharply reduced the Ruthene and Ukranian population. Nazi depredations had killed many of the Jews and Gypsies. The Czechoslovak attempt to expel the Hungarian minority failed, and the alternative of forced dispersion had only limited success. Hence the objective of a state of only two nationalities, Czechs and Slovaks, was not achieved, but the percentage of minorities was sharply reduced.[8]

The communist takeover in February 1948 seemed to consolidate the restoration of a unitary Czechoslovakia, as arguments for federalism were suppressed and the independent-minded Slovak Communist Party was incorporated into the Communist Party of Czechoslovakia. Prague's dominance was thereby ensured. Some Slovak communist leaders such as Gustav Husák had indicated that incorporation into the Soviet Union might be preferable. In Stalin's eyes they must have appeared as dangerously nationalistic, promoting tendencies that he was actively engaged in suppressing at home. In 1950 Husák, Laco Novomeský and Vladimir Clementis were compelled to confess publicly to 'bourgeois nationalist tendencies', manifested against Czechs, Jews and Hungarians. Clementis was to be tried on this charge and executed. The other two were imprisoned in 1952, ironically alongside Rudolf Slanský and other Jewish communists accused of being Zionist agents. This demonstrative trial was followed by purges of Slovak intellectuals in public life, paralleling attacks on those concerned to promote national identity in other parts of Stalin's empire. Slovak communists who favoured a unitary state were installed in power.

THE PRAGUE SPRING AND FEDERATION

It was not until 1963 that some Slovak communists were sufficiently emboldened by Khrushchev's earlier and selective exposure of the misdeeds of Stalin to build openly on Slovak resentment of insensitive dominance by Prague in an attempt to rehabilitate the 'Slovak bourgeois nationalists' and to laud the 'Slovak national uprising', which had fallen under a cloud by association with them. This pressure led to significant changes in the leadership of the Slovak Communist Party, and in particular to the appointment of Alexander Dubček as its first secretary. Dubček's later success in replacing Antonin Novotny as the head of the Czechoslovak Communist Party was a victory not just for reform and liberalisation but also for the federal idea. The 'Prague Spring' of 1968 had a Bratislava sub-plot with the acceptance of a new federal constitution in October 1968. Opinion polls had revealed overwhelming Slovak support for a federal solution once it had been openly proposed in March. The Soviet invasion of 21 August had suppressed liberalisation and 'socialism with a human face' but it tolerated the revival of the concept of two nations within one state and the leadership of the previously reviled 'bourgeois nationalist' – Gustav Husák.

The thrashing out of a constitutional agreement revealed substantial differences of view between Czechs and Slovaks, not to mention a Moravian bid for recognition via a tripartite solution. In order to safeguard their national rights and interests in a state in which they were numerically a distinct minority, the Slovaks pressed for parity in the legislature, in the government and in government posts. Only a limited number of areas, notably defence and foreign affairs, should be retained as the preserve of the federal government. Czechs protested against such an 'undemocratic' solution, which would allow a minority to block legislation and government decisions and to enjoy a privileged position. In the final compromise Czechoslovakia was called 'a voluntary union of equal national states'. Many powers were reserved for the two states: others were to be 'common affairs'; defence, foreign affairs and a limited range of other concerns were reserved for the federal organs. The national assembly had wide legislative powers, but the presence of two chambers of equal authority, with the chamber of nations divided into Slovak and Czech sections, gave the Slovaks significant protection against abuse by the majority. However the retention of a unitary Czechoslovak Communist Party and the denial of democratic choice in voting made such safeguards nominal rather than real.[9]

Husák's leadership from 1969 to 1987 did ensure that Slovak economic interests were not neglected in Prague. Investment in heavy industry and armaments manufacture polluted the valleys of Slovakia with smoke but also raised consumer spending per head to 93 per cent of the Czech level in 1983, as opposed to 68 per cent in 1953.[10] There was greater Slovak participation in the federal ministries in Prague, and at least the appearance, if not to any great degree the reality, of some devolution of authority to Slovakia. Cultural life was less repressed than in the Czech republic, and its national base became even more apparent. Czechs and Slovaks nevertheless gave the appearance of reasonably harmonious coexistence within a federal structure that was deprived of genuine meaning by the domination of a unitary and exclusive political party.

THE REVOLUTION OF 1989

Communist rule collapsed with impressive suddenness in November 1989. The forces of the opposition did not have a specifically national base. Intellectuals clustered around Charter 77, a basic document of the opposition, and were especially fired by human-rights issues. Catholic activists dwelled heavily on religious repression. Students, actors and professionals had specific grievances related to their work. They shared with the general populace a contempt for the moral corruption and inefficiency of the regime. There was cooperation between the opposition forces in the Czech lands and in Slovakia, even if coordination was far from perfect. The movements were national in being an overt rejection of foreign domination by the Soviet Union as well as of foreign-inspired ideology, which provided a creed for the regime that was decisively rejected. They were national in the sense that they were essentially separate, with differing emphases and characteristics. For instance environmentalists were more prominent in Slovakia, and political dissidents more in evidence in Prague.

But separation into two independent states and the rejection of federalism was not on the political agenda in 1989. Nor was it a real issue in the general election of June 1990. Only one minority party openly advocated this course; the major parties were united in supporting the maintenance of a union of sorts. Nevertheless there were already clear signs that this issue would become more prominent in political debate, even if very few would have predicted that by 27 August 1992 the political leaders of the Czech and Slovak republics would have decided to go their separate ways towards total independence on 1 January 1993.

THE MOVE TOWARDS SEPARATION

The elections of June 1990 made it apparent that the Czechs and Slovaks had distinct political cultures. The dominant forces were the two broad church movements of the former opposition: the Civic Forum in the Czech lands and Public against Violence in Slovakia. The fact that they proved unable and unwilling to coalesce presaged a separate political existence for the two nations. The political scene was even more divided on national grounds than it had been during the first republic. Even the Christian Democrats found it necessary to form separate national parties. The strength of feeling on the national issue soon became apparent in a fierce renewal of the hyphen debate. The compromise that ensued, whereby the federation could be described as Czechoslovakia on one side of the divide and Czech-Slovakia on the other, was symptomatic of a lack of common purpose.

The dissolution of the broad political movements into rival political parties, in itself a move towards a properly functioning political democracy, only strengthened separatist tendencies. Václav Klaus's Civic Democratic Party, to be far and away the most successful Czech political party, was committed to the continuation of the federation. However it and its leader tended to see issues from a Czech perspective and to be uncompromising in defence of Czech interests. In Slovakia, Public against Violence split asunder acrimoniously when the politically talented and charismatic but also abrasive and controversial Slovak prime minister, Vladimír Mečiar, seceded from the movement to form his own organisation and was as a result dismissed from office along with seven of his cabinet.

The issue that led to the formation of his Movement for a Democratic Slovakia was his insistence that Slovak national interests should be given a significantly higher political priority. He was careful to keep himself aloof from the popular demonstrations in Bratislava by the minority of fervent nationalists who raucously demanded the rehabilitation of Tiso and his wartime government. He also did not join the Slovak National Party, which had won about 11 per cent of the vote on the election of the federal assembly and nearly 14 per cent in that of the Slovak national council, in its openly separatist demands. He was nevertheless able to tap the rich vein of resentment and frustrated national aspirations of Slovaks who, in Václav Havel's words 'wanted to stand on their own two feet and be masters of their own fate, because for a thousand years their nation was always ruled over by someone'.[11]

Shrugging off allegations that he had collaborated with the secret police, Mečiar's effective populist style made him Slovakia's leading political figure and was to secure him electoral victory in June 1992.[12] The extent to which separate statehood had become the main issue in Slovak politics was shown when even Jan Čarnogursky, the new Christian Democrat prime minister, posited that Slovakia should achieve full independence by 2000 and membership of the European Community as a sovereign state.[13]

The constitution that had been inherited from the old regime was a major obstacle to proper functioning of the federation. The system of checks and balances it incorporated made it possible for belligerent Slovak deputies to obstruct the work of the federal government. The federal assembly was divided into two chambers, of the people and of the nations, and the chamber of nations was sub-divided into Czech and Slovak halves. Bills had to pass all three hurdles by a clear majority, and constitutional amendments needed a three fifths majority. Constitutional reform was thus difficult to achieve. But in constitutional terms the major source of contention was the relationship between the federal assembly and government on the one hand and the national governments and elected councils or parliaments on the other. On the Czech side there was a clear wish to have clear and firm federal foreign, defence and economic policies. On the Slovak side there was increasing pressure for the maximum devolution of powers in all areas to the national governments. The passage of the law on competencies through the federal assembly in December 1990 was a significant landmark in this context since it opened the way for Mečiar as Slovak prime minister vigorously to promote the devolution of competence in decision making from the federal to the national level. The Slovaks thus set up their own foreign ministry in Bratislava, and increasingly challenged the economic policies being pursued by Klaus from Prague.

The arguments over competencies were symptomatic of genuine differences of interest and policies between Prague and Bratislava. Klaus's emergence as the head of his own political party strengthened his hand in pushing through a vigorous programme of economic reform, including rapid privatisation, the promotion of a market economy and stringent monetary controls. Mečiar and his supporters, whilst not opposing the concept of a market economy, wanted more attention to be paid to the social impact of these reforms and demanded a much slower pace of transition. The truth was that Slovakia was very much harder hit by the reforms than the Czech lands. Husák's largesse had developed uneconomic heavy industrial and armaments plants in Slovakia, and these were adversely affected by the new policies and by the arms-limitation agreements enthusiastically championed from Prague. Unemployment had reached 12 per cent in Slovakia by May 1992, as opposed to only 4 per cent in the Czech republic. Slovaks complained bitterly that only 5 per cent of Western investment had gone to their republic, and accusations of manipulation were made against Prague. Slovakia was hard hit by the collapse of markets to the east as the countries of the former Soviet Union became unable to afford imports when terms of trade were converted into US dollars. Slovak defiance of federal injunctions by continuing foreign arms sales publicised the real conflict of interests.

These clashes strengthened the view that Slovakia was not being treated as an equal partner in the federation but as a subordinate province. Fears grew that Slovakia's interests could never be properly safeguarded in a federation in which it had only a third of the total population. A vigorous debate on the issue developed within Slovakia. The concept of a unitary state had little support. Alexander Dubček's definition of the federation as an alliance of two republics, each with a distinct national identity, had strong support. But Mečiar and his movement for a democratic Slovakia were also widely backed for their notion of a confederation in which Slovakia would be not just a nation but also a sovereign state, enjoying independence but loosely linked in a mutually agreed cooperative arrangement with the Czechs. It was argued that this would be an arrangement without precedent, but in line with what the countries of the European Community were trying to achieve in their Maastricht Agreement.[14]

Formal separation and complete independence as such were not issues in the June 1992 elections, except for the Slovak National Party, which gained only nine of the 75 seats in the Slovak half of the chamber of nations. Neither of the main contenders, Klaus or Mečiar, campaigned openly for separation. To have done so would have been electorally harmful since public-opinion polls indicated that most voters in both republics did not want separation. Nevertheless their positions were so irreconcilable that a continued union after their victories was hardly possible without significant concessions that neither side was prepared to make. Klaus was insistent that his reform programme was immutable and that confederation was unacceptable. Convinced of the rightness of his views, he appears to have decided that more autonomy to the republics would compromise his radical economic proposals and that its recent track record showed that it was impossible to work with the Slovak nationalist camp. Mečiar was possibly more ready to compromise in order to avoid separation, but needed significant concessions to Slovakia in economic and social policies and sufficient autonomy to give some realism to his claims that Slovakia should be a sovereign state within a confederation. Neither was willing to hold a referendum on the issue. Only a strong president might have enforced a truce, but Havel's powers and influence were limited even before his resignation after the Slovak national council had adopted Slovakia's declaration of sovereignty on 17 July 1992. Despite all his efforts he had been regarded as a Czech favouring the Czech side by Slovak nationalists, who were suspicious of his Prague base and regarded the Slovak element in his advisory council to be relatively too weak.

CONCLUSIONS

It would be easy to depict the separation of the Czech and Slovak republics as the inevitable consequence of a tide of history that had produced a multitude of new and often small nation states in Eastern Europe and the former Soviet Union. The swift international recognition of states smaller and less obviously viable than Slovakia showed that independence was feasible and encouraged nationalist aspirations. Slovaks and Czechs had a separate history, distinctive cultures and languages, and clearly defined national identities. Historical trends certainly made separation more rather than less likely, but at all stages of the story individuals made decisive contributions, whether it be Štúr adopting the central Slovak dialect as the basis for literary language, or Klaus and Mečiar preferring quick divorce to the slow and painful process of conciliation.

Separation has not removed nationalism from the scene as a live force in Czech and Slovak relations. The heightened sense of nationality increases the possibility of tensions between the two new states, and the position of the Slovak minority in the Czech republic will be watched with eagle eye from over the border. Moravians have twice voted in sufficient numbers for their Movement for Self-Governing Democracy – the Society for Moravia and Silesia to make incipient Moravian national self-consciousness a potential destabilising force if significant concessions are not made to their aspirations in the new Czech constitution, even if their movement is wracked by internal tensions. National problems are likely to be more intense in Slovakia: 10.8 per cent of Slovakia's population are Magyars, concentrated close to the Hungarian border. They are politically organised, sensitive on the issues of language educational rights, and are likely to be defended in any conflict by Hungary, which has strained relations with Slovakia as a result of the protracted dispute over the building of the Gabčikovo dam on the Danube, a project rejected by the post-communist Hungarian government on environmental grounds but continued by the Slovaks out of economic necessity. The small

Ruthenian minority on the eastern frontier could become involved in a Ruthenian movement in Ukraine. The Gypsies are seen as a problem by many Czechs and Slovaks as human-rights issues compound social problems. No early end to the problems caused by actual and potential nationalism seems likely in the former Czechoslovakia.

Notes and References

1. Quoted by Hugh Le Caine Agnew, 'Slovak Linguistic Separation', in John Morison (ed.), *The Czech and Slovak Experience* (London: Macmillan, 1992), p. 51.
2. For more detail on this point see Z. A. B. Zeman, *Pursued by a Bear* (London: Chatto and Windus, 1989), pp. 25–32.
3. Cited in Joseph F. Zacek, *Palacký: The Historian as a Scholar and Nationalist* (The Hague and Paris: Mouton, 1970), pp. 84–5.
4. For a detailed discussion of this thesis, see Miroslav Hroch, *Social Preconditions of National Revival in Europe* (Cambridge: Cambridge University Press, 1985), pp. 44–61, 98–106.
5. Cited in Barbara A. Kohak Kimmel, 'Karel Havlíček and the Czech Press before 1848', in Peter Brock and H. Gordon Skilling (eds), *The Czech Renascence of the Nineteenth Century* (Toronto: University of Toronto Press, 1970), p. 122.
6. Joseph F. Zacek, 'Nationalism in Czechoslovakia', in Peter F. Sugar and Ivo Lederer (eds), *Nationalism in Eastern Europe* (Seattle: University of Washington Press, 1969), p. 193.
7. James Felak, 'Slovak Considerations of the Slovak Question: the Ludak, Agrarian, Socialist and Communist Views in Interwar Czechosloavakia', in John Morison (ed.), *The Czech and Slovak Experience* (London: Macmillan, 1992), p. 143.
8. For detailed analysis, see Ludvík Němec, 'Solution of the Minorities Problem', in Victor S. Mamatey and Radomir Luza (eds), *A History of the Czechoslovak Republic 1918–1948* (Princeton: Princeton University Press, 1973), pp. 416–27.
9. H. Gordon Skilling, *Czechoslovakia's Interrupted Revolution* (Princeton: Princeton University Press, 1976), pp. 457–89, 858–77.
10. Martin Myant, *The Czechoslovak Economy 1948–1988* (Cambridge: Cambridge University Press, 1989), p. 261.
11. Interview with Adam Michnik and Andrzej Jagodzinski in *Gazeta Wyborcza*, reprinted in the *Guardian* on 25 September 1992.
12. Jan Obrman, 'Slovak Politician Accused of Secret Police Ties', *RFE/RL Research Report*, 10 April 1991; Jiri Pehe, 'Political Conflict in Slovakia', *RFE/RL Research Institute Report on Eastern Europe*, 10 May 1991; Jiri Pehe, 'The Realignment of Political Forces', *RFE/RL Research Institute Report on Eastern Europe*, 24 May 1991.
13. Bernard Wheaton and Zdeněk Kavan, *The Velvet Revolution: Czechoslovakia, 1988–1991* (Boulder Co: Westview Press, 1992), pp. 177–8.

14.   For a clear analysis of this debate, see Stanislav J. Kirschbaum, 'Les Slovaques et le droit des peuple à disposer d'eux-mêmes: a le recherche d'une solution', in André Liebich and Andre Reszler (eds), *L'Europe centrale et ses minorities: vers une solution européene* (Paris: Press Uiversitaire Française, 1993), pp. 83–102.

6 Hungarian National Identity: Definition and Redefinition

Rebecca Ann Haynes

HISTORICAL BACKGROUND

Hungarian national identity today closely resembles that of interwar Germany. This is not to say that Hungarians, as their detractors would sometimes have us believe, are about to launch an aggressive war for living space on their neighbours. For Hungarians today, however, as for interwar Germans, state and nation do not coincide. As a consequence there exists among Hungarians a sense of thwarted nationhood and of lost national greatness. In addition, while the sense of national community is strong in Hungary, this communal identity lacks a firm underpinning in the mythology of nationhood. As a consequence of its weak structural content, Hungarian national identity is constantly open to redefinition. In precisely the same way as German identity this century, the ascriptive qualities of Hungarian nationhood may be associated alternately with democratic values and with exclusive and intolerant varieties of nationalism.

The history of the Hungarian people in Europe goes back to the late ninth century when Magyar tribesmen from the steppes crossed the Carpathian mountains and settled in Pannonia. The invaders spoke a Finno-Ugrian language unrelated to the Indo-European languages used in their areas of settlement. The newcomers were rapidly converted to Christianity. During the reign of St Stephen (1000–1038) a Hungarian kingdom was founded that was firmly in the orbit of Catholic Christendom. An independent Hungarian state flourished in the middle ages and extended over an area roughly three times that of modern-day Hungary. Medieval Hungary included the territories of western Romania (Transylvania), Slovakia, Transcarpathian Ukraine (Ruthenia), Croatia and parts of northern Serbia.

In 1526 the king of Hungary was slain by the Turks on the field

87

of Mohács. While the Turks subsequently occupied the central portion of the kingdom, the Habsburg rulers of Austria claimed the vacant throne. Over the succeeding two centuries the Habsburgs pushed the Turks out of Hungary, eventually incorporating the entire kingdom within the Habsburg monarchy of central Europe. The Habsburg kings of Hungary were seldom, however, mindful of the feudal privileges of the Hungarian nobility; moreover they persecuted the kingdom's Protestants. Hungarian resistance to Habsburg overlordship led to a succession of rebellions that culminated in the 1848 revolution. Although the Hungarian uprising was suppressed by the Habsburgs with Russian help, Hungary was awarded home rule in 1867. The Habsburg monarchy was refashioned as the Dual or Austro-Hungarian monarchy, and Hungary was permitted its own parliament.

Although proclaiming itself a national state, nineteenth-century Hungary was in reality multinational, as ethnically diverse as the Habsburg monarchy itself. Only half the population comprised Hungarians, the remainder consisting of Romanians, Slovaks, Serbs, Croats, Germans, Ruthenes and Jews. Despite the state's ethnic diversity, it was regarded by Hungarians as their historic territory since it corresponded roughly to the area the Magyars had settled in the ninth century, and from which the medieval kingdom had developed. Furthermore the creation of the dual monarchy in 1867 reinforced a sense of 'mission' amongst Hungarians to rule over and 'civilise' the national minorities in their half of the Habsburg monarchy.[1]

Until the nineteenth century the Hungarian nation was understood to comprise only the nobility. The nobles constituted the *natio* and *populus*; the peasantry ranked only as the *misera contribuens plebs*. They were excluded by Hungary's antique constitution from any share in the country's political life. Under the impact of the French Revolution, romanticism and liberalism, a new concept of the nation emerged during the middle decades of the century. The nation was defined no longer in terms of status but in terms of nationality. Membership of the political nation now belonged to all those of Hungarian nationality and nationality was almost entirely defined by language. Hungarian policy towards the nationalities is frequently criticised for its intolerance. However, because nationality was understood almost entirely by reference to linguistic criteria, it proved relatively pervious. In this respect it bears closer resemblances to

Western models of civic nationality (particularly the French variety) than to the more exclusivist types typical in East Central Europe.[2]

Hungary entered the First World War on the side of the central powers. She thus emerged in 1918 diplomatically isolated as a defeated belligerent. Under the terms of the 1920 Treaty of Trianon, Hungary lost two-thirds of her prewar territory, which was awarded to Austria and Romania and newly created Czechoslovakia and Yugoslavia. As a result of these territorial arrangements, over three million Hungarians were left outside the borders of the new Hungarian state.

The Treaty of Trianon had two important effects on traditional notions of identity. Firstly, by dismembering the prewar state the link between the nation and a historic territory was shattered. Moreover the effect of the treaty was to undermine the notion of a Hungarian 'mission' to govern the nationalities in the Danube basin. From being joint guardian of an empire that had taken centre stage in European affairs, Hungary was now merely one amongst many Central European states.

With traditional concepts of identity thus undermined, the notion of Hungarians as a community of suffering gathered strength. Hungarians now perceived themselves as the victims of foreign aggression that had thwarted Hungary's national development. The notion of a community of suffering was reinforced by a brief but bloody period of Bolshevik rule in 1919. The severity of the regime, particularly towards the landed nobility and peasantry, created a lasting distrust of left-wing, 'internationalist' politics.

Following the collapse of the Bolshevik regime, Hungary's traditional ruling elite – the gentry – reasserted themselves. In 1920 a counter-revolutionary and conservative majority was returned to the national assembly. From this majority the 'Government Party' was created and retained a majority in the national assembly throughout the interwar decades. This was an important factor in maintaining gentry interests. The Government Party, together with all major political parties, espoused patriotism and a policy of territorial revisionism.

During the 1920s and early 1930s, however, the ruling elite failed actively to reinforce the traditional notion of Hungarian identity based on equating the nation with a historic territory. A search for a Hungarian identity based on alternative foundations began. This often took the form of emphasising ethnic or presumed racial differ-

90 *Hungarian National Identity*

ences between Hungarians and members of national minority groups who had assimilated into Hungarian society (see Table 6.1). These assimilated minorities then became the 'outsiders' against whom the boundaries of a renewed Hungarian nation could be measured.

It was the Jews in particular who were often taken as the yard-stick against which the 'true' Hungarian could be measured. Following the collapse of the Bolshevik regime, a Numerus Clausus was introduced in 1920 to limit the number of Jews attending Hungarian

Table 6.1   Ethnic composition of Hungary (per cent)

Ethnic group	1930	1949	1970	1980
Magyars	92.1	98.6	98.5	98.8
Germans	5.5	0.2	0.4	0.3
Slovaks	1.2	0.3	0.2	0.1
Romanians	0.2	0.2	0.1	0.1
Croats	0.5	0.2	0.2	0.2
Serbs	0.1	0.1	0.1	0.0
Wends and Slovenes	0.1	0.1	0.0	0.0
Gypsies	0.1	0.2	0.3	0.3
Others	0.2	0.1	0.2	0.2

Notes: Statistics taken from Glatz, Ferenc, 'A kisebbségi kérdés Közép-Európában tegnap es ma', *história plusz*, no. 11 (1992), p. 43. The fall in the German and Slovak populations between 1930 and 1949 is due to the population transfers that took place after the Second World War. The figures above are based on ethnicity by mother tongue. The Jewish population has not, therefore, been recorded separately since the Jews are regarded as a Magyar-speaking religious group rather than a national group. According to Joseph Rothschild, the 'Israelite' population of Hungary in 1930 was 444 567, or 5.1 per cent of the total population. See his *East Central Europe between the Two World Wars* (Seattle: University of Washington Press, 1974), p. 192. In 1991 there were between 80 000 and 100 000 Jews in Hungary. There is a similar problem in calculating the number of Gypsies in Hungary. The figures above are almost certainly an underestimate since the Gypsy population was calculated at between 600 000 and 700 000 in 1991. These figures are quoted in Alfred A. Reisch, 'Hungary: First Law on Minorities Drafted', RFE/RL Research Report, 13 December 1991, p. 15.

universities, although this was later revoked. In 1923 the Race Protection Society was formed to protest against the high number of Jews in the recent Bolshevik regime and in the economy and professions. A number of such 'patriotic' associations existed throughout the 1920s and 1930s, some of which espoused 'Turanianism'. According to this obscure ideology, the Hungarians were an Asiatic race, akin to the Japanese, whose ancestors had been the so-called Turanians. A biogenetic element was thus introduced as a 'true' Turanian was marked out from Semitic and European interlopers by the existence of a curious yellow streak across the back.[3]

During the interwar decades a populist ideology also emerged in Hungary.[4] This was both a literary and a political movement that aimed at the renewal of Hungarian society through the articulation of the needs of Hungary's peasant masses. For the populists, it was the 'true' Hungarian peasantry who, as the repository of traditional and 'unique' Hungarian values, constituted the core of the nation. For the populists, the Hungarian 'rural' nation stood in danger of contamination and destruction by the Jewish and German 'urban' middle class. The populist movement therefore had a strong anti-German and anti-Semitic element. The populist belief in the 'uniqueness' of Hungarian values and traditions led many of its adherents to revive the prewar notion of a Hungarian mission. This often took the form of a Hungarian 'Third Road' whereby both Western and communist forms of political development were rejected as alien to Hungarian traditions. Rather, an independent, peasantist democracy was advocated: a 'Garden Hungary', which was to take its place in a federation of free Danubian states.

The interwar decades witnessed considerable flux in Hungarian notions of identity. Traditional concepts based on equating the nation with a specific territory and the Hungarian mission to govern the peoples of the Danube area had been undermined by the postwar settlement. A theoretical vacuum therefore existed behind the strongly felt sense of Hungarian community, which provided considerable room for the creation of new national myths and identities.

THE SECOND WORLD WAR

Only in the late 1930s, when the diplomatic initiative had passed to the Axis powers, could Hungary's ruling elite embark on an active pursuit of revisionism. With the rise of Axis power in Europe, the ruling Government Party moved increasingly to the right of the political spectrum. Axis diplomacy eventually led to the return to Hungary of southern Slovakia in 1938, Ruthenia in 1939 and northern Transylvania in 1940. The need to secure herself in Germany's favour in order to retain her newly regained territories was a major factor in Hungary's decision to join Germany in the war against the Soviet Union in June 1941.

The Government Party's pro-Axis shift in foreign policy also had implications for Hungary's internal policies. For the first time since 1920 anti-Semitic legislation was passed. A law of 1941 prohibited marriages between Jews and non-Jews. This introduced into Hungarian legislation for the first time a racial rather than a purely religious definition of Jewishness. Further anti-Semitic legislation was to culminate in the destruction of the vast majority of Hungary's Jews following the German occupation in March 1944. Of the 725 000 Jews who lived within the expanded wartime borders of Hungary, only 260 000 survived the war.[5] The destruction of Hungary's Jewish community cannot be blamed entirely on the policies of the occupying Germans, it also represented the culmination of the xenophobic nationalist ideologies that had developed in interwar Hungary.

In October 1944 the occupying Germans placed the fascist Arrow Cross movement in government in place of the Government Party. With the green shirt and the arrow cross as its symbols, the movement had preached a nebulous mixture of Marxism, nationalism, anti-Semitism and revisionism during the 1930s. Central to the movement was the ideology of 'Hungarism', according to which the Hungarian destiny was to create and govern over a federation to be known as the 'Carpatho-Danubian Great Fatherland'. The Arrow Cross movement thus attempted to revive the notion of a Hungarian mission to govern the nationalities of the Danube basin. But in this renewed Hungary there was to be no place for the Jews.[6]

THE COMMUNIST PERIOD

The Hungarian Communist Party, which held power from 1949 to 1990, was almost unique amongst East European communist parties in not exploiting nationalism. The communists' failure to address questions of national identity was based in the first instance on their dependence upon the Soviet Union. The 1947 Paris Peace Treaty, which settled the territorial questions arising from the Second World War, reaffirmed Hungary's Trianon losses. During the negotiations the Soviet Union had made her preference for Czechoslovak and Romanian claims against Hungary very clear. Since the Hungarian Communist Party was unpopular amongst most Hungarians, it was dependent on Soviet backing to maintain power. The Party was not, therefore, in any position to revive revisionism as a policy. A Hungarian identity based on equating the nation with a historic territory was effectively dead.

With revisionism moribund as an official policy, it could no longer be invoked as a means of reuniting the Hungarian diaspora within the Hungarian state. Revisionism therefore gave way to a direct interest amongst the Hungarian population in the fate and treatment of the Hungarian minorities now permanently 'exiled' in neighbouring states. These were perceived as being in danger of 'disappearance' through assimilation, forced or unforced, into the majority populations in their respective countries.

Nevertheless the experience of communist rule itself served to provide a redefinition of Hungarian identity based in particular upon the 1956 revolution. Although its ideals lacked coherence, calls for national sovereignty, neutrality in foreign policy and solidarity with the Hungarian minorities provided a 'national' dimension to the revolution. A number of opposition populists who had survived the Second World War and the communist takeover were instrumental in providing an intellectual foundation for the revolution, based upon the so-called 'Petőfi Party'. The populists' stress on the importance of Hungary's 'unique traditions' was invoked by István Bibó in a reworking of the interwar populist idea of the Hungarian 'Third Road'. This time, however, the 'Third Road', a mixture of communism and capitalism, was to include guarantees for individual rights and parliamentary democracy based on 'Western' models.[7] The 1956 revolution thus relocated Hungary's 'traditional values' within the mainstream of Western liberal history. A Hungarian identity based on 'Western traditions' could, therefore, be contrasted with Soviet 'Eastern' totalitarianism. This was to be an important factor by the late 1980s when opposition groups were demanding that Hungary should be allowed to 'rejoin' her Western neighbours – in a so-called 'return to Europe'. Since it was Soviet power that had ensured both the victory of communism in the late 1940s and the suppression of the 1956 revolution and had thus cut Hungary off from her 'Western traditions', the entire communist period came increasingly to be seen as an aberration in Hungary's national development.

The populists were particularly concerned about the fate of Romania's two million Hungarians. Pressure had been placed on the Transylvanian Hungarians throughout the era of Nicolae Ceauşescu's rule in Romania. In particular, Ceauşescu hoped to eliminate the Hungarians as a distinct ethnic group by the suppression of separate language facilities. Ceauşescu's 'systematisation' policy, involving the destruction of traditional villages and the movement of the villagers into urban settlements, was also an attempt to destroy ethnic Hungarian communities. As a result of a meeting held in September 1987, the populists founded the Magyar Democratic Forum (MDF) under the protection of the reform-communist minister of state, Imre Pozsgay. Prime Minister Károlyi Grósz' failure to secure any changes in Ceauşescu's 'systematisation' policy in August 1988 was an important factor in the MDF's decision to proclaim itself a formal movement the next month. The question of Hungarian minorities thus was a factor in eroding the communist regime's last vestiges of legitimacy.

HUNGARIAN NATIONAL IDENTITY AFTER COMMUNISM

Following the free elections of March 1990, the MDF established a coalition government with the Independent Smallholders' Party and the Christian Democratic Party. The coalition was based upon a common espousal of Christian and conservative values, with the MDF in particular stressing the importance of Hungarian 'national values'. These 'national values' were, however, ill-defined.[8] Indeed, although a sense of a unique identity remains strongly felt amongst Hungarians, the fall of communist power has not resulted in the creation of a new and coherent sense of nationhood.

The principal marker of Hungarian identity remains primarily linguistic. Ethnic minorities continue to be assimilated with relative ease into Hungarian society. Of Hungary's 100 000 citizens of Slovak descent, for instance, only 15 000 continue to speak Slovak as their first tongue.[9] The gradual assimilation of the Slovak community into Hungarian society seems assured. Ease of assimilation suggests that, apart from language, further ethnic criteria are not necessarily a bar to the assumption of a Hungarian identity. More particularly, notions of identity currently lack the racial underpinning provided by exclusivist, interwar ideologies such as 'Turanianism'.

The interwar notion of Hungarians as a community of suffering still exists and has been strengthened by the period of communist rule. In particular, the Party's inability to deal with the problems faced by the Hungarian minorities has served to intensify the feeling of belonging to a common nation amongst the Hungarian population both inside and outside the Hungarian state. Furthermore, since it was Soviet power that ensured the victory of communism after 1947 and the suppression of the 1956 revolution, Hungarians regard themselves as the victims of an unwanted communist regime much as they did after the 1919 Bolshevik experiment.

To these interwar concepts of nationhood, however, a new element has been added. Based on the experience of the 1956 revolution, a conviction has developed that the Hungarians are would-be democrats looking to Western Europe. This is symbolised by the 'return to Europe' slogan used by virtually all political parties during the 1990 election campaigns. Indeed the concept of a Hungarian 'mission' has even been revived in this context. In a recent interview, Bertalan Andrásfalvy, minister of culture and education, stated that 'Every people has a mission, so do the Hungarians. . . . The full respect of the individual and the collective liberty of conscience is a part of the Hungarian role'.[10] Even the Hungarian 'Golden Age' of St Stephen has been used as an example of Hungary's 'Western' credentials. According to Foreign Minister Géza Jeszensky, St Stephen wanted Hungarians 'to fall in line with the most advanced ideas then prevailing in the West'.[11]

Beyond these convictions, however, there is little other intellectual foundation to the Hungarian sense of identity. In particular, Hungarian nationhood lacks any coherent sense of a religious underpinning. In a recent interview Géza Jeszensky stated that 'Hungary's ideal continues to be religion as an important moral force'.[12] Since religious affiliation in Hungary is divided between Catholicism and Calvinism, religion as such cannot provide an underpinning to notions of identity beyond a vague loyalty to a broadly based 'Western' Christianity. Furthermore, while the majority of the Hungarian population is Catholic, it was the Calvinism of the gentry class that was identified with the national struggle against Habsburg domination. The strength of religious loyalties have, additionally, been eroded by communist secularisation.

The present-day Hungarian identity has shed the identification of the nation with an 'ancestral territory' and the historic Hungarian kingdom. There have been no calls for revisionism by any major political party since 1947. On the seventieth anniversary of Trianon in June 1990, the main political parties reaffirmed Hungary's adherence to the 1975 Helsinki Final Act, which fixed European borders. At the same time the Hungarians have but an infirm grasp of the concept of the nation-state, since a considerable part of the Hungarian ethnic nation lives beyond the borders of the Hungarian political state. As Hungary's president, Árpád Göncz recently stated, Hungarian culture may be regarded as 'almost a regional culture'.[13]

Similarly, the sense of Hungarian nationhood based on the mythology of the nation's unbroken historical development has also been eroded. This is evident in the commonly held belief that Hungary has a 'lost history'. President Göncz recently stated that due to the imposition of communism, postwar Hungary was 'unable to pursue its own national aspirations' and has consequently 'missed its own modern history'.[14] Géza Entz, state secretary for Hungarians abroad, has referred to the Habsburg Empire and the interwar nation-state as 'distortions of our national development'.[15] This sense of a 'lost history' has led to an obsession amongst present-day Hungarians with Hungary's past.

Paradoxically therefore, although Hungarians have a strongly felt sense of national identity, the intellectual, mythological and historical underpinnings are weak. As in the interwar period, a theoretical vacuum exists that provides considerable room for national myth-making or the recreation of 'outgroups' by which to measure Hungarian identity.

CSURKA AND THE REVIVAL OF INTERWAR NATIONALIST IDEOLOGY

A start has already been made in redefining Hungarian identity based on the creation of 'outgroups' by István Csurka, who heads the populist wing of the MDF and is the party's former vice-president. In August 1992 he produced an article in which he stated that the MDF needed to construct a new programme and that its priority should be the survival of the Hungarian nation.[16] He claimed that through its links with the liberal opposition and the Western business world, Jews and former communists were clinging on to power. Indeed this was part of an 'international plot' to destroy the MDF.[17] Csurka went on to suggest that the destruction of the MDF would mean the end of the Hungarian nation.

Csurka further suggested that the deterioration of the Hungarian population had genetic causes and, in a possible reference to Hungary's approximately 700 000 Gypsies, he stated that the underprivileged 'have been living amongst us for far too long'. He suggested that the MDF should support only economically productive families and what he called a 'national middle class'. Csurka went on to refer to the Treaty of Trianon as an injustice. He claimed that the 1945 Yalta Declarations were due to expire in 1995, with the implication that territorial revisionism would once again be a possibility. He asked whether Hungarians could 'live with the new possibility of creating a Hungarian living space', thus reviving the notion of a Hungarian identity based on the nation being coterminous with ancestral territory. He closed his article on a note of almost religious fervour, by stating that the new MDF programme should be drawn up 'in the sign of the trinity . . . the Hungarian spirit, justice and populism'.

The publication of Csurka's article appeared to presage a growing nationalist radicalisation in Hungary. A large rally was held in Budapest in support of Csurka in September 1992, while an attack on Gypsy households was carried out in Ketegyhaza during October.[18] The MDF, however, failed to issue a whole-hearted condemnation of Csurka's position, despite a storm in the international press. This reluctance was due not so much to general agreement with his position as a need to prevent a split in the MDF.

For the party's Christian democratic wing the nation is regarded as a moral unit, and 'moral regeneration' is thus seen as the most important aspect of the party's role. The liberal wing, on the other hand, regards Westernisation of the Hungarian economy and government as the priority. The populist wing, headed by Csurka, however, is wary of economic and social policies that could be alien to Hungary's traditions. The MDF prime minister, Jószef Antall, presides as a 'trimmer' over the three groups. An ambiguous response to Csurka's article was deemed necessary to keep the party united. Consequently, however, the party's overall response to questions of national identity remain confused. Antall's self-description as a 'liberal Christian Democrat of national commitment who believes in a united Europe'[19] reflects just this confusion.

A strong sense of Hungarian unity as a community of suffering, however, still prevails and the national question, as in the communist period, continues to centre almost entirely around the issue of the Hungarian minorities. Following his election victory in April 1990, Antall stated that the 'Hungarian nation stands united regardless of the citizenship that some Hungarians may have acquired in the tempest of history'.[20] In August of the same year he declared himself 'in spirit' the prime minister for all fifteen million Hungarians who live world-wide.[21]

Despite the fears of Hungary's neighbours, however, there seems no reason to believe that these comments presage attempts at territorial revision. There have been no revisionist calls since the 1947 Paris Peace Treaty. A rally organised by the extra-parliamentary Christian National Union in June 1990 to demand the return of Transylvania received little support, while all the political parties represented in parliament reaffirmed their commitment to Hungary's Trianon borders.

At the same time, however, the existence of the Hungarian diaspora means that Hungarians do not believe that the nation-state is necessarily the best means of solving the region's ethnic disputes. In March 1992, for instance, state secretary for foreign affairs, Tamás Katona, stated that the solution to the minorities issue lay not in redrawing borders but in 'rendering borders permeable'.[22] András Gergely, former chief secretary of the Foreign Ministry, invoking what he called 'the St Stephen ideology', declared that 'Hungarian statehood . . . called for creating a common homeland for the nationalities living there'.[23] In particular, Hungary hopes to ensure the assertion of minority rights on a collective rather than an individual basis. This would give minorities a right, for instance, to education in the mother tongue.

Concern is still particularly centred on the fate of the two million Transylvanian Hungarians who constitute the largest of the Hungarian minority groups. The early promises given by the Romanian National Salvation Front following the 1989 revolution to ensure Hungarian language facilities and collective rights have been broken. Since the interethnic clashes in Tîrgu-Mureş in March 1990, Hungarians have often been the victims of judicial malpractice.[24] Hungary has used its position within the Council of Europe (which it entered in 1990) and the Conference on Security and Cooperation in Europe to draw attention to their plight and to bring pressure to bear on the Romanians over the issue of collective rights. The Romanians, however, have repeatedly denied the legality of collective rights, asserting that rights can only be asserted by individual citizens. Calls by the Hungarian Democratic Union of Romania (HDUR) for cultural and local autonomy have inevitably, therefore, fallen on deaf ears.[25]

The break up of the Czechoslovak federation in January 1993 has renewed concerns amongst the MDF for the fate of Slovakia's 600 000 Hungarians, who make up 11 per cent of the new state.[26] Slovakia's nationalist prime minister, Vladimír Meciar, has ruled out any assertion of collective rights or autonomy advocated by the main Hungarian political party in Slovakia – Coexistence. Like the Romanian government, Meciar has stated that members of the Hungarian community should exercise their rights as individual citizens rather than collectively and that the Slovak nation alone is the 'state-building' nation of the new Slovakia. Indeed this concept was incorporated into the new Slovak constitution of September 1992.

The outbreak of the war in Yugoslavia in 1991 and the break up of the Yugoslav federation has also affected the status of the 400 000 Hungarians in the Serbian province of Vojvodina. Autonomy granted to Vojvodina under the 1974 constitution was abolished and in July 1991 Serbian was made the sole official language. Following Hungary's arms sale to Serbia's Croatian enemies in October 1990, Serbia has intensified pressure on the Hungarians of Vojvodina, including drafting them into the Federal Army in numbers disproportionate to their population. Matters have not been helped by Antall's somewhat tactless remark in July 1991, with the break up of Yugoslavia imminent, that Hungary ceded Vojvodina to the Yugoslav state in 1920 and not to an independent Serbia.[27] Demands made by the Democratic Community of Hungarians in Vojvodina for collective rights and autonomy have been no more successful than those made by fellow Hungarians in Slovakia and Romania.

Ukraine alone has accepted the principle of collective rights and that Hungary has an obligation to Hungarians abroad. In December 1991 the Transcarpathian Oblast, where most of the Ukraine's 160 000 Hungarians live, voted for autonomy. Preparations were then put underway for Hungarian self-government through the Hungarian Cultural Association of Subcarpathia, and there has been considerable progress in the provision of Hungarian language facilities. In a visit to Ukraine as early as September 1990, President Göncz referred to the creation of a borderless economic zone between Oblast and Hungary. He also referred to the possibilities of regional co-operation between the western Ukraine, eastern Slovakia, southern Poland, north-east Hungary and Transylvania.[28]

CONCLUSION

The events of the twentieth century have profoundly weakened the mythological and intellectual underpinnings that gave Hungarian identity its coherency before the First World War. The Treaty of Trianon destroyed the sense of a Hungarian mission to govern the nationalities of the Danube basin. In addition, the loss of two thirds of the historic Hungarian kingdom undermined the notion that the Hungarian nation was coterminous with an historic or ancestral territory. There were calls for territorial revisionism throughout the interwar period. Of the prewar mythology of Hungarian identity, therefore, language alone remained as a marker. A number of altern-ative 'myths' subsequently developed during the interwar period to buttress this linguistic criterion. These included the idea that Hungar-ians constituted a unique community of suffering, peasant populism, anti-Semitism and even biogenetic concepts. These ideologies sought to differentiate between 'true' Hungarians and members of assimi-lated national minorities. At the same time, the presence of three million Hungarians outside the post-Trianon state meant that Hun-garians never developed an ideological commitment to the notion of the nation-state. Vague ideas of Danubian federations and a peasantist, East European 'Third Road' emerged as alternative concepts.

During the Second World War the more extreme, exclusivist nationalist ideologies that had developed during the interwar period reached their conclusion in the destruction of Hungary's Jews. At the same time, the territorial concept of nationhood based on 'ancestral territory' and the Hungarian 'mission' to govern the nationalities of the Danube basin was briefly revived as a result of successful revi-sionist diplomacy.

The communist period saw general acceptance of the Trianon borders following the 1947 Paris Peace Treaty. Calls for territorial revisionism came to an end. As a consequence, however, attention became focused directly on the fate of the Hungarian minorities now permanently outside the Hungarian state. The inability of the Hun-garian Socialist Workers' Party to act on their behalf eroded what little remained of the party's legitimacy. It was partly as a result of this that power began to slip away to the MDF by the late 1980s. But despite the regime's failure to exploit nationalism, the communist period saw the development of a new notion of Hungarian identity based around Hungary's supposed 'Western credentials'. This was a result of the calls for democracy and guarantees for individual rights that had emerged during the 1956 revolution. The communist period failed, however, to provide any other redefinitions of Hungarian identity.

It is opposing attitudes towards the concept of the nation-state that lie at the heart of Hungary's current conflicts with her neighbours. Romania and Slovakia in particular fear that Hungarian talk of regional cooperation could simply be a Trojan horse for separatism by the Hungarian minorities or expansionism by the Hungarian state. Although these fears are currently largely unfounded, they remain fanned by tactless Hungarian remarks such as Prime Minister Antall's questioning of the legal status of Vojvodina in an independent Serbia or Csurka's reference to a 'Hungarian living space'. At the same time, the failure of governments to provide adequate safeguards to protect the distinct identities of the Hungarian minorities could well in itself lead to separatist moves or even the return of revisionist ideas. There are unconfirmed reports of moves afoot amongst the Hungarian Democratic Union of Romania to establish a Hungarian parliament.[29] In a recent statement, the Hungarian mayor of Komarno in Slovakia said that if the situation worsened for the Hungarian community, 'it could well be that our people will seek reunification with Hungary'.[30]

It remains to be seen to what extent the minorities issue, together with the growing problems within Hungary itself, will result in the reemergence of the type of nationalist intolerance visible during the interwar period and Second World War. It seems certain that Hungarian identity today, although strongly felt, is as weak in its intellectual and mythological underpinnings as it was in the interwar period. In particular the effects of economic marketisation, which are resulting in increasing unemployment and social dislocation, could also result in populist demagogues directing discontented elements of the population against 'outgroups' such as Gypsies or Jews. The publication of Csurka's article may foreshadow a move in this direction. On the other hand there can be little doubt that the majority of Hungarians at the present time equate Hungarian nationhood with at least some idea of democratic and broadly 'Western' values. Hungary thus has the potential to emerge, like postwar Germany, as a model of democratic virtue despite her totalitarian, communist past. The present reemergence of nationalist disputes throughout East Central Europe and the problems of the Hungarian diaspora may, however, impede the realisation of this goal.

Notes and References

1.	For the history of the Magyars from earliest time to the 1930s, see C. A. Macartney, *Hungary* (London: Ernest Benn, 1934), pp. 13–126.
2.	For an interpretation of Hungarian nationalism during the nineteenth century and up to the 1956 revolution, see George Barany, 'Hungary: From Aristocratic to Proletarian Nationalism', in Peter F. Sugar and Ivo J. Lederer (eds), *Nationalism in Eastern Europe* (Seattle: University of Washington Press, 1969), pp. 259–309.
3.	For more information on the patriotic associations and interwar nationalism, see, for instance, A. Janos, *The Politics of Backwardness in Hungary 1825–1945* (Princeton: Princeton University Press, 1982), pp. 238–312 and C. A. Macartney, *October the Fifteenth, A History of Hungary 1929–45*, vol. 1 (Edinburgh: University Press, 1956–7), and in particular pp. 25–45 for the patriotic associations. The Etelköz Association, for instance, set up in the wake of the Bolshevik experiment, was organised on the pattern of primitive Hungarian society. Rituals included an invocation of Hadúr (the God of War), believed to have been worshipped by the early Magyars. See Macartney, *October the Fifteenth*, p. 31.
4.	For the history of Hungarian populism, see G. Borbándi, *Der Ungarische Populismus* (Mainz: Hase and Koehler, 1976).
5.	J. Rothschild, *East Central Europe Between the Two World Wars* (Seattle: University of Washington Press, 1974), pp. 197–9.
6.	For a discussion of the Arrow Cross movement and the 'Carpatho-Danubian Great Fatherland', see E. Weber, *Varieties of Fascism: Doctrines of Revolution in the Twentieth Century*, (Princeton: Robert E. Krieger Publishing, 1982), pp. 88–96, 157.
7.	For the populist contribution to the 1956 revolution, see Borbándi, pp. 283–96. For the revolution and its background, see B. Kovrig, *Communism in Hungary: From Kun to Kadar* (Stanford: Hoover Institution Press, 1979), pp. 267–316.
8.	Despite the lack of definition, however, the MDF's populists are extremely sensitive on the issue of 'national values'. Hungarian Radio in Budapest reported a meeting of MDF populists held on 9 January 1993. At the meeting the minister of culture, Bertalan Andrásfalvy, was reported as saying that: 'In [his] opinion, there are those who subject to ridicule the values of centuries established by the whole nation. When this phenomenon became evident here, he understood why the writer Salman Rushdie was condemned to death by the Muslims, because he had committed sacrilege' (*BBC Summary of World Broadcasts*, Third Series EE/1584, 12 January 1993).

9. Alfred A. Reisch, 'The Difficult Search for a Hungarian–Slovak Accord', RFE/RL Research Report, 23 October 1992.
10. *The Hungarian Observer*, vol. 5, no. 8 (1992, Budapest), p. 13.
11. *The Hungarian Observer*, vol. 5, no. 8 (1992, Budapest), p. 2.
12. *The Hungarian Observer*, vol. 5, no. 8 (1992, Budapest), p. 3.
13. 'Culture and Society in Contemporary Hungary', address given by President Goncz at the University of London, 18 November, 1991.
14. Goncz address in London.
15. *The Hungarian Observer*, vol. 5, no. 8 (1992, Budapest), p. 8.
16. The text of Csurka's manifesto, 'Néhány gondolat a rendszerváltozás két esztendeje és as MDF új programja kapcsán', was published in *Magyar Fórum*, 20 August 1992. No English translation of the text is yet available, although extracts have been published. For the quotations that follow see Judith Pataki, 'Istvan Csurka's Tract: Summary and Reactions', RFE/RL, 9 October 1992.
17. On 25 November 1992 Csurka replied to criticisms that his statements had been anti-Semitic. In 'Some Words on a Single Issue' he stated that 'I do not see any united "international Jewish plot", but I do see signs of a plot for a return to communism. Those involved in this plot happen to include Jews without any strong identity and murderous gunmen in the Balkans' (*BBC Summary of World Broadcasts*, Third Series EE/1550, 28 November 1992).
18. See *The Independent on Sunday*, 25 October 1992. There has also been a rise in neo-Nazism in Hungary. István Györkös, who leads the neo-Nazi Hungarian National Front, is demanding a historical reappraisal of the interwar Arrow Cross movement. He recently stated: 'Why shouldn't it be accepted? Romanian society is prepared for Marshal Antonescu and the Slovaks have named a square after Tiso. . . . The Hungarist idea of Ferenc Szalasi, the leader of the Arrow Cross movement, will remain topical as long as Hungary exists' (*BBC Summary of World Broadcasts*, Third Series EE/1560, 10 December 1992).
19. As quoted in Judith Pataki, 'New Government Prefers Cautious Changes', RFE/RL, 13 July 1990.
20. As quoted in Zoltan D. Barany, 'The Hungarian Democratic Forum Wins National Elections Decisively', RFE/RL, 27 April 1990.
21. Edith Oltay, 'Hungary: Minorities Within and Without. Minorities as Stumbling Block in Relations with Neighbours', RFE/RL, 8 May 1992.
22. Oltay, 'Hungary: Minorities Within and Without'.
23. *The Hungarian Observer*, vol. 5, no. 8 (1992, Budapest), p. 5.
24. Edith Oltay, 'Hungary: Minorities Within and Without'.
25. For further information regarding the problems of the Hungarian minority in Transylvania, see Dennis Deletant, 'The Role of "Vatra Romaneasca" in Transylvania', RFE/RL, 1 February 1991.
26. Statistics quoted from Alfred A. Reisch, 'Meciar and Slovakia's Hungarian Minority', RFE/RL, 30 October 1992.
27. Edith Oltay, 'Hungary: Minorities Within and Without'.
28. Alfred Reisch, 'Hungary and Ukraine Agree to Upgrade Bilateral Relations', RFE/RL, 2 November 1990.
29. Moreover, Béla Markó, a Hungarian Democratic Union of Romania (HDUR) presidential candidate, apparently 'considers conceivable that in the future

the HDUR . . . would become – in accordance with the Hungarian community's demand for autonomy – a self-government body too' (*BBC Summary of World Broadcasts*, Third Series EE/1590, 19 January 1993).

30.   As quoted in Jan Obrman, 'Czechoslovakia: Minorities Not a Major Issue Yet', RFE/RL, 13 December 1991.

7 Nationalism in Poland
Frances Millard

INTRODUCTION

Polish nationalism has evolved over nearly two centuries, much of its development moulded by experience of foreign domination. Yet the Polish nation of the 1990s is not the Polish nation of the partition era, nor even that of the 1930s. The content of Polish nationhood, its scope and its territory have undergone profound changes (see Table 7.1 for changes in the ethnic composition). In brief, we can identify a shift from a civic–territorial model of the nation to an ethnic model.[1] This process also entailed a growth in mass consciousness of ethnic identity. In the late eighteenth and early nineteenth centuries the peasants, who constituted the majority of the population, displayed little sense of national consciousness. By the end of the nineteenth century they had begun to develop an ethnic–linguistic identity, and political parties based on nationalist ideology emerged to mobilise and channel that identity. The twentieth century saw the extension and consolidation of this ethnically based Polish nationalism, which also retained elements of both the gentry tradition and romantic nationalism.[2]

THE ORIGINS AND DEVELOPMENT OF POLISH NATIONALISM

The Polish Commonwealth (*Rzeczpospolita*) came into being in 1569, but its origins lie in the dynastic tie of 1386 between the Kingdom of Poland and the Grand Duchy of Lithuania. It covered a large and heterogeneous area, which varied over time but broadly encompassed modern Lithuania, Belorussia, Ukraine and most of modern Poland. It was highly decentralised, with six official languages, several judicial codes and considerable variety of local customs. The late sixteenth century saw the consolidation of the 'gentry democracy', which provided one element of the developing national tradition. Every member of the gentry (*szlachta*) was enfranchised, from the great aristocratic magnates to the impoverished petty gentry

Table 7.1　Ethnic composition of Poland

Ethnic group	1921 Census		1980s Estimates	
	Number	%	Number	%
Poles	18 814 239	69.2	–	95–98
Ukrainians	3 898 431	14.3	200 000	–
Jews	2 110 448	7.8	3 000	–
Belorussians	1 060 237	3.9	300 000	–
Germans	1 059 194	3.9	100 000	–
Lithuanians	68 667	0.3	20 000	–
Russians	56 239	0.2	–	–
Czechs	30 628	0.1	–	–
Total	27 176 717	100.0	35 700 000	100

Sources: The 1921 census statistics are as cited in Joseph Rothschild, *East Central Europe Between the Two World Wars* (Seattle: University of Washngton Press), p. 36. Accurate official or unofficial statistics of minorities in Poland are difficult to find. Generally, reference works indicate that minorities represent a negligible proportion of the overall population of Poland. The figures cited are taken from the following sources: Andrzej Albert [Wojciech Roszkowski], *Najnowsza historia Polski 1918–1980*, 4th ed. (London: Puls Publications, 1991), pp. 1051–2; 'Bialorusini u wicepremiera', *Rzeczpospolita*, 2 February 1993; R. F. Leslie (ed.), *The History of Poland since 1863* (Cambridge: Cambridge University Press, 1980), p. 444.

tilling tiny holdings. They possessed a shared consciousness of membership of the *natio* and loyalty to the commonwealth and its 'golden liberty'. It was thus not ethnic but political identity and shared privilege that united members of the 'nation'. Yet the great magnate families were not averse to seeking aid from foreign powers in order to enhance their own political influence.[3] Moreover this concept of national identity excluded the mass of the population. The peasants especially remained heterogeneous in language and religion, while their economic lot was one of virtual enslavement in conditions of serfdom.

The shock of the first partition, coupled with the spread of the radical ideas of the Englightenment and the French Revolution, generated a burst of modernising activity to save Poland by a regenerative internal reform. Conservative opponents, however, wished to return to the conditions of 'golden liberty' and found the reformist notions of hereditary monarchy, the abolition of the famous *liberum veto* and a strong standing army equally abhorrent. The reformers' victory was symbolised by the Constitution of the Third of May (1791), an attempt to limit the obstructive powers of the anarchic *szlachta* by strengthening the power of the monarch.

The new regime lasted just fifteen months. A group of conservatives secured the support of Catherine the Great, under whose protection they organised the Confederation of Targowica (1792). The Act of Confederation considered the May Constitution an 'audacious crime' that had abolished the liberty and equality of the nobility and 'imposed the shackles of slavery' upon the nation (that is, the *szlachta*).[4] Prussian guarantees proved meaningless in the context of a new Russian offensive. The result was the Second Partition (1793) and two years later the Polish state ceased to exist. Targowica subsequently became a symbol of national betrayal. It had the immediate consequence of dividing the interests of the aristocracy from those of the lesser *szlachta*. 'Whatever else the Confederation did', notes Leslie,

> it destroyed the divine right of the aristocracy to a monopoly of political power . . . even those aristocrats who had not been party to the Confederation were discredited. . . . The lesser *szlachta* convinced that in moments of crisis the aristocrats would prefer their own private interest to the welfare of the state, saw themselves as inheriting the cause of Poland.[5]

Many magnates adapted themselves to foreign rule, which maintained their economic power intact. 'In a certain sense we are now better off', wrote one; 'although without Poland, we are, nevertheless, in Poland and are Poles'.[6] Another echoed this view: 'We Polish landlords in Ukrainian provinces can only praise the new regime; we are free to live by our old Polish customs and . . . we are no longer afraid (of peasant risings)'.[7] It should not be forgotten that many ethnic 'Poles' increasingly identified with Russian or German culture.

For the petty gentry, however, especially the landless, the loss of statehood was catastrophic. They lost their political privileges, and there was little room for them in the new administrative machinery. Many, already compromised by the abortive Kościuszko Uprising of 1794, went into exile, where they continued to work for the resurrection of the state. The formation of Polish legions in 1797 to fight with Napoleon's army reflected their hope that Napoleon would help regain Polish independence. Indeed he set up the Duchy of Warsaw in 1806, but the debacle of his Russian invasion brought the collapse of Polish hopes. Nonetheless the patriotic fervour of the last days of the Republic, and its traditions of independence and active citizenship, continued to influence the development of Polish national consciousness.[8]

At the Congress of Vienna (1815) much of the Duchy of Warsaw became the Kingdom of Poland, linked to Russia by a common monarch. This solution found favour with conservative Polish forces; they saw Tsar Alexander I as an enlightened reformer who might well countenance the revival of a Polish state under his aegis.[9] The gain of a separate administration providing for self-rule under the supervision of Grand Duke Constantine already appeared significant. This was also a period of support for Slavophilism, one current of which emphasised the importance of a united Slav effort, under Russian leadership, to resist the influence of the decadent West. 'By association with the one great Slav power, by fusing Poland's efforts with the enormous collectivity of the Slav peoples, compensation was sought for their own nation's weakness.'[10] Nationalist feelings, then, were far from dominant.

At the same time the influence of that same decadent West was also becoming apparent, particularly on the young emergent intelligentsia, largely of *szlachta* origin. European Romanticism exerted a profound impact on Polish culture, which came to echo its themes of individualism, lyricism and emotion and its use of national and folk themes. Historians, painters, ethnographers and poets sought inspiration in the countryside and recreated an idealised past; some stressed the peasant's role as the true bearer of national culture. A new emphasis on the community of language began to take its place alongside territorial–political concepts of the nation. Gradually 'nation' assumed its modern ethnic connotation, though the territorial–historical dimension remained important, especially for Poles from the eastern borderlands (*kresy*). The embodiment of Polish Romantic nationalism, the poet Adam Mickiewicz, began his epic poem *Pan Tadeusz* with the words 'Lithuania! My Fatherland!'. The prominent historian Joachim Lelewel wrote in 1836, 'Already for centuries the Ruthenian, Polish and Lithuanian languages have been brothers; they constitute no national divisions among themselves'.[11] The historic claim to the 1772 boundaries recurred in nationalist discourse, even while the ethnic concept of the nation gained currency.

Romanticism increased the sense of a Polish cultural community, especially for the young intelligentsia. It evolved into a political movement focused on numerous secret societies that 'proclaimed the freedom of all nations and their own right to express the spirit of the Polish nation'.[12] Disgruntled young army cadets met the *literati* and imbibed their ideas. Their main inspiration was the Kościuszko uprising and the myths surrounding Napoleon's Polish legions. Their activities culminated in the abortive 1830 insurrection, which soon escalated into a full-blown war against Russia. However the conspirators lacked a social programme. The peasants, mistakenly equating the concept of 'liberty' with freedom from their compulsory labour obligations, were quickly disillusioned.[13] The uprising was quelled and Congress Poland's autonomy lost.

In the interlude lasting to the outbreak of the 1863 uprising, Russian Poland was quiet. Emigré circles nurtured a messianic concept of Poland, articulated by Mickiewicz as the 'Christ of Nations'. This was a spiritual concept of the nation, developed from a 'conviction that defeat in heroic struggle for a just cause is essentially a moral victory, while great suffering is an essential cleansing force in the great process of collective human redemption and salvation'.[14] In Prussian and Austrian Poland, however, there was a renewal of activity, though the Springtime of Nations proved yet another disappointment. In 1846 Galician peasants rose against their Polish masters in a bloody *jacquerie*. In 1848 antagonism between Germans and Poles undermined their common cause and the Poles succumbed to Prussia's military might. Polish nationalism then remained weak in Prussian Poland until stimulated by Bismarck's *Kulturkampf*, which (among other things) banned the use of Polish in state schools, and his Prussian Colonisation Commission (1886) to encourage German settlers in the eastern provinces. The anti-Catholic elements of Bismarck's policy stimulated a strong identification of Polishness and Catholicism. Thus, paradoxically, Bismarck's measures 'succeeded in stimulating the very feelings which they were designed to suppress. . . . Without them, there might have been no Polish movement in Prussia'.[15]

Political life in Russian Poland was reactivated with the accession of Alexander II in the period known as 'the Thaw' after the long reign of Nicholas I. However the 1863 uprising put paid to hopes of reform, while its failure weakened the romantic national impulse. The terms of peasant emancipation were more liberal than elsewhere in the empire, and many *szlachta* estates were confiscated. Poles were removed from the administration, the school system and the judiciary. Displaced employees competed with new arrivals from the countryside, creating a large labour surplus aiding industrial development.[16] Industrialisation and urbanisation proceeded rapidly. Part of the *szlachta* merged into the new proletariat; more significant was the entry of declasseé *szlachta* into the free professions. The *szlachta* formed the basis of the modern urban intelligentsia, which became the bearer of national culture.[17]

The watchword after 1864 was 'organic work', a rejection of heroic romantic activism for peaceful economic and cultural activity to augment the health and strength of the social organism. The Warsaw positivists, as they were known, believed that the nation could thrive by ignoring politics for economics.

Gradually two alternative strategies emerged in response to the absence of a positivist political programme to deal with government policies of russification and repression. The first was not based on nationalism; it advocated conciliation or tri-loyalism, urging Poles in the three partitions to come to terms with partition and be loyal to their respective governments. This strategy attracted support from the conservative magnates and the emerging big bourgeoisie. The second was a new radicalism among the young intelligentsia. This took the form of small socialist groupings in the mid-1870s, which rejected national independence as a diversion from class struggle; and later, nationalist-socialists and nationalist-populists who saw liberation of the nation as a prerequisite of working-class and/or peasant liberation. The latter cooperated in clandestine organisations such as the Zet (*Związek Młodzieży Polskiej*) and the Polish League (*Liga Polska*, 1887), the latter founded abroad to prepare a new insurrection.

By the late 1880s influential journals were expressing a concept of the nation that was firmly ethnic and linguistic, albeit leavened with notions of civic duty and romantic idealism. Continuing repression in the 1880s and a period of resurgent loyalism on the accession of Tsar Nicholas II created strategic problems for the young activists. Gradually a division of labour emerged: the newly founded Polish Socialist Party (PPS, *Polska Partia Socjalistyczna*) agitated among the workers, while the National League (*Liga Narodowa*, 1897), successor to the Polish League, sought to develop the peasants' sense of national consciousness. The National League, and later the National Democratic Party (*Stronnictwo Narodowo-Demokratyczne* or 'Endeks'), were initially populist and radical, but the party evolved under its leader, Roman Dmowski, into an elitist, authoritarian and chauvinist organisation, imbued with an explicitly nationalist ideology: ' . . . men are first and foremost members of a nation; only secondly are they divided into social classes within the nation . . . the first commandment of the citizen's catechism is solidarity, a sense of union with the entire nation', wrote Dmowski.[18] His close colleague Zygmunt Balicki elevated 'self-conscious national egoism' to the supreme moral principle: 'The social ethic demands that each man feel himself to be a member of his nation . . . that he fuse his whole social being with its being and live its life'.[19] The Endeks stressed national characteristics such as language and religion, but they also maintained a notion of the spiritual quality of the nation, and they applied Spencerian notions of the survival of the fittest to the incipient nationalism of the Lithuanians and Ukrainians. Each should pursue its national interests; where conflict arose, the stronger would triumph.[20] The idea of struggle was extended to the Jews in 1903, when National Democratic anti-Semitism made its first official appearance.[21]

Clear divisions between the two main pro-independence camps were well developed by 1905, when the PPS supported revolution but the Endeks took an anti-insurrectionary stance. Dmowski became convinced that the crumbling Russian empire no longer constituted a threat to the survival of the Polish national identity; the empire was disintegrating and anyway, Polish culture was superior to Russian culture. His increasing preoccupation with geopolitical considerations, the continuing growth of German nationalism, and the Polish population's new receptivity to National Democratic ideas in Prussian Poland persuaded Dmowski that the German *Drang nach Osten* represented the greatest danger to the Polish nation.

Thus the Endeks saw unification under the tsar as a likely next step before independence, and they remained firmly in the Allied camp during the First World War, while the PPS itself split, with Józef Piłsudski and his associates opting for the central powers as the best route to independence. In fact, of course, independence came with the collapse of the partitioning powers and the victors' commitment to the principle of national self-determination. However the territorial configuration of the restored Polish state was not based on ethnographic Poland. The Germans lost territories that had not been under Polish rule for centuries; they were never reconciled to the loss of Silesia or the corridor through Pomerania giving access to the Baltic Sea.

In the east, too, the state was ethnically mixed. Military confrontation with the Bolsheviks determined the eastern border such that the new state incorporated too few Ukrainians, Lithuanians and Belorussians to make Piłsudski's federalist plans workable, and far too many for the assimilationist centralism of the Endeks. Approximately one third of the population of the interwar Polish state were non-Poles, yet they played no part in the running of government. In the eastern borderlands class and ethnic cleavages overlapped and reinforced one another, as the non-Polish peasants confronted Polish landlords. Broadly speaking, Polish policies towards the minorities in the interwar period had the effect of stimulating national consciousness among peoples whose prime loyalties had not hitherto been 'national' but regional or religious. In the 1920s policies were either chauvinistic or thwarted by 'the chauvinism and incapacity of local officials'.[22] Piłsudski's 1926 coup failed to resolve these problems,[23] while his successors in the Camp of National Unity (*Obóz Zjednoczenia Narodowego*) adopted a number of openly fascist themes.[24]

The tragic demise of Poland and its wartime occupation by Nazi Germany brought a renewal of the romantic, heroic strand of Polish nationalism. Nationalists, liberals, socialists, peasantists and conservatives united in defence of the nation. The underground Polish resistance movement was not only the largest in Europe; it was also a movement to protect and preserve the nation by means of a parallel, underground Polish state, with its own institutions, press and education system.[25] Its main element was the *Armia Krajowa* (AK, Home Army), which was loyal to the government-in-exile. A smaller, communist resistance movement, the AL or *Armia Ludowa*, also operated. In 1944 the National Armed Forces (NSZ, *Narodowe Siły Zbrojne*) detached itself from the AK and began to cooperate with the Gestapo against Jews and communists, who were seen as a greater threat than the Germans.[26] The war had a searing effect. To the massive physical losses of some six million citizens, mass dislocation, psychological degradation and exhaustion were added a sense of national betrayal by the Western Allies.

NATIONALISM IN COMMUNIST POLAND

When the Polish communists came to power they took control of a new territorial entity. The Soviet Union had incorporated the ethnically mixed eastern borderlands. In return Poland acquired German lands, now known as 'the recovered territories'. This new Poland was largely homogeneous, both in regard to ethnicity and religion. Ninety-seven per cent of its population was now Polish and most Poles were Roman Catholic. The multi-ethnic interwar state was now genuinely a nation-state, its civic bonds strengthened by the shared experience of Nazi occupation.

The Communist Party began its rise in July 1944; by 1948 it had secured an effective monopoly of political power.[27] There is little doubt that it could not have succeeded without Soviet support. The party was tiny and unpopular: it was widely perceived as the instrument of a foreign power and the bearer of an alien ideology. There remained a strong residue of anti-Russian sentiment dating from tsarist occupation. For the then largely peasant population Soviet-style socialism was indelibly associated with collectivisation, atheism and the lost territories of the east. The gentry and the intelligentsia, much reduced in numbers by the war, were also predominantly anticommunist. They were still reeling from the shock of the defeat of the Warsaw Uprising in August 1944 and the virtual crushing of the non-communist resistance movement, the AK. What is more, the survivors blamed the Red Army, at the outskirts of Warsaw, for standing by while the capital was reduced to rubble and the cream of the AK perished.[28] Popular anti-communist sentiment was also fed by the assumption, proved correct with the release of Soviet documents in 1992, that the Soviet Union had been responsible for the murders of several thousand Polish officers discovered in mass graves at Katyń in 1943, as well as thousands more who had disappeared.

With Soviet aid the Polish communists established their power through a combination of terror and patronage. After 1945 groups of disparate nationalist anticommunist partisans continued to fight in isolated areas against communist forces. Some were linked to the AK, some to the ultra-right NSZ, others to the Peasant Party. By late 1948 armed resistance was at an end. The Communist Party (the PZPR, *Polska Zjednoczona Partia Robotnicza* or Polish United Workers' Party) was firmly in control.

In these circumstances it proved impossible openly to articulate a concept of Polish nationalism. Mass arrests of non-communists gradually took their toll. No organisation could function autonomously, without communist direction and control. Rigid censorship effectively prohibited the expression of alternative views about Poland's future and about the nature of the Polish nation. Official political discourse focused on the centrality of the working class and the fraternal ties of proletarian internationalism, protected against the threat of Western imperialism by the Soviet Union and Stalin.

The communist elite was not, however, indifferent to national concerns. For many communists, alliance with the Soviet Union was not only a way of ensuring principles of social justice. It was also the only certain guarantor of the integrity of the state within secure boundaries. A limitation of sovereignty was a necessary concomitance of that guarantee, for without Soviet support Poland would again risk becoming the prey of German imperialism. The notion of a German threat was (once again) a powerful unifying factor, and Stalin's concession that the Polish–German boundary should lie on the Oder (Odra) and western Neisse (Nysa) rivers was seen as vital in protecting Poland's strategic interests.

Polish communist elements also tried to limit Soviet interference in domestic politics. Even Bolesław Bierut, regarded by some as Stalin's puppet, reported to his colleagues on 28 August 1944 that he had raised with Stalin the matter of the arrest of Poles by the Red Army on the ground that it infringed Polish sovereignty.[29] There was considerable criticism within the party of the behaviour of Soviet forces. Gradually the so-called 'locals', who had spent the war years in Poland, crystallised their view that the path to communism could be adapted to meet Polish needs by recognising the specificity of Polish conditions. The party leader Władysław Gomułka represented this approach. Gomułka was concerned that the pace of collectivisation should not be forced, and he understood the significance of the Catholic Church and the depth of anti-Soviet and anti-Russian feeling.

As the Cold War intensified, so Stalin drew the East Central European countries closer. Tito's insistence on an independent stance led to Yugoslavia's expulsion from the Cominform in June 1948. Soon the hunt for 'Titoists' was on, as the East European states emulated the Stalinist show trials of the 1930s. Gomułka, one of few genuine Titoists, was duly dismissed for the sin of 'nationalist deviation'. Until Stalin's death in 1953 the expression of any form of

Polish nationalism, whether the 'nationalist deviation' of the left or
the 'bourgeois counterrevolutionary nationalism' of the right, was
stifled. Repression became a central feature of the political system.
History was rewritten, for example denying the central role of the
AK in the wartime resistance. National symbols were altered, the
Polish eagle deprived of its crown and cross. The party intensified
the collectivisation of the peasantry, while a mass industrialisation
drive rapidly transformed the social structure. At the same time
the party launched a bitter campaign against the Catholic Church.
The new Constitution of 1952. mimicked Soviet institutions and
procedures.

After Stalin's death and some hesitant steps towards de-Stalinisation
in the Soviet Union, Nikita Khrushchev impelled the process forward with his famous Secret Speech to the Twentieth Party Congress
(1956). While Khrushchev could blame Stalin for the Soviet terror
of the 1930s, the East European communists were placed in a difficult position, for their current leaders had been prime movers and
beneficiaries of the purges. However in Poland there had been no
show trials and less violence, because so many Polish communists
had perished in Stalin's purges of the 1930s; because the party felt
its own weakness in a hostile environment; and because of the
personalities involved. Gomułka was quietly freed and rapidly became a symbol of repressed Polish nationalism for communists and
non-communists alike, for his defiant refusal to repent his 'nationalist sins' was widely known. The death of the party leader, Bierut, in
March 1956 provided a convenient scapegoat for Polish Stalinism.
His successor, Edward Ochab, set a steady de-Stalinising course,
though the Stalinist faction of the PZPR remained uneasy about
continuing intellectual ferment. Ochab proved a rarity among political leaders when he graciously stepped aside later that year.

In June, however, liberalisation appeared threatened by workers'
discontent. Although economic grievances were the major cause of
the Poznań riots, the national dimension also surfaced, for among the
protesters' slogans were calls for a withdrawal of Soviet troops. The
protests were suppressed by force and blamed on antisocialist provo-
cateurs. However this view quickly yielded to the recognition that
the workers had legitimate grievances. Increasingly the party looked
to Gomułka, who demanded inter alia the departure of the Polish-
born but russified minister of defence, Marshall Konstanty
Rokossovsky, along with numerous Soviet 'advisers'. An attempted
coup by the Stalinist wing was successfully thwarted, and the way

was paved for the now dominant reformers to reinstate Gomułka as party leader. Khrushchev's arrival with a high-powered Soviet delegation and the mobilisation of Soviet military units increased the level of tension, but Gomułka reassured the Soviets of his unswerving loyalty to the socialist camp. On 21 October Gomułka became leader and reaffirmed the legitimacy of a Polish 'national road to socialism'.

The exhilarating sense of national unity under a popular, reformist leader gave the communists a brief period of genuine legitimacy. Certainly there were enduring consequences, including a *modus vivendi* with the Church and acknowledgement of the spontaneous decollectivisation of the peasantry that had occurred. Also, until the rise of Solidarity the Polish communists ran domestic affairs without Soviet interference, although they remained subordinate in foreign-policy matters. However rapid popular disillusion set in with Gomułka's failure to implement a thoroughgoing reform programme. During the 1960s he became increasingly unpopular in the country at large, which lost the outlet for its national and patriotic emotions. At the same time new factions claiming to represent the national interest developed within the PZPR.

In March 1968 protest erupted again, this time among students and intellectuals. It centred on issues of censorship but also reflected a broad desire for wider political reform. Demonstrations provided the opportunity for the 'Partisan' wing of the Communist Party, led by Interior Minister Mieczysław Moczar, to launch a bid for power. This right-wing variant of Polish communist nationalism began to orchestrate a campaign of virulent anti-Semitism, thinly disguised as an attack on the 'Zionism' that was allegedly pervading the universities. Gomułka rode the storm, but his position was further weakened. There were signs that Moczar had struck a chord among part of the population, as well as rank and file communists, elements of which enthusiastically embraced the campaign. Large numbers of Polish Jews were expelled from Poland, including reformers from within the PZPR itself.[30] Gomułka's loss of touch was amply confirmed by major political blunders two years later, leading to his replacement by Edward Gierek. Gierek sought to base his rule on expectations of material progress rather than appeals to sentiment. The nationalist strand within the PZPR sank into temporary abeyance. However nationalist feelings intensified in Polish society.

In December 1970 Gomułka made his first major political mistake by increasing the price of basic foodstuffs just before Christmas. The second error was in responding with force to the strikes that shook the Baltic coastal region. The political impact of dozens dead and thousands wounded not only ensured Gomułka's removal but reinvigorated powerful collective memories of communist repression. After a brief period of prosperity the economy began to decline. The gap between party and society again loomed wide, fuelled by resentment of the privilege of the ruling elite. In 1976 a new attempt to increase prices led to another outburst of working-class discontent, cut short by a hasty political retreat.

1976 was important because of this new test of working-class strength against the authorities. It also saw successful resistance to a proposed constitutional amendment that would deeply wound national sensibilities. The draft promised the strengthening of 'indissoluble ties of friendship' with the Soviet Union. Open letters of protest came from outraged intellectuals and the episcopate, criticising this formulation as limiting Poland's sovereignty and inviting interference in her internal affairs. The revised version referred only to the strengthening of 'friendship and cooperation with the Soviet Union and other socialist states'. The protest helped stimulate the development of political opposition. Later that year the Workers' Defence Committee (KOR, Komitet Obrony Robotników) emerged to provide legal assistance and material support for striking workers. KOR provided the first real linkage between disaffected workers and the intelligentsia.[31]

The severity of the situation by the late 1970s was obvious to all but, apparently, the party leadership. The sole effort made to recover a semblance of popular credibility was Gierek's attempt to renew a truce with the Catholic Church. The economy was in dire straits. There were drastic shortages, endless queues and a deterioration in social services. A party-sponsored group of experts produced reports analysing the bankruptcy of the polity, the moral exhaustion of society and the wide gulf between the two.[32]

Two factors worked against the prolongation of social paralysis and malaise. Dissent was spreading and providing the basis of an active alternative culture, notably but not exclusively among the intelligentsia. Discussion groups and illegal publications proliferated. The Flying University, whose name echoed national resistance to tsarism and the underground Polish state of the Second World War, challenged the party's monopoly of scholarship and education. The Confederation for Independent Poland (KPN, Konfederacja Polski Niepodległej), the first modern underground political party, preached a bitter anticommunist and anti-Soviet message. The regime see-sawed between repression and uneasy tolerace.

The second factor was the resurgence of a renewed sense of spiritual community, further stimulated by the election of the Polish Pope John Paul II in October 1978, and culminating in the first papal visit in June 1979. It was 'a psychological earthquake. . . . A whole generation experienced for the first time a feeling of collective power and exaltation'.[33]

Solidarity arose a year later, in August 1980. A wave of industrial unrest was yet again triggered by rising prices and spread rapidly. The culmination of the 'hot summer' was the negotiation of the Gdańsk Agreement with the government. The workers succeeded because of support and advice from representatives of the intelligentsia; because they did not protest in the streets but occupied their workplaces; and because they forestalled the traditional divide-and-rule tactic by refusing to negotiate on a factory-by-factory basis, instead establishing a single negotiating committee. They achieved far-reaching, fundamental concessions, in particular the right to establish an autonomous trade-union movement free of party control and buttressed by the right to strike. This was an unprecedented departure from communist practice.

Solidarity rapidly developed not only as a trade union but as a mass social movement some nine million strong.[34] It aimed for change within the framework of the existing system, not only of PZPR political domination but of the alliance with the Soviet Union; this reflected the notion of a 'self-limiting revolution'. Yet it also represented a unified national challenge of society against the polity, in which about one third of rank and file party members also took part. National and religious symbolism was pervasive. The PZPR proved unable to cope with an independent mass movement commanding the disciplined support of its members. The vestiges of authority drained from the party, which was divided over strategy and tactics despite a continuing formal commitment to conciliation (Stanisław Kania replaced Gierek in September 1980 and General Wojciech Jaruzelski succeeded Kania in October 1981). There is also no doubt that the leaders faced unremitting Soviet pressure, nor that they feared Soviet intervention. It is also true that the party's leaders were unable to contemplate the radical changes needed to cope with the deteriorating economy.

As the stalemate appeared to generate a paralysis of both sides, Solidarity itself became increasingly divided, its more radical elements becoming bolder in their anticommunist rhetoric. Initially Solidarity was nationalist *faute de mieux* by very virtue of its unified challenge to communist authority and its recognition as the legitimate representative of the national community. Its main concerns were with workers' rights, including principles of self-management and social justice. By autumn 1981, however, a more specific political agenda was being articulated, including calls for free elections. The ability of Solidarity's leader Lech Wałęsa to control the escalation of demands was also being called into question.

The introduction of martial law in December 1981 was primarily a result of the impotence of the PZPR in the face of this social challenge. The military under Jaruzelski moved into the political vacuum, not to displace the party but to make possible its ultimate restoration. Senior leaders perceived increasing civil strife at home and the imminence of Soviet intervention. They tried to justify martial law in terms of *raison d'état*, as the lesser evil and the last chance to preserve some elements of the reform programme, despite the banning of Solidarity.

Jaruzelski remained indelibly associated with what was widely seen as an act of national betrayal. Although he moved relatively quickly to restore a strategy of controlled participation, including amnesties in 1983 and 1986 and certain institutional innovations, the rhetoric of democratisation and renewal had been heard too often before. The policies constituted 'a vastly asymmetrical process with an active state courting a passive population'.[35] Nor were they uniformly supported by the party, which remained divided even after a major purge. An attempt to coopt elements of the dissident intelligentsia also failed. Alternative foci of national loyalties remained in Solidarity and the Church. Solidarity maintained a tenuous underground existence but the mythologised memory remained strong. When the turning point came in 1988, it was not Solidarity but a new generation of young workers whose strikes finally convinced the exhausted regime that dialogue was the sole remaining option.

NATIONALISM IN THE POST-COMMUNIST PERIOD, 1989–93

When the communist authorities sat down at the Round Table early in 1989 they aimed to find a way to share power with the opposition, not to relinquish it. In fact the agreements reached over partially free elections led to their defeat and a peaceful transfer of power. Gorbachev's 'new thinking' was important in Soviet acceptance of change. It was symbolised by the replacement of the Brezhnev doctrine, a justification of armed intervention when socialism was 'threatened', with the Sinatra doctrine, which envisaged the possibility of cooperation among neighbours without their need for a common political system. This was not altogether obvious in mid-1989. There was considerable anxiety regarding the Soviet attitude when it became clear that Solidarity had won the June elections and that a non-communist prime minister was a real possibility. However the Soviet leadership made it plain that the days of intervention were past.

The Soviet acceptance of a broad coalition under Tadeusz Mazowiecki altered the Soviet–Polish relationship dramatically and fundamentally. The disintegration of the Soviet Union and its final demise in December 1991 changed the entire basis of postwar international and inter-European relations. Poland could at last perceive itself as a truly sovereign state. In autumn 1992 two events symbolised this new sense of independence: the final withdrawal of Russian troops and the handing over by Boris Yeltsin of documents proving Stalin's authorisation of the Katyń massacre. The conflict between those who saw Poland's national security and integrity as violated by the Soviet alliance and those who saw the alliance as a vital guarantor of that security had resolved itself. The nationalism welded by hostility and anger to the Soviet Union, by the perceived forced subordination of Poland to an alien, exploitative power, did not disappear. However, in the absence of clear and present external danger much of the argument has shifted to a focus on the 'enemy within', the agents of that power. Demands for a historical reckoning, a national cleansing process, became a crucial issue for the new political elites.

The lines of division within Polish politics were fluid after 1989. New political parties were still in their infancy. They neither reflected clear cleavages nor represented consistent ideological positions. Neither did they develop stable constituencies. Nonetheless one could broadly identify strands of nationalism moving along a continuum marked at one end by a nationalism based on concepts of the organic unity of the nation, which in its most extreme version was highly xenophobic, and at the other by a pragmatic, rational, patriotic approach, conceiving the nation as an association of common laws and shared history and culture. Both claimed to act in the service of the Polish national community, both affirmed the centrality of national identity, and there were certain elements of broad consensus, as over Poland's new name (the Polish Republic) and the reintroduction of the national emblem, the crowned eagle. Nevertheless the differences loomed large.

In the parliamentary elections of October 1991 the small right-wing nationalist parties failed to gain representation.[36] Most of these had attempted to revive prewar political formations and claimed links with the National Democratic Party (Endeks) of Roman Dmowski, but with notable lack of success. A partial exception was Bolesław Tejkowski's Polish National Party–Polish National Commonwealth (Polskie Stronnictwo Narodowe–Polski Związek Wspólnoty Narodowej). Although tiny, it made its extraparliamentary presence felt, especially in the street activities of its youth wing ('Tejkowski's skinheads'). It was a quasi-fascist grouping, vehemently nationalist, anticommunist, anticapitalist, anticlerical, antidemocratic and anti-Semitic.

Within parliament the best known parties with overtly nationalist ideologies (those for whom the nation constituted the primary focus of identity) were the ZChN (the Christian National Union, Zjednoczenie Chrześcijańsko-Narodowe) and the Confederation for Independent Poland (KPN). For the ZChN the concept of national identity remained closely linked to Catholicism, and the party was overtly clerical and antiliberal in its orientation. The ZChN joined Jan Olszewski's government in January 1991 and was also a member of Hanna Suchocka's coalition from July 1992. The KPN, which established its nationalist credentials on the basis of a committed anticommunism from 1979, remained outside government. It lacked the clericalism of the ZChN and was more openly populist in its appeals.

In contrast Mazowiecki's Democratic Union (Unia Demokratyczna) and Jan Krzysztof Bielecki's Liberal Democratic Congress (Kongres Liberalno-Demokratyczny) were liberal parties in the classic European sense, with their focus firmly on the individual. Both favoured Poland's 'return to Europe'. In particular, they saw accession to the European Community as a means of enhancing Poland's status, security and economic position. They viewed accession to the EC not as a sacrifice of sovereignty but as a recognition of Poland's links with Western civilisation and of the changes to the concept of sovereignty wrought by the process of increasing globalisation; they saw no conflict in simultaneously asserting a

'Polish' and a 'European' identity. Yet the signing of the association agreement with the EC in December 1991 also generated resentment, directed at both the specific terms of accession and the principle of European integration.

The most fervent opponents of this 'return to Europe' argued that joining the EC would once again limit Poland's sovereignty and its ability to defend its national interests. For certain groups this was coupled with anxiety about perceived IMF diktats and about the penetration of foreign capital and foreign ownership of Polish land. The Christian-National Union (ZChN) shared this view with former Prime Minister Olszewski's Movement for the Republic (Ruch dla Rzeczpospolitej, RdR); it caused tensions within the Suchocka government (July 1992), to which the Democratic Union and the liberals also belonged.

Another issue where nationalist sentiments were evident was that of decommunisation or lustration (formerly a religious term meaning purification, lustration now refers to the issue of revealing communist files). The proponents of lustration argued that Poland could not be secure so long as former communists, Soviet agents and collaborators were still able to occupy positions of importance within the state apparatus, particularly the military. Secondly, decommunisation was essential to rid Poland of this alien implant. Poland, argued the 'decommunisers', should refuse to acknowledge the People's Republic; it should excise the forty odd years of communist rule and rejoin the path from which it had departed in 1944, notably by reverting to the interwar Polish Constitution. At the same time, those who committed crimes against the nation, including the Stalinist terror and the introduction of martial law, should be brought to book. The Confederation for Independent Poland (KPN) was the most vociferous of all parties in its view that communism was virtually synonymous with national betrayal. It joined Olszewski's supporters in a policy of ostracising the former communists, now the Social Democratic Party (SDRP, Socjaldemokracja Rzeczpospolitej Polskiej) and refusing to regard their elected deputies as genuine representatives of the nation.

Opponents argued that decommunisation would occur as a natural consequence of system transformation. They saw explicit procedures of lustration are divisive and threatening to civil liberties, chiefly because of the known existence of falsified and misleading files; the ultimate victory of the secret police, said President Wałęsa, would be the requirement that they should provide certificates of moral rectitude for their erstwhile victims.[37] The opponents of lustration also argued that no one could be seen as free of complicity with the communist system; all Poles would continue to bear its taint. Nor could one automatically equate communism with a lack of patriotism. The Democratic Union was associated with this view, as were the communist system's successor parties.

Jan Olszewski and his colleagues were in turn labelled 'Olszewiks' or 'White Bolsheviks' and were accused of willingness to condone violation of the rule of law and due process. The lustration issue came to a head in June 1992, when Olszewski lost a vote of confidence over his government's drafting of a list of politicians allegedly guilty of collaboration with the communists. The list, which included the president himself, the speaker of the *Sejm* and KPN leader Leszek Moczulski, was immediately compromised; but the issue continued to rumble on, including numerous attacks on Wałęsa's patriotism and integrity from those claiming better to represent the national interest. 'Whose Poland is it to be?', asked Olszewski metaphorically: 'ours' or the communists?[38]

Lustration was not the only conflict to reflect different conceptions of national identity. The issue of the relationship between Church and state was also one of continuing political confrontation in the period up to the second free election of September 1993. On the one hand were those who stressed the links between national identity and the Catholic Church. The strongest version of this view was found in the tiny ultranationalist parties, which equated the two; only a Catholic could be a 'true Pole'. Other, mainstream parties, however, notably the ZChN, came very close to this concept, though less explicitly and without the overt anti-Semitism of the former. A leading ZChN spokesman, Stefan Niesiołowski, argued eloquently that Catholicism should be embodied in the state: otherwise the majority would be forced into a metaphorical ghetto of exclusion from their own political community. The Solidarity trade union and the numerous peasant parties also stressed the significance of the religious dimension, albeit supporting principles of religious toleration. The policy implications of such an attitude were numerous: strongly anti-abortion, in favour of Catholic education in schools, hostile to divorce, favourable to state use of religious symbols, sympathetic to censorship (especially of 'pornography') and endorsing the position that the media should reflect Christian values.[39] In contrast the liberal secular view supported a separation of Church and state and took a more subjective view of nationality: it recognised objective factors such as language and religion are elements of national identity, but saw them as contingent rather than necessary features. Furthermore, the liberals stressed the state's role in safeguarding the cultural identities of minority groups, whether religious or ethnic. The state should not seek to impose a particular morality through legislation.

These debates were fought out bitterly in parliament after 1989. They are not necessarily echoed in society, though their effects helped shape the new political and social system and its ethos. According to opinion polls, the population felt that many of these issues bore little relation to their everyday economic tribulations. The popularity of all institutions fell significantly, including that of the Church, which was thought to interfere too much in politics.[40] Yet the vast majority felt secure within their state boundaries; they no longer feared their neighbours (though levels of anxiety increased with outbreaks of xenophobia in Germany); and they retained confidence in their armed forces.

Indeed the September 1993 election represented a catastrophic defeat for the nationalist parties. Neither the ZChN, nor Olszewski's group, nor the Centrum of Olszewski's rival Kaczyński passed the 5 per cent threshold needed to obtain parliamentary representation. Even the KPN, widely tipped to do well, polled only 5.77 per cent of the vote. Attempts to mobilise nationalist sentiments failed. The successor parties, the Social Democrats and the Polish Peasant Party, scored a resounding victory for economic interventionism, the principles of the welfare state, secularism and a willingness to bury the past.

We cannot necessarily regard Polish nationalism as peacefully and finally interred by the 1993 election. Before the war the right-wing variety of Polish nationalism was very strong, and nationalism can become more attractive in circumstances of profound economic dislocation. Although few Jews remain in Poland, traditional anti-Semitism still surfaces in diverse ways.[41] The relationship with Germany is not fully resolved, and this has implications for the German minority. One cannot be entirely confident that an aggressive, xenophobic mood will not take hold if large numbers of Poles become marginalised and alienated. However, historically Polish nationalism has taken various forms, but its nationalisms have been shaped mainly by the need to resist external domination and encroachment. Now, in the late twentieth century, the national identity is clearly ethnic and linguistic, and the nation's right to statehood is unquestioned and threatened by none. No Polish parties have territorial aspirations. Nostalgia for the historic cities of Wilno and Lwów remains just that – nostalgia. This is an enormous gain. Indeed, given the ethnic hatreds of the past and their rekindling elsewhere in Eastern Europe, it may be that the communist commitment to an homogeneous nation-state will come to be seen as a vital, positive contribution to the development of a secure, tolerant Polish nation.

Notes and References

1. See Anthony D. Smith, *National Identity* (London: Penguin, 1991), pp. 8–15.
2. See Andrzej Walicki, *Trzy patrjotyzmy* (Warsaw: Res Publica, 1991).
3. See, for example, the intrigues surrounding the election and kingship of Stanisław Poniatowski in Adam Zamoyski, *The Last King of Poland* (London: Jonathan Cape, 1992); Herbert Kaplan, *The First Partition of Poland* (New York: Columbia University Press, 1962), pp. 36–45.
4. Quoted in R. H. Lord, *The Second Partition of Poland* (Cambridge, Mass: Harvard University Press, 1915), p. 275.
5. R. F. Leslie, *Polish Politics and the Revolution of November 1830* (London: Athlone Press, 1956), pp. 30–1.
6. Quoted in Peter Brock, 'Polish Nationalism' in Peter Sugar (ed.), *Nationalism in Eastern Europe* (Seattle: University of washington Press, 1969), p. 312.
7. Quoted in S. Kieniewicz, *The Emancipation of the Polish Peasantry* (London: University of Chicago Press, 1969), p. 33.
8. Walicki places heavy emphasis on this point; see Walicki, pp. 10–41.
9. Leslie notes that the tsar's aim in granting Poland some representative institutions was 'not to conciliate all groups of the population, but to bind the propertied classes more closely to him' (Leslie, p. 45).
10. Brock, p. 314.
11. Brock, p. 322.
12. Leslie, p. 106.
13. Kieniewicz, pp. 82–6.
14. Walicki, p. 54.
15. Norman Davies, *God's Playground. A History of Poland*, vol. II (Oxford: Clarendon Press, 1981) p. 130.
16. J. Leskiewiczowa, *Warszawa i jej inteligencja po powstaniu styczniowym 1864–1870* (Warsaw: PWN, 1961), pp. 36, 43–4.
17. See Aleksander Gella, 'The Life and Death of the Old Polish Intelligentsia', *Slavic Review*, vol. xxx (March 1971), pp. 1–20.
18. Narodowiec (Roman Dmowski), 'W naszym obozie', *Przegląd Wszechpolski*, vol. VII (February 1901), p. 76.
19. Z. Balicki, *Egoizm narodowy wobec etyki* (Lwow: Gubrynowicz, 1914) p. 57 (reprinted from 1902 edition).
20. See, for example, Jan Ludwik Popławski, 'Sprawa ruska', *Przegląd Wszechpolski*, vol. VII (December 1901), p. 711.

21. *Program stronnictwa demokratyczno-narodowego w zaborze rosyjskim* (Kraków: Przegląd Wszechpolski, 1903), paragraph 12, p. 22.
22. A. Polonsky, *Politics in Independent Poland 1921–1939* (Oxford: Oxford University Press, 1972), p. 139.
23. For an assessment of Piłsudski, see J. Rothschild, *Piłsudski's Coup d'État,* (New York: Columbia University Press, 1966), pp. 359–71; and Davies, pp. 53–6.
24. On the period 1935–39, see Edward Wynot, *Polish Politics in Transition* (Athens, Georgia: University of Georgia Press, 1974).
25. Stefan Korboński, *The Polish Underground State* (New York: Hippocrene, 1978).
26. K. Kersten, *The Establishment of Communist Rule in Poland, 1943–1948* (Oxford: University of California Press, 1991), pp. 126–7.
27. The best monograph on this period is Kersten.
28. This view is too facile, however; see Jan Ciechanowski, *The Warsaw Uprising of 1944* (Cambridge: Cambridge University Press, 1974).
29. See A. Polonsky and B. Drukier, *The Beginnings of Communist Rule in Poland* (London: Routledge and Kegan Paul, 1980), document 29, p. 268.
30. M. Checinski, *Poland, Communism, Nationalism, Anti-Semitism* (New York: Karz Kohl, 1982), pp. 156–73.
31. On KOR see Jan Józef Lipski, *KOR: A History of the Workers' Defense Committee in Poland 1976–1981* (Berkeley: University of California Press, 1985).
32. The English version is *Poland. The State of the Republic* (London: Pluto Press, 1981).
33. B. Szajkowski, *Next to God . . . Poland* (London: Frances Pinter, 1983), p. 72.
34. The literature on Solidarity is vast. Among the most readable works are those of Neal Ascherson, *The Polish August: The Self-Limiting Revolution* (London: Penguin, 1981), and Tim Garton Ash, *The Polish Revolution: Solidarity 1980–82* (London: Jonathan Cape, 1983).
35. G. Kolankiewicz, 'Poland and the Politics of Permissible Pluralism', *East European Politics and Societies*, vol. ii (winter 1988), p. 157.
36. Jan Zamoyski was elected as a Senator for Zamość, the seat of his aristocratic family; but this was due largely to his personal popularity rather than to his membership of the National Party (*Stronnictwo Narodowe*).
37. See *Rzeczpospolita*, 127, 30–1 May 1992; also J. Snopkiewicz, *et. al., Teczki, czyli widma bezpieki* (Warsaw: BGW, 1992), pp. 39–41.
38. See Jan Olszewski, *Olszewski Przerwana Premiera* (Warsaw: Tygodnik Solidarność, 1992).
39. The ZChN's electoral programme in October 1991 stressed all these themes.
40. See, for example, M. Deis and J. Chin, 'Roundup: Life in Poland', *RFE/RL Research Report*, vol. i (22 May 1992), p. 63; *Rzeczpospolita*, 7–8 November 1992.
41. See, for example, K. Gebert, 'AntiSemitism in the 1990 Polish Presidential Election', *Social Research*, vol. lvii (winter 1991), pp. 723–55.

8 Nationalism and Nationality in Romania[1]

Martyn Rady

CEAUŞESCU AND ROMANIAN NATIONALISM

Ceauşescu's Romania was brilliantly anticipated by Bellu Silber, a Romanian communist imprisoned in the 1950s, who predicted that 'socialism in Romania will bear the seal of two combined geniuses: Iosif Vissarionovich Stalin and Ion Luca Caragiale'. (The nineteenth-century playwright, Ion Caragiale, was a main source of inspiration for the absurdist dramas of Eugene Ionesco.)[2]

Ceauşescu's despotism united all the elements identified by Friedrich and Brzezinski as typical of totalitarian regimes: ideological uniformity, a single party under a single leader, the use of terror, and the state control of society, communications and the economy.[3] These elements operated, however, on a highly exaggerated level and almost as caricature features: from 'socialism in one family'; to the deliberately cultivated myth of the *securitate*; to the grandiose but pointless social, economic and architectural programmes; to the increasingly implausible epithets that attached to the name of the ruler.[4]

One of the principal aspects of Ceauşescu's rule was the leader's self-conscious espousal of nationalist motifs and symbols. From the start of his office as first secretary in 1965, Ceauşescu broke away from the slavish conformity to Soviet models that had marked all but the very last years of his predecessor's (Gheorghiu-Dej) leadership. Ceauşescu restored the Latinate spelling of the country's name to 'Romania', which in deference to the Soviet Union had been previously altered to the Slavonic form 'Romînia', and he affirmed the equality of nations under socialism. In 1968 Ceauşescu, alone among East-bloc leaders, broke rank with Moscow by condemning the Warsaw Pact invasion of Czechoslovakia as 'a flagrant transgression of national independence and sovereignty . . . as an action in full contradiction with the fundamental norms of the relations that must reign among the socialist countries'.[5] Thereafter his public utterances were often critical of Soviet policy and he was increasingly preoccupied with the role of the nation in the building of socialism. In Ceauşescu's speeches, nation came to replace class as the main dynamic of socialist development in Romania, while the history of the party was depicted as being no different from the history of the nation.[6]

During the 1970s, however, the personality of the ruler and of his family was added to the equation of socialism, party and nation. In the official media Ceauşescu was portrayed as the last in a long line of Romanian statesmen and he was frequently photographed posturing beside the statues of national heroes. A whole floor of the National Museum in Bucharest was dedicated to his achievements. His wife and, on occasion, his children were likewise fêted as champions of Romanian socialism and symbols of national prestige. The identification of the leader with the historic greatness of the Romanian people was completed in 1976, when Romanian archaeologists discovered 'evidence' of the earliest *homo sapiens* in Europe at a site near Ceauşescu's home village; his wife's place of birth yielded in its turn human remains from the palaeolithic period.[7]

The exaggerated nationalist ideology that fed the Ceauşescu-cult carried, however, tragic consequences for the Romanian people. In order to fulfil the leader's schemes of national renewal and demographic regeneration, the population was obliged to forego basic human comforts, including the right to contraception. National minorities suffered particular hardship. The 1970s and 1980s witnessed a vicious xenophobia directed principally against Romania's Hungarian and Jewish populations. A series of scurrilous publications accused Jews of drinking the blood of gentile children and blamed Hungarians both for excesses committed during the Second World War and for 'illegalities' perpetrated during the early years of communist rule. The slogan 'Romanians must be masters in their own home' was frequently employed to justify discriminatory policies aimed against the 'cohabiting' minorities.[8]

Interpretations of Ceauşescu's recourse to nationalist propaganda often involve the notion of 'mythologic overcompensation'. As his economic and social policies stalled in the 1970s and 1980s, Ceauşescu turned to nationalism as a way of making up for the failure of his regime. Nationalism was, moreover, a powerful legitimating tool for a government that was increasingly perceived as illegitimate and, because of its defiance of Moscow, in need of new ideological symbols. In this respect it should also be recalled that the communist party in Romania had acted throughout the interwar years as a pliant tool of Comintern and had been overwhelmingly led by 'foreigners': Jews, Hungarians and Ukrainians. Thus the party, like Ceauşescu himself, had to establish solid national credentials.

Beyond this there is the role of nationalism in communist states more generally. Having destroyed civic institutions, the Communist Parties of Eastern Europe were confronted with an increasingly atomised society. Nationalism was all that was left to build a collective identity. Most communist states exploited nationalism in one guise or other, and the least successful did so the most.[9] One is tempted to suggest that the espousal of a vigorous nationalism eventually proved as much a feature of total states as the points elaborated by Friedrich and Brzezinski.

Although analysts have been right to stress the influence of the ruler and the problems of late communism in the development of modern Romanian nationalism, there is plainly a need to place our understanding of Romanian national identity within a broader historical framework. As will be suggested in much of what follows, the exaggerated notions of nationalism employed by Ceauşescu had as much to do with deeply rooted attitudes in Romanian society as with the needs of his regime and of 'system-maintenance' in communist states. In short, Ceauşescu's nationalism was a product of a historic nationalism; it was not invented by him, but was discovered and exploited by him instead. For this reason the more extreme manifestations of Romanian nationalism did not perish with Ceauşescu, but continue to beset post-revolutionary Romanian politics.

HISTORICAL BACKGROUND

The Romanian people are the descendants of the original Thracian population of the Balkans who were 'Romanised' by intermarriage and cultural contact during the first centuries of the Christian era. During the middle ages, the Romanian principalities of Moldavia and Wallachia enjoyed several centuries of independence before eventually succumbing to the Ottoman Turks in the fifteenth and sixteenth centuries. Until the nineteenth century, Moldavia and Wallachia were vassal states of the Turkish Empire and their rulers were designated by the sultan. In 1859 Moldavia and Wallachia were joined together under a single prince. By the terms of the Treaty of Berlin (1878), the two principalities were declared fully independent of the Ottoman Empire and merged together to become the state of

Romania. Seven years later Romania acquired its own monarch and kingdom status.

At this stage the new kingdom did not, however, include the entirety of the Romanian people, for a substantial body of Romanians still dwelled outside the state's boundaries. In Transylvania, a part of the kingdom of Hungary, the largest national group consisted of Romanians, who were largely deprived of political influence. Bessarabia, once a part of the principality of Moldavia but under Russian occupation since 1812, also included a substantial Romanian population. Only in 1918 were these two regions joined to the Romanian state. Bessarabia, which now forms part of the independent state of Moldova, was, however, incorporated into the Soviet Union in 1940 and renamed the Moldavian Soviet Socialist Republic. The presence in Moldova of large Russian and Ukrainian minorities has ensured the continuation of Moldovan distrust of the policies pursued in Bucharest, and a political condition verging on civil war makes its early reunification with Romania unlikely.[10]

Before the First World War Romania had been a largely homogeneous national state. The largest minority group, the Jews, although significant by reason of their extensive representation in commerce and the professions, numbered only 250 000 in a population of over seven million. The acquisition of Bessarabia and Transylvania had the consequence of transforming Romania from a national to a multinational state. The Romanians of Bessarabia, although they constituted the region's largest single group, formed less than half the total population, the remainder comprising Jews, Ukrainians and Russians. In Transylvania Romanians made up a bare majority, the rest being Hungarians and Germans who had moved into the region during the middle ages. Interwar censuses indicate that of the total population of 'Greater Romania', just over 70 per cent were Romanian by nationality.

Despite the loss of Bessarabia, wartime persecution and emigration, Romania retains today the character of a multinational state (see Table 8.1). Out of a population of just under 23 million persons, there are 1.6–2.0 million Hungarians and (until recently) at least 350 000 Germans. There may also be as many as a million Romani Gypsies.[11] The Hungarian and German minorities are overwhelmingly concentrated in Transylvania, where they make up about a third of the region's overall population. In the two easternmost Transylvanian counties, Harghita and Covasna, Hungarians make up respectively 85 per cent and 75 per cent of the total population.[12]

Table 8.1   Ethnic composition of Romania (per cent)

Ethnic group	1930	1948	1977	1992
Romanians	71.9	85.7	88.0	89.4
Magyars	7.9	9.4	7.9	7.1
Germans	4.1	2.2	1.6	0.5
Jewish	4.0	0.9	0.12	–
Ukrainian/Russian	5.5	0.4	0.4	0.5
Gypsies	1.5	0.3	1.0	1.8

Sources: Statistics taken from official census data and Michael Shafir, 'Preliminary Results of the 1992 Romanian Census', RFE/RL Research Report, 24 July 1992, p. 65. All the official censuses have been challenged on the ground that for nationalist purposes they deliberately under-record the size of the minority population and, in particular, the number of Gypsies. It is hard to prove or disprove these allegations – see Andre Liebrich, 'Minorities in Eastern Europe: Obstacles to a Reliable Count', RFE/RL Research Report, 15 May 1992, pp. 32–9.

ORIGINS OF ROMANIAN NATIONAL IDENTITY

The distinction between Western and Eastern variants of nationalism is frequently addressed in the literature on national identities.[13] In Western Europe notions of nationhood were grafted on to older concepts of citizenship, natural rights and popular sovereignty. This development was facilitated by the existence of strong unitary states that operated very much as the forcing-houses of national consciousness. In Eastern Europe, in contrast, the concepts of individual rights and citizenship were less well developed and they often lacked an enabling framework of political and civic institutions. Under these circumstances the nation itself became the collective repository of rights. The nation thus subsumed the individual, and civic rights took second place to a doctrine of national rights.

Because of its historical experience, Romanian nationalism has come to be paradigmatic of the Eastern variety of nationalism. During the long period when the principalities were ruled as satellites of the Ottoman Empire, neither Wallachia nor Moldavia possessed civic institutions comparable in any way to those found in

Western states or even across the border in Hungary. There was no parliamentary life of any description, nor any conviction that the state might owe some form of reciprocal obligation to its members. The type of state structure operating in the Romanian principalities was characteristic of that found almost universally outside Europe: the 'floating' or tribute state. The state existed solely to collect taxes to fund a military–bureaucratic elite that held exclusive authority. The only point of contact between government and people was the tax collector; and the law was the caprice of the ruler – be this the vizir, sultan or vassal prince.

The type of nationalism this variety of government engendered could not be rooted in notions of civic rights and individual freedoms. For these ideas were entirely lacking in a political structure that designated the population as *reaya*, or cattle. Furthermore, until this century the Romanian state and nation did not coincide. As a consequence national identity was understood as being quite distinct from the legal character of citizenship. The nation was instead understood in a purely ethnic sense as a tribal *Volk* that transcended political and legal identities.[14]

National identities that rest on an ethnic formulation tend by their very nature to exclude rather than accommodate minorities. In view of the multinational character of the Romanian state after 1918, the predominance of an ethnically derived notion of nationality was bound to lead to domestic tension. Conflict was, and still is, most apparent with regard to the large Hungarian minority in Transylvania, who, on account of the proximity of the Hungarian state, have been considered not only an alien presence on Romanian soil but also a focus of political disloyalty.

CHARACTERISTICS OF ROMANIAN NATIONALISM

The definition of nation in Romania rests overwhelmingly on linguistic criteria. The definition has been sharpened by the fact that Romania is a Romance island set in the heart of a Slavic sea, with Hungarians as both neighbours and 'cohabitants'. In addition, the connection established in Romania between language and historic descent has made the linguistic badge of ethnic affiliation an all the more potent symbol of identity.

The association of nationhood with language has led to repeated tension between the majority Romanians and the country's minority populations. In the interwar period compulsory schooling in Romanian was enforced on members of the minorities, and penalties were imposed for submitting accounts in any language other than Romanian.[15] Under Ceauşescu the publication of non-Romanian placenames was prohibited and minority-language facilities were drastically pared. Attempts were even made to cleanse Moldavia by forcing members of the Hungarian *csangó* minority to speak Romanian in public. Leaders of the Hungarian community suffered imprisonment and worse at the hands of the *securitate* Office for the Study of Nationalists, Fascists and Hungarian Irredentists.[16]

Even after Ceauşescu's fall, linguistic affiliation continued to be a source of rivalry. The interethnic violence in Tîrgu Mureş in March 1990, which left at least six dead, arose over the issue of Hungarian-language schools and was sparked off by a shopkeeper putting up a notice in Hungarian. (The incomprehensibility of this incident to outsiders led to speculation that the sign had insulted Romanians. In fact all the notice said was 'Chemist', but this, being written in Hungarian, was considered sufficient to justify the subsequent violence.) Notwithstanding the bloodletting of 1990, there has been continued resistance in Transylvania to the establishment of a private Hungarian university and to broadcasting through the medium of the Hungarian language.[17]

Language is by itself a convenient mark of ethnic identity. Nevertheless language is seldom felt by any nation to be a sufficient explanation of its special identity. This is particularly the case in Romania, where because of its Latin roots the language retains unwelcome connotations of 'cosmopolitanism' and of 'European-ness'.[18] There is therefore a consistent need to add substance to language, usually through an interpretation of the nation's particular history and culture.

The process of national myth-making often involves ascribing to the nation a common ancestry and an ancient homeland, which is invariably coterminous with the existing or aspirational boundary of the nation-state. In Romania much stress has been laid on the common origin of the nation, either in the period of Roman colonisation or, more fashionably, in the distant Geto-Thracian past preceding the period of 'Romano-European' colonisation. Likewise much effort has been expended on laying an historic claim to Transylvania on the grounds that the Romanians have always lived in the region and that its soil is therefore drenched with the blood of many past generations. The uniqueness of language (and, after all, every language is unique) is thus reinforced by reference to the unique and exceptional qualities of the nation's history and territory, both of which are considered to be virtually interchangeable ideas.

The doctrine of exceptionalism is a common feature of nationalism and is implicit in its more exclusive varieties. In Romania exceptionalism is tied up with the concept of a certain destiny and with a belief in the inherent and future greatness of the people. The special qualities of the Romanian people are thus made evident in every history book. Romanians, we are assured, were inventors of the laser beam and the jet engine; a Romanian was one of the first pilots; and a Romanian scientist was one of the pioneers of space navigation.[19] The conviction common among Romanians that they are a great people was exploited and fostered by Ceauşescu, most notably in the interminable 'Song of Romania' celebrations, used to demonstrate 'the talent, sensitivity and creative genius of our people'.

Notions of exceptionalism and national destiny may be found in varying degrees in every form of nationalism, whether this be in the supposed British *sang-froid* or the American commitment to liberty. Where Romanian nationalism reveals its exceptionalism the most plainly is in respect of its relationship with neighbouring civilisations. The ambiguity of this relationship explains many of the contradictory elements of both Ceauşescu's brand of nationalism and that of his successors.

On the one hand there has been historically a feeling of frustration in Romania at the backwardness in which an allegedly great people have been stuck. This conviction expressed itself most notably during the eighteenth and nineteenth centuries, when exponents of the 'Latinist' school argued that the Romanian principalities should wholeheartedly embrace Western norms and standards. The culmination of pro-Western, 'Latinist' sentiment was reached in 1859, when the Cyrillic alphabet was replaced by the Latin script. A modest enthusiam for 'Westernisation' was apparent in the influential journal *Viata Românescá*, but found its fullest expression this century in the work of such literary critics as Filotti and Lovinescu. According to the former, writing in 1924, '[We seek] the affirmation of our genius and specific character in the forms of European culture, in the harmonious and shining framework of the culture of the West. . . . We have faith that soap, comfort and urbanism, the telegraph and civil law in no way threaten the purity of our race'.[20] The desire for rapid modernisation impelled desperate attempts to engineer an industrial breakthrough, both in the interwar period and during the communist decades. This trend reached a high point under Ceauşescu, when roughly 30 per cent of national income was reinvested in industrial projects and plans were put in train to replace over half the country's villages with urbanised 'agro-industrial centres'.[21]

On the other hand there has traditionally been a profound resentment of modernisation in Romania, and this sentiment has generally proved to be the more powerful and persuasive. For modernisation has been perceived as Westernisation, and thus a betrayal of indigenous, national values. A strong antagonism towards modernisation and Westernisation was particularly apparent in the peasant–populist movement of the nineteenth century and in the 'Dacian' school, which emphasised the native Thracian as opposed to Roman elements in the national character. The Dacianist peasant–populists decried the 'falsehood' of industrialisation and capitalism and were fiercely critical of the new urban culture adopted by Romania's emergent middle class. They declared the village to be 'all that was real' in Romanian society: everything else was a sham that ate away the fabric of traditional virtues. In their rejection of Western values a number of populists embraced a strongly orthodox and 'orientalist' position. Nichifor Crainic, theologian at Bucharest University, put it thus between the wars:

> A great river of orientalness flowed in the riverbed of our people's soul. Byzantium and Kiev took their toll of it as it passed by, flowing underneath Orthodoxy – that import, which in time dissolves into the reservoir of our primitive forces. . . .Westernisation means the negation of our orientalness; Europeanising nihilism means the negation of our creative potential. Which means to negate in principle a Romanian culture, to negate a destiny proper to Romanians, and to accept the destiny of a people born dead.[22]

Crainic, together with twentieth-century exponents of the peasant populist movement, sought the regeneration of Romanian culture by founding it upon the peasantry. They idealised the rural masses as the embodiment of all that was true and natural in the population, as opposed to the alien veneer of urban and European civilisation. Although no 'orientalist', Constantin Rădulescu-Motru, writing in 1936, summed up a widely shared viewpoint:

Our whole social life is shot though with illusions. We have adopted civil and political laws unsuited to our traditions; we have organised a public education useless to the large majority of the people; we have imitated the bourgeois technique of economic production in which neither the qualities of our people nor the wealth of our country can bear fruit; we have done everything in our power to falsify the traditions and the aptitudes given us by nature . . . [thinking] ourselves obligated to be to Europe's taste. . . . For better than a century, the Romanian people has not been faithful to itself.[23]

An identical rejection of 'European' values was powerfully manifested in the quasi-fascist Iron Guard, the legionary movement of the interwar period and the first political mass-movement in Romanian history. The legionaries rejected capitalism and foreign models and espoused instead what they understood to be traditional rural values: the 'peasant with his hectare' and illiteracy. Their ceremonies and rituals borrowed heavily from orthodox religious practices; and the target of their violence was invariably the Jewish population, which was perceived as urban, cosmopolitan and inherently perfidious.[24]

Antipathy towards foreign models also informed Ceauşescu's brand of nationalism. On the one hand he urgently sought to modernise the country, and to make manifest the inherent greatness of the Romanian people in terms of industrial development, military capacity and architectural vision. On the other he believed in a specifically Romanian road of development, known as 'Towards a Multilaterally Developed Socialist Society', which uniquely promised to bring his people to communism. In the 1980s Ceauşescu sought to free Romania entirely from its economic commitments abroad by embarking on the repayment of the country's foreign debt. The avowed purpose behind this measure was to save Romania from the 'financial and banking oligarchy' that 'purloined the people's income and, what is truly tragic, that of entire nations'.[25] Ceauşescu's rejection of the West was reflected in the espousal by Romanian historians of an emphatically 'Dacian' position with regard to the national past and, later on, in the circulation of a board game 'Dacians and Romans', which presented the 'European' Romans as the baddies against the 'native' Dacians.[26] Under these circumstances it is hardly surprising that the revolt of the old communist guard against Ceauşescu in the spring of 1989 and the more effective revolution at the end of the year should have been accompanied by slogans pressing for a 'return to Europe'.[27]

The revolution of December 1989 may have effected a change of government, but it did little to transform the underlying assumptions in Romania about the nature of national identity. The propaganda put forward by the National Salvation Front (NSF) during the 1990 election campaign involved a simultaneous rejection of market capitalism and democracy. These were portrayed as specifically Western inventions that were inappropriate for Romania. Instead the NSF leadership recommended that the country embrace a specifically Romanian road from communism, for which it was duly rewarded with two-thirds of the national vote.[28] (In the same poll, Ion Iliescu, leader of the NSF, was overwhelmingly elected president.)

Faced with the necessity of obtaining Western aid and investment, the National Salvation Front subsequently curbed many of the excesses of its propaganda. Nevertheless a strongly nationalist position was maintained by the parties of the far right, most notably by the Vatra Românească (Romanian Home) organisation, which is a pressure group set up on behalf of Transylvania's Romanian majority. Although the Vatra's statutes are hedged around with references to the benefits of European civilisation, references to the unity of state and nation and to the inspiration of Dacian origin and oriental culture indicate the persistence of older attitudes.[29] Unsurprisingly the Vatra has been responsible for some of the worst tribal violence in Transylvania.

A xenophobic nationalism is also embraced in post-revolutionary Romania by România Mare (Greater Romania), a party that acts as the Vatra's counterpart in Moldavia and Wallachia. Besides Gypsies, Jews, Hungarians and intellectuals, the targets of România Mare's venom include advocates of market reform, who are characterised as agents of international Jewish and Freemasonic conspiracies. România Mare has additionally called upon the government to repudiate 'false democracy' and to restore an authoritarian dictatorship.[30] It supports reunification with Bessarabia and nurses territorial ambitions in eastern Hungary. Its newspaper has a circulation of about half a million copies.

On the far right, România Mare and the Vatra are challenged by the newly emergent Movement for Romania, led by the former student leader Marian Munteanu. The Movement for Romania embraces a mystical nationalism and has close ideological links with the interwar legionary movement. Repudiating social democracy and liberalism as contrary to the 'cultural and spiritual nature' of the Romanian people, the Movement advocates values deemed to be inherent in a transcendental community of the nation. These are defined as an 'harmonious, unitary and stable set of traditions, as well as of cultural, judicial, artistic, economic and political values'. By embracing these traditions Romania would be empowered to fulfil its 'historical destiny' and 'civilising mission' in Europe.[31]

Although the Movement for Romania has yet to make itself felt as a political force, in 1992 the parties of the far right commanded the allegiance of an eighth of the Romanian electorate. As a consequence of the continued infusion of powerful nationalist sentiment into Romanian politics, all the main political parties have consistently felt it necessary to maintain a nationalist edge to their propaganda. Even representatives of the liberal opposition have, therefore, considered it politically advantageous to affirm the traditional unitary character of the state, the interchangeability of state and nation, the essential 'Romanian-ness' of Transylvania and speedy re-unification with Bessarabia.

In summary, Romanian nationalism is unmitigated by civic notions of national identity. It is rooted in ethnicity rather than in a concept of citizenship and of rights. The *Volk* is defined by linguistic affiliation and its identity is reinforced by national myths regarding culture and achievements. Romanian nationalism, being ethnically derived, is furthermore an exclusive and excluding form of nationalism that cannot accommodate those whose first language is other than Romanian. Notions of exclusivity and separateness express themselves in concepts of exceptionalism, native genius and national destiny, and in a 'Dacian' ambivalence towards foreign models and methods. These are the historic features of Romanian nationalism that Ceauşescu exploited and used to underpin his tyranny, and they are still apparent in Romania today.

PROSPECTS

Can a new type of national identity be constructed in contemporary Romania? Or is Romanian nationalism inescapably caught in a culturally determinist trap?

Ever since the 1990 election Western commentators have been predicting that the liberal opposition, presently gathered together in the Democratic Convention, would soon triumph over the NSF. Despite the appointment of a liberal, non-party prime minister in October 1991 and a split between reformers and conservatives in the NSF, President Iliescu and his party (now renamed the Democratic NSF) held on to power in the election of September 1992. In the same poll the presidential candidate, backed by the Vatra and România Mare, obtained 11 per cent of the vote, mainly from Romanians living in Transylvania. The combined vote of România Mare and the Vatra amounted to just under 12 per cent of the poll.[32] The problem would appear to be that foreign journalists, having confined their observations largely to the cities, overlooked the strength of traditional attitudes prevailing in the countryside.[33] In this respect it is telling that while the city vote has tended to go the opposition, Iliescu and the Democratic NSF continue to command the loyalty of the rural electorate.

As a consequence of the election a new government was formed that depended for support in the legislature upon a left–right coalition made up of the Democratic NSF, România Mare, the Vatra and the reconstituted Communist Party (Party of Socialist Labour) headed by Ceauşescu's brother-in-law. A Vatra MP was appointed to the sensitive post of minister of education. The left–right coalition was cemented in October 1992 by a pact between România Mare and the Party of Socialist Labour. The accusation that Romania was once again ruled by a 'national communist' government was not slow to follow.

Despite the poor electoral performance of the opposition and its continued exclusion from government, the parties gathered together in the Democratic Convention as well as the non-party Group for Social Dialogue have contributed to a sophistication of perceptions and expression in contemporary Romania. Romania now has over 900 newspapers and political weeklies, only a handful of which are pro-government. Today there is discussion, debate and institutions, and a civil society is gradually taking shape. This development should be assisted by Romania's admission to associate membership of the European Community and the Council of Europe. Although still largely confined to the cities, it can only be a matter of time before the vocabulary of liberalism and rights starts to spill over into the countryside to affect the political discourse of the rural population.

Romania, like most of Eastern Europe today, stands at a critical moment in the process of transition from communism. At this point the question is whether Western concepts of citizenship can be grafted on to Eastern concepts of nationality in such a way as to transform national identity and make it less exclusive and ethnically biased. In the solution to this question lies the possible fate not only of Romania and its minorities, but also of the whole region.

Notes and References

1.　An earlier version of this paper was delivered at the summer school of the Centre for the Study of the Transformation of Eastern and Central Europe held at Brioni (Croatia), September 1992.
2.　Noted by Vladimir Tismaneanu, 'The Tragicomedy of Romanian Communism', in Ferenc Fehér and Andrew Arato (eds), *Crisis and Reform in Eastern Europe* (New Brunswick: Transaction Publishers, 1990), p. 155.
3.　Carl J. Friedrich and Zbigniew K. Brzezinski, *Totalitarian Dictatorship and Democracy*, 2nd revised edition (New York–Washington–London: Praeger Publishers, 1966), pp. 21–2.
4.　For this and much of what follows, see Martyn Rady, *Romania in Turmoil: A Contemporary History* (London: IB Tauris, 1992), pp. 44–71 and *passim*.
5.　Nicolae Ceauşescu, *Romania, Achievements and Prospects. Reports, Speeches, Articles. July 1965–February 1969* (Bucharest: Meridiane, 1969), p. 663.
6.　George Schöpflin, 'Romanian Nationalism', *Survey*, vol. xx, nos 2–3 (1974), p. 93; Anneli Ute Gabanyi, 'Nationalismus in Rumänien: Vom Revolutionspatriotismus zur chauvinistischen Restauration', *Südosteuropa*, vol. xli, no. 5, p. 277.
7.　Rady, pp. 46–53.
8.　Rady, pp. 46, 71–2; political responsibility for the anti-Semitism of the period probably lay more with the president's wife and son than with Ceauşescu himself: Michael Shafir, 'Men of the Archangel Revisited: Anti-semitic Formations among Communist Romania's Intellectuals', *Studies in Comparative Communism*, vol. xvi, no. 3 (1983), p. 240.
9.　On nationalism as a symbolic–ideological mode of control in weak states, see Katherine Verdery, *National Ideology Under Socialism: Identity and Cultural Politics in Ceauşescu's Romania* (Berkeley–Los Angeles–Oxford: University of California Press, 1991), pp. 83–7.
10.　The Soviet Republic of Moldova, with a population of 4.2 million and with its capital at Chisinau, proclaimed its sovereignty in June 1991 and its full independence within the Commonwealth of Independent States in August the same year. The population of Moldova is only 65 per cent Romanian-speaking, the remainder comprising Ukrainians (14 per cent), Russians (13 per cent) and Gagauz Turks (3.5 per cent). In September 1990 leaders of the Russian community dwelling east of the Dniestr River proclaimed the independent state of the Dniestr Republic with a capital at Tiraspol. Armed conflict broke out in 1992 between the Dniestr Republic and Moldova, with the Russians being supported by Don Cossacks and the ex-Soviet 14th Army. The Moldovan government in Chisinau, besides claiming the lands east of the Dniestr, also has unsatisfied territorial claims with regard to southern

Bessarabia and the Northern Bukovina, both of which were assigned to Ukraine in 1940. Moldova's close economic integration with the former Soviet Union makes its reunification with Romania unlikely. Moreover, the Moldovan population has an historic suspicion of Bucharest caused by memories of the region's neglect and exploitation when it was part of interwar Romania. Tentative estimates suggest that 80 per cent of the Moldovan population oppose reunification. The formula now officially embraced in both Chisnau and Bucharest is 'one nation, two states'. Within Moldova, however, a recent 'Moldavian' nationalism has been recently detected, which aims at reunifying Bessarabia with Romanian Moldavia.

11. Obtaining precise figures from the official census data is hard. The statistics given here are based on Andre Liebich, 'Minorities in Eastern Europe: Obstacles to a Reliable Count', *Radio Free Europe/Radio Liberty Research Report*, 15 May 1992, pp. 32–9; George Schöpflin and Hugh Poulton, *Romania's Ethnic Hungarians* (London: Minority Rights Group Report, 1990), p. 5; Michael Shafir, 'Preliminary Results of the 1992 Romanian Census', *Radio Free Europe/Radio Liberty Research Report*, 24 July 1992, pp. 62–8.

12. During the 1980s the number of ethnic Germans in Romania declined because of the government's policy of permitting their emigration to the Federal Republic of Germany in return for 'head money' in hard currency. After the 1989 revolution a large number of Germans emigrated. There are less than 120 000 Germans remaining in Romania today. The figures for Harghita and Covasna are taken from the 1992 census, as given in Shafir, 'Preliminary Results', p. 65.

13. Hans Kohn, *The Idea of Nationalism* (New York: Collier Books, 1967) (first published 1944), esp. pp. 329–31; John Plamenatz, 'Two Types of Nationalism', in Eugene Kamenka (ed.), *Nationalism: The Nature and Evolution of an Idea* (New York: St Martin's Press, 1976), pp. 22–35; Anthony D. Smith, *The Ethnic Origins of Nations* (Oxford: Basil Blackwell, 1986), pp. 134–44, *National Identity* (London: Penguin Books, 1991), pp. 11–13, 'National Identity and the Idea of European Unity', *International Affairs*, vol. LXVIII, (1992), p. 61.

14. The term *Volk* amply fills the same meaning as the fashionable neologism *ethnie*.

15. C. A. Macartney, *Hungary and Her Successors 1919–37* (London: Oxford University Press, 1937), pp. 276, 297–8, 308.

16. Schöpflin and Poulton, *passim*; Rady, pp. 72, 87.

17. Rady, pp. 148–58.

18. Verdery, pp. 36–40.

19. Dinu Giurescu, *Illustrated History of the Romanian People*, (Bucharest: Editura Sport-Turism, 1981), pp. 451, 541; Andrei Otetea, *A Concise History of Romania* (London: Robert Hale, 1985), pp. 530–1; Constantin Giurescu and Dinu Giurescu, *Istoria Românilor Din Cele Mai Vechi Timpuri Pînă Astăzi* (Bucharest: Editura Albatros, 1975), pp. 898–9.

20. Verdery, p. 51.

21. Ceauşescu's 'cult of industrialisation' is explained by Mark Almond, *Decline Without Fall: Romania Under Ceauşescu*, European Security Studies no. 6 (London: Institute for European Defence and Strategic Studies, 1988), pp. 11–16.

22. Verdery, p. 48.
23. Verdery, p. 49.
24. The literature on the Iron Guard is remarkably slim: see however, Eugen Weber, 'Romania', in Hans Rogger and Eugen Weber (eds), *The European Right: A Historical Profile* (London: Weidenfeld and Nicholson, 1965), pp. 501–74; R. A. Haynes, *Germany and the National Legionary State 1940–41*, unpublished MA Dissertation, School of Slavonic and East European Studies, University of London, 1992.
25. Shafir, 1985, p. 115.
26. Dennis Deletant, 'The Past in Contemporary Romania: Some Reflections on Current Romanian Historiography', *Slovo*, vol. I, no. 2, pp. 77–91.
27. Verdery, pp. 1–2.
28. Rady, pp. 164–5.
29. *Uniunea Vatra Românească. Proiect de Statut şi Declaratie-Program*, 1990, p. 3.
30. România Mare is financed by the emigré industrialist Iosif Constantin Dragan, who is not only honorary president of the Vatra but also a former youth leader in the Iron Guard: Anneli Ute Gabanyi, 'Nationalismus in Rumänien. Vom Revolutionspatriotismus zur chauvinistischen Restauration', *Südosteuropa*, vol. XLI, no. 5 (1992), p. 288.
31. Michael Shafir, 'The Movement for Romania: A Party of "Radical Return" ', *Radio Free Europe/Radio Liberty Research Report*, 17 July 1992, pp. 16–21.
32. Vatra was represented in the election by the Party of Romanian National Unity.
33. Much the same mistake was made with regard to Yugoslavia: see Misha Glenny, *The Fall of Yugoslavia: The Third Balkan War* (London: Penguin Books, 1992), p. 3.

9 Nationalism in Former Yugoslavia*

John R. Lampe

The multi-ethnic mosaic of former Yugoslavia had undoubtedly generated a series of competing nationalisms by the last decade of its existence. What was undoubtedly true by the 1980s does not, however, prove the oft-cited presumption that any Yugoslavia was a misalliance of ethnic groups divided by a list of 'age-old antagonisms' whose very numbers doomed any common state. Was it the sum total of all these mutually antagonistic nationalisms that brought down the federal structure that the Tito regime had erected after the Second World War? I will argue that it was not, despite the clear evidence that all the major ethnic groups, with the ironic exception of the Bosnian Moslems, had come to believe by the 1980s that the existing federation worked against their ethnic interests and to the advantage of others.

Only one ethnic antagonism was fatal to former Yugoslavia, or to the first Yugoslavia of the interwar years – the Serb–Croat conflict. Here we find two peoples closer in socio-cultural profile and language than any other pair, save Serbs and Montenegrins from former Yugoslavia, and yet also possessed of the only fully articulated *and* mutually exclusive 'nationalisms'. The medieval distinction between Catholic Croats and Orthodox Serbs and their early modern division between the Habsburg and Ottoman Empires admittedly put them on separate tracks, but it was not until the nineteenth century that they entered onto a collision course. Charting that course will be one major purpose of this inquiry.

The other major purpose will be to identify the principal alternative to Serbian and Croatian nationalism that was available to hold either the first or the second Yugoslavia together. This was not some federal idea that would find separate places for two or more separate peoples in a common framework, as is frequently assumed. It was instead a Yugoslav nationalism that proceeded from its own nineteenth-century roots to see the various ethnic groups as drawing on enough existing commonalities to comprise or be able to create a single Yugoslav identity. Tito's communist Yugoslavia was indeed established on the assumption that such a single nationality already existed. That state's belated search for some genuinely federal institutions in the 1960s culminated in constitutional amendments and then a new constitution in 1974. These endeavours only created an unworkable *con*federation whose failures did much to fan the aforementioned disaffection of all ethnic groups by the 1980s.

Let us briefly recall the positive commitments of the Slavic peoples other than Serbs and Croats to some sort of Yugoslavia before the 1980s. The readiness of Slovenes, Bosnian Moslems, Macedonians and Montenegrins to forego a separate state in favour of a wider Yugoslav entity in which their representatives would have a fair say rests in part on the promise that separate republics and the rising prosperity of Yugoslavia as a whole seemed to hold, and actually began to be fulfilled during the 1960s.[1] The evolution of their modern nationalisms from the nineteenth century onward provided a second source of support. Each has a distinct history, but each also came to prefer a wider Yugoslav entity either to the unrealistic prospect of full independence or to the virtual incorporation into Serbia that Macedonia experienced after the First Balkan War in 1912 and again during the interwar period.[2] We may even speculate that the disparate commitments of these four Slavic peoples would have been sufficient to create a genuinely federal structure that could also have accommodated the largest non-Slavic minority, the Albanians of Kosovo, if the unitary principles of Serbian, Croatian and alas Yugoslav nationalism had not stood in the way. The next largest non-Slavic minority, the Hungarians of the Vojvodina, were reasonably well accommodated under the confederal system of the 1970s.

The demographic weight of these six groups other than Serbs and Croats was in any case growing throughout the postwar period, although the latter still comprised a majority. That majority had however shrunk from 65.5 per cent in 1948 to 56.1 per cent by 1981. Table 9.1 reveals that the still largest Serb share had declined only slightly more than the Croat proportion, from 41.5 per cent to 36.3 per cent versus from 24 per cent to 19.8 per cent. Small losses of less than a percentage point were recorded by the Slovenes to 7.8 per cent, Montenegrins to 2.6 per cent and Hungarians to 1.9 per cent, while Macedonians made a similarly small advance to 6 per cent. Bosnian Moslems, boosted by their reclassification from a religious to an ethnic group in the 1971 census, and the largely Kosovar Albanians, accounted for most of the proportional increase

Table 9.1 Ethnic composition of Yugoslavia, 1921–81

Ethnic group	1921 (1000s)	(%)	1948 (1000s)	(%)	1961 (1000s)	(%)	1971 (1000s)	(%)	1981 (1000s)	(%)
Serbs	–	ca.40[1]	6547	41.8	7806	42.3	8143	39.7	8140	36.3
Croats	–	ca.23[1]	3784	24.0	4294	23.1	4527	22.1	44428	19.8
Bosnian Moslems	–	ca.6	809	5.1	973	5.2	1730	8.4	2000	8.9
Slovenes	1020	ca.8.5	1415	8.8	1589	8.6	1678	8.2	1753	7.8
Macedonians	–	ca.5[1]	810	5.1	1045	5.6	1195	5.8	1340	6.0
Montenegrins	–	ca.2[1]	426	2.7	514	2.8	509	2.5	579	2.6
Albanians	440	3.8	750	4.5	915	4.9	1309	6.4	1730	7.7
Hungarians	468	3.9	496	3.1	504	2.7	477	2.3	427	1.9
Yugoslavs[2]	–	–	–	–	317	1.7	273	1.3	1219	5.4
Others[3]	–	ca.8[1]	735	4.6	495	3.2	945	4.6	809	3.6
Total	11985	ca.100	15722	100	18549	100	20523	100	22425	100

Notes:
1. As roughly calculated from the 1921 census data for Serbs, Croats, Bosnian Moslems, Macedonians and Montenegrins as a single category by language (Serbo-Croatian) and religious categories for Orthodox, Catholic and Moslem in Markert (ed.), *Jugoslawien*.
2. A category introduced in 1961 for those considering themselves Yugoslav; in 1981, primarily used by individuals from mixed marriages.
3. Consisting of 16 other ethnic groups, of which Bulgarians, Czechs, Gypsies, Italians, Romanians, Rothenes, Slovaks, Turks and Vlachs numbered over 15000 in 1981, and Austrains, Germans, Greeks, Jews, Poles, Russians and Ukrainians numbered less than 10000.

Sources: Savezni Zavod as Statistiku, *Jugoslavija, 1945–1985* (Belgrade, 1986), p. 56; Werner Markert (ed.), *Jugoslawien* (Cologne: Böhlau, 1954); Michael B. Petrovich, 'Population Structure', in Klaus-Detlev Grothusen (ed.), *Jugoslawien* (Göttingen, 1975), pp. 330–2.

at Serb and Croat expense. Bosnian Moslems rose from 5.1 per cent to 8.9 per cent and Albanians from 4.8 per cent to a probably understated 7.7 per cent between 1948 and 1981.

The Albanian ascendancy and the Serbian reaction to it contributed mightily to the breakup of Yugoslavia in 1991, as did the Bosnian Moslem increase to 44 per cent of that republic's population versus 31 per cent for the Bosnian Serbs play its part in the civil war that erupted there in 1992.[3] Yet neither the Albanian nor the Bosnian Moslem populations, growing in numbers and national consciousness but devoid of any measurable political connection to make them a united force, could have triggered the terrible events of the past few years had not the long-standing Serb–Croat antagonism been there to rise up and sweep aside the commitment of both of their political and intellectual elites to preserving some sort of single state acceptable to the other. Let us therefore return to that antagonism and its interrelation with the failed alternative of a single Yugoslav nationalism.

THE IRRELEVANCE OF RELIGIOUS DIFFERENCES

Conventional wisdom assigns to religious differences the central role in what is assumed to be centuries of Serb–Croat antagonism that preceded (and therefore precluded) any Yugoslav idea that would have placed the two peoples within a single state. These differences have been used repeatedly since the nineteenth century by religious as well as political figures to justify ethnic antagonisms between Orthodox Serbs and Catholic Croats. Both sides have claimed Bosnian Moslems as ethnic fellows lost through Islamic conversion, but either redeemable or, for the Serbs, eternally damned for cooperating with the Ottoman conquest. The limited evidence available from the early modern centuries supports neither the thesis of widespread religious antagonism nor that of general animosity between Serbs and Croats. Eve Levin has identified the religious teachings of a number of Orthodox churchmen that were indeed hostile to the Catholic faith as a threat to the very survival of Orthodoxy.[4] But she also finds that Catholics, that is, Croats, in local communities who showed themselves friendly ceased to become dangerous 'Latins' and became simply 'Christians'. Official hostility did not in any case prevent local cooperation with Catholic or Islamic authorities, nor did local communities accept official hostility in their daily lives. The intermingling of religious customs and holidays from all three faiths that became typical of Bosnia in particular testifies to the absence of antagonism, rather than to Moslems seeking to preserve their Serbian or Croatian origins, as later nationalists have argued. In short, Levin concludes, 'the actual religious milieu in the pre-modern Balkans was much less sharply delimited than either modern politicians or medieval churchmen would like to suggest. The sharp distinction between Croat Catholics, Orthodox Serbs, and Slavic Muslims in the western Balkans seems to have been an outgrowth of modern nationalism, rather than ancient loyalties'. It is noteworthy, too, that the Orthodox clergy of Serbia did not play the leading role ideologically, let alone militarily, that subsequent Serbian historiography has sometimes ascribed to them in the First Serbian Uprising of 1804–13. Neither, according to the late American Slavicist, Michael Petrovich, was the uprising primarily a crusade against Islam and for the 'venerable cross'.[5]

On the Croatian side, the distinguishing feature of its early modern churchmen was their training in and commitment to the canons of European humanism. Petrovich devoted a half dozen journal articles to these fifteenth- and sixteenth-century clerics, their Italian university education, and their devotion to the study of classical antiquity as a common human heritage. Their patriotism was confined to a non-political loyalty to their native Dalmatian towns and to European civilisation in which Slavs should be included. None of this, Petrovich repeatedly points out, 'has anything to do with modern Croatian nationalism'.[6] Even Pavao Ritter Vitezović (1652–1713), the nobleman that Ivo Banac has rightly called 'the first Croat national ideologist to extend the Croat name to all the Slavs', based his ideas on historical, largely anti-Venetian arguments that 'paid almost no attention to the cultural, linguistic, and religious attributes of nationhood'.[7] It is also worth recalling that the principal Catholic presence in the Croatian military border throughout the early modern period was not the proselytising Jesuit order, but rather the Franciscan order whose work for religious accommodation had already spread to Bosnia by 1340 and endured until the present civil war broke out in 1991. The Serbs that came to the military border in large numbers from the sixteenth century forward were attracted in part by the full freedom to follow Orthodox rituals with their own priests and to erect their own churches. Their attachment to some

exclusivist version of the Serbian national idea came into being only
after the events of the two world wars, the second more than the
first, made the local Croatian presence, clergy included, appear genuinely threatening.

THE ILLYRIAN IDEA OF A SINGLE YUGOSLAV
NATIONALITY, 1806–66

A Yugoslav national idea has surfaced several times during the past
two centuries, before and during the formation of each of the two
Yugoslavias, and even earlier in a sixty-year period significantly
bounded by the two Napoleonic regimes in France. This initial
'Illyrian' period began with the French occupation of Dalmatia between 1806 and 1813, and was extended to civil Croatia, the military
border, and some of Slovenia in 1809. That Napoleonic regime is
remembered in most Western and Yugoslav accounts for trying to
implement some measure of peasant emancipation, general equality
under the law and freedom of speech. The latter included the publication of a native-language newspaper for the first time. Of greater
political significance, however, was the single administrative structure and the centralising assumption about national identity that the
French regime introduced. The unitary state government of the French
départments were presumed modern and efficient in contrast with
the backward feudal structure of the Habsburg monarchy. *Départments*
demanded a single people to serve as *la nation*. Acting as 'veritable
commissars of the Enlightenment and the French Revolution', the
French administrators of the Illyrian Provinces rejected the legitimacy not only of the old empires, but also of all medieval entities,
the Croatian and Serbian states included.[8] They saw Croat and Serb
peasants speaking virtually the same language and displaying enough
ethnic similarities to consider them as one people. Thus did the 'new
nationalism' that Benedict Anderson has identified with the French
and American Revolutions, starting from a blank historical slate,
bring forward for the first time the idea of a single Yugoslav state
and people.[9]

   The subsequent impact of this brief period of French theory and
practice is to be found primarily in the leftist Yugoslav ideologies of
the early twentieth century and the administrative structures introduced after both world wars by the new Yugoslav governments. Yet
even this influence has been debated, and historians are in general

agreement that the two native revivals of what was called Illyrianism, in the period 1830–48 and again in the 1860s, had no political connection with the brief French regime or its administrative system. Nor do we find any traces of the French commitment to an individual's constitutional rights and obligations that promised to assimilate all loyal citizens regardless of ethnic origins in particular.

Prompting the first revival and shaping its content was the challenge of the Hungarian language law of 1827. This official start to the transition from Latin to Magyar across all of the Hungarian crown lands naturally included Civil Croatia. A single Slavic language that would tie Civil Croatia to as much non-Hungarian territory as possible was the goal that led forward Ljudovit Gaj and writers familiar with Czech Panslavism. Gaj's Croatian-language newspaper, *Danica ilirska*, and other Zagreb publications succeeded in creating a movement, but one that was essentially apolitical. It was instead a cultural and linguistic movement for a single literary language, owing its wider debts to German Romanticism and Russian Slavophilism as well as Czech Panslavism.[10] Its one concrete achievement was the so-called Vienna Accord of 1850, which produced temporary agreement on a common literary language by choosing a dialect, from the several Croatian variants, that was closest to Serbian.

In the meantime a separate Serbian state had emerged with considerable autonomy from its titular Ottoman rulers. This internal independence drew Serbian linguists, led by Vuk Karadžić, and politicians, led by Ilija Garašanin, away from any prospect that would compromise their newly won power. A memorandum drafted in 1844 for Garašanin by a Panslavic Czech advisor spoke of such power-sharing among representatives of all the South Slavic peoples under Ottoman or Habsburg rule in concert with Serbia. But Interior Minister Garašanin would not sign his name to this *Načertanije* until he had changed the text to remove all references to non-Serbian peoples. Garašanin's text seems to base Serbian preeminence on the cold judgement that the one real state existing among the south Slavs could bargain better with the great powers, who would otherwise subsume everyone's sovereignty under their own authority.[11] Its references to historical rights for a Greater Serbia derived, of course, from the medieval empire, but this memorandum was the work of a state official who spoke from Bismarckian first principles of current geopolitics and a politician courting domestic support.

Garašanin was both prime minister and foreign minister in the

1860s, when Louis Napoleon's readiness to challenge Habsburg legitimacy in Italy and the Russian retreat after the Crimean War opened the way for international maneuver in the Balkans. A new Serbian prince with the credentials of an educated European ruler, Michael Obrenović, allowed the principality to conduct its own foreign policy, at least informally, for the first time. These opportunities for *realpolitik*, rather than romantic cultural nationalism, guided Garašanin in rejecting the proposal of the more political Illyrians, who had succeeded Gaj in Civil Croatia, to create a *pair* of presumably unitary Yugoslav states. Bishop Josip Strossmayer and his Zagreb colleagues at the newly founded Yugoslav Academy took advantage of the Austrian defeat at German hands in 1866 to propose a single state of south Slavs, consisting of former Habsburg lands ruled from Zagreb, and a Serbian state that would take new territory from the Ottoman Empire. Garašanin countered with a demand for Serbian state domain over the Habsburg Serbs, but then declined to pursue the project as too risky both diplomatically and militarily.[12] Croatian prospects soon vanished in any case with the Hungarian extraction from Vienna of autonomous rights over all its crown lands, Civil Croatia again included. Garašanin's Serbian statecraft came to terms first with Hungary, abandoning the Vojvodina Serbs, and with Ottoman authorities, abandoning the Bosnian Serbs as well in return for control of the Belgrade fortresses.

The Illyrian prospect of a multi-ethnic South Slav state also faced attack from another direction by the 1860s. The reclusive philosopher and publicist, Ante Starčević, emerged as the articulate and persuasive purveyor of a full-blown concept of Croatian national identity that disputed the Illyrian assumptions of the previous generation about a common Yugoslav culture. This was the first statement of Croatian states rights that rested not just on the medieval polity, but also on a cultural identity that was explicitly separate from and, ominously, superior to the Serbian one. Starčević went so far as to postulate coopting the Serbs into what he called the superior Croatian culture, although the later Croatian nationalist emphasis on religious conversion, from Orthodoxy to Catholicism, is not to be found in his writings.[13]

Thus ended the original Illyrian movement in the Croatian lands. It had first failed to find a significant echo in the emerging Serbian state. Now it was also under intellectual siege from within, an attack made difficult to resist by the growing European ascendancy of nation-states and the cultural nationalism that supported their political claims during the last decades of the nineteenth century.

NARODNO JEDINSTVO: THE IDEA OF NATIONAL UNITY AND THE CROATIAN–SERBIAN COALITION, 1905–14

After the turn of the century and during the last decade before the First World War, the idea of a single Yugoslav people reemerged, this time without the search for a single language or cultural framework that had bedeviled the Illyrian idea in its later stages. But the fear of foreign pressures that called it forth also created a political framework for cooperation between Croatian and Serbian political parties in Habsburg Croatia that was confederal at best. The Croatian–Serbian coalition of 1905–14 was originally a Dalmatian enterprise organised by local politicians Ante Trumbić and Frano Supilo. One motive was to resist the German–Austrian expansionism that they feared would flower after the humiliating Russian defeat in the brief war with Japan. The coalition's founding meeting in Rijeka took advantage of the greater freedom of assembly in Hungary proper to attract support from Croatian parties, including Starčević's Party of Croatian Rights, that were demanding relief from the Magyarisation of language and official symbols in Croatia–Slavonia. These impositions had continued even after the imperious Hungarian *ban*, Khuen-Héderváry, had ended his twenty-year term in 1903. At this time Serb representatives also gave up their temptation to accept Hungarian favours and keep the Croat nationalists isolated. The principal Serb parties joined the new coalition, but only on the understanding that they represented a separate 'nation', not just another religion.[14] This confederal coalition won the 1906 elections and remained in office until 1910, and powerful until 1914.

There also emerged, inside and outside the coalition groups of Croats and Habsburg Serbs, a belief that their two peoples were one. Among the Croats, the Progressive Youth movement accepted religious differences, but argued that these were of no greater significance than those of Bavarian Catholics and Wuerttemburg Protestants in what had become a united Germany.[15] A faction within the Party of Croatian Rights fastened on the Rijeka resolution's reliance on natural rather than historical rights to put Serbs in the same category as Croats as potential citizens of a new South Slavic state or, at least, a new 'trialist' entity within the Habsburg monarchy. (The restoration of the medieval Croatian state thus became a secondary issue for this faction.) Among the Serbs, social democrats there and in Serbia proper were attracted to what became known as *narodno jedinstvo*, or national, if not religious, unity.

The rapid modernisation and growing democratisation of Serbia proper during this last prewar decade made it a more attractive partner or even model for the advocates of *narodno jedinstvo* than it ever had been for the proponents of Illyrianism during the nineteenth century. Following the assassination of one native ruler in 1903, the head of the rival dynasty agreed to take the throne, but only after his election by the National Assembly. King Peter Karadjordjevic became a constitutional monarch, insisting on the immediate reinstatement of the never-honoured 1888 constitution. This liberal, Belgian-based document guaranteed equality before the law and an independent judiciary, freedom of religion and speech to Serbian citizens. These individual rights were soon buttressed by a two-party system of government, a free press and an independent university. Belgrade rapidly became a European capital city with the cultural freedom to match. But such modernisation, as celebrated by Ernest Gellner, ironically discouraged any widening belief in *narodno jedinstvo*.[16] The country as a whole was over 90 per cent ethnically Serbian, with minorities concentrated in Belgrade. There a mixture of Jews, Romanian Tsintsars, Armenians and Croats increasingly adopted the Serbian language and state identity, not because of conscious cultural campaigns, but by their own desire to be part of the modern, European world as residents of Belgrade and citizens of Serbia.

The stage was well set for a positive nationalism based on modernisation and citizenship as vehicles for patriotism on the French or American pattern. But it was the German (and Hungarian) pattern of exclusive ethno-nationalism that prevailed. The flowering of pre-1914 Serbia appeared to their citizens to be a process of irresistible ethnic assimilation that would succeed anywhere conationals were found, and perhaps even where they were not. Belgrade newspapers fed their readers with that dangerous presumption during the decade's several confrontations with Austria–Hungary, most ominously when they disputed the monarchy's annexation in 1908 of already-occupied Bosnia–Hercegovina and its Serb plurality. That the press raised such alarms for commercial as well as patriotic reasons did not alter the impact on public opinion.

Perhaps the greater effect on public opinion came from geography and history textbooks that simply presented heroic myths as fact and omitted references to any south Slav peoples other than Serbs. American historian Charles Jelavich has surveyed primary and secondary texts from Serbia, Croatia and Slovenia and found neither support for *narodno jedinstvo* nor recognition of a multi-ethnic heritage.[17] Nor did the Serbian textbooks devote any emphasis, even much space, to the ethnically color-blind constitutional base or on which the Serbian state rested, in theory after 1888 and in practice after 1903. This refusal to admit any other south Slav heritage plus the overconfidence bred by the Serbian state's emergence as the apparent vehicle for modernisation left little room for the idea of a distinct Yugoslav state in Serbia. In its place, the idea of Serbia as the Balkan Piedmont leading the south Slavs to liberation from Ottoman and Habsburg dominion appeared again as the foreign policy of an independent state.

Government ministers Cedomil Mijatović and Nikola Pašić, joined intellectuals in basing Serbia's claim to leadership not on its liberal, Western constitution, but rather on the Kosovo myth as propagated by Vuk Karadžić in the 1830s. From 1889, with Mijatović's celebration of the 500th anniversary of the lost battle that ended the medieval Serbian empire, up to the province's recapture from the Ottomans in the 1912 Balkan War, Kosovo as the center of that medieval empire became the Greater Serbian precedent by which any further territorial gains would be defended.[18] The Kosovo myth, reinforced by its acquisition and the great losses suffered in losing and regaining it during the First World War, confused the distinction in the minds of Serbian nationalists between a Serbian and a Yugoslav state. Before the First World War there was also confusion, but the irredentist demand for uniting all Serbs was less pronounced. Only rarely did those supporting a Greater Serbia, even when starting with Bosnia–Hercegovina rather than Kosovo, espouse anti-Croatian sentiments or advance arguments for Serbian ethnic superiority.[19]

The same could not be said, however, for the Croatian nationalist minority that gathered around Josip Frank, the young disciple of Starčević. Frank emphasised that cultural as well as religious differences set Croats above Serbs. Frank founded a separate political party in 1899, the Party of Pure Croatian Rights, and split away from Starčević and his rejection of the Habsburg monarchy. The Serbian danger in Croatia–Slavonia or elsewhere was too great to risk a break. The Serbian nationalist reaction to the racist challenge of the *Francovci* did not materialise until after the First World War. Before 1914 the largest opposition group in Croatian politics collected around the peasant movement led by the Radić brothers, Stjepan and Antun. Their Croatian People's Peasant Party (HPSS – Hrvatska Pucka Seljacka Stranka) was founded in 1904 on egalitarian, but not internationalist, principles. The teachings of Tomaš Masaryk in Prague led the brothers and other party leaders to base their claim to a universal franchise and other democratic institutions on the natural rights of the peasant majority rather than on the historic rights of the medieval Croatian state.[20] The Croatian peasantry had 'no history', as Stjepan Radić was fond of saying. No respect for the political legitimacy of either the Habsburg or the Serbian monarchies followed from this philosophy.

FOUNDING THE FIRST YUGOSLAVIA, 1917–29

Precious little philosophy was present during the three events that decisively shaped the first Yugoslavia. These events were the Corfu agreement of 1917, which created a confederal state under the Serbian monarch; the 1921 unitary constitution of the Kingdom of Serbs, Croats and Slovenes, which was signed in Belgrade without Croatian representation; and King Aleksandar's proclamation of the Kingdom of Yugoslavia in 1929. Once more a Yugoslav national idea emerged the 1920s, but it did not survive the 'royal dictatorship' that in 1929 ironically changed the country's name to Yugoslavia for the first time.

The meeting of a beleaguered Serbian regime with the London-based Yugoslav Committee of Trumbić and Supilo in July 1917 made the first plans for a postwar south Slav state, one that reflected the relative strength of the two parties at the time.[21] Nikola Pašić's regime faced internal turmoil stemming from the Black Hand organisation's usurping control of military intelligence before the war. Pašić's generals saw little hope for the army that had barely survived its expulsion from Serbia to break out of the Salonika front and return to Serbian soil, let alone Croatia in the near future. Hence Pašić agreed to the same sort of confederal rights that Masaryk's Czech representatives granted the Slovaks in Pittsburgh the following year (only to revoke them in Washington when their position improved). The Serbian position was in fact diametrically reversed by the war's end. Not only had the Serbian army, together with the Allied expeditionary force, retaken all of its post-1912 territory, but the emigré Yugoslav Committee had been replaced by a National Council formed in Zagreb as the Habsburg monarchy was disintegrating in October 1918. The new council was obliged to ask for Serbian military assistance to restore local order and, more importantly, to repel Italian advances that would otherwise have swallowed all of Slovenia and the Dalmatian coast.

A combination of external threats from all the surrounding states (save Romania and Greece) and internal disorder, especially in Kosovo and Macedonia, persisted into the early 1920s. As a result the Serbian army continued its role as a guarantor of the new state's existence. Nikola Pašić and other leaders of the prewar Radical Party also counted on public opinion in Serbia proper to support their proposal for a unitary constitution on the French model. This was not a continuation of prewar overconfidence, but rather the sense of past victimisation and present injustice that returned to haunt Serbian politics in the late 1980s. In the post-1918 period this sense was fed by the immense losses (up to one third of the pre-1912 population) that were seen as a sacrifice to create the new state and by the perceived unfairness of the postwar settlement. Promised reparations from the central powers to Serbia to rebuild a largely destroyed economy were never delivered, while Croatia and Slovenia, with essentially undamaged facilities plus proximity to the prostrate Austria and Hungary, recovered much more quickly.[22] The Belgrade press took the lead in suggesting, with no reliable evidence, that early profiteering in the war effort against Serbia had gotten the Croatian and Slovenian economies off to a fast start.

This was the atmosphere in Belgrade when the constituent assembly, elected in 1920, convened the following year to ratify the constitution put forward by Pašić and his allies. The Croatian delegation representing the Radić brothers' Peasant Party abstained, as did the new Communist Party, which had the fourth largest number of seats. Ratified not surprisingly on 28 June, the Vidovdan anniversary of the Kosovo defeat, this constitution created a centralised state composed of thirty-three districts, whose legal authorities, including the police, were to be appointed by the Interior Ministry in Belgrade. The powers reserved for Aleksandar as king and for the essentially all-Serb army reinforced this unitary framework.

In spite of a start that excluded a substantial number of non-Serbs and gave the former Serbia's political leaders a proprietary stake, the first Yugoslavia still attracted several sources of support during the 1920s that took seriously a specifically Yugoslav national idea. All of them saw that idea as advancing the process of modernisation as well as responding to it in Gellnerian fashion. Yet all were unfortunately grounded in the assumption that a single Yugoslav national identity could still emerge, making unnecessary a federal redistribution of power outside Belgrade.

The first of these supports was the cultural life of the capital city itself. The largest city by far in the new state, Belgrade had been freer to develop its own intellectual and artistic life than Zagreb or other provincial Habsburg towns. Unlike Belgrade, their cultural life had laboured without full freedom from censorship, and perhaps most importantly without any chance to keep talented locals from moving away to the world cities of Vienna or Budapest. After the war, Vienna in particular ceased to be such a cultural centre, except in music. Belgrade quickly became a cultural magnet that attracted writers and artists from across the new state, especially from the Dalmatian coast. The members of this disparate and largely apolitical group did have one political sentiment in common: they thought of themselves as Yugoslavs, more as a way of scorning the narrow nationalism of any one ethnic group than of affirming any set of coherent principles. The brilliant but erratic Croatian poet, Tin Ujević, typified both the optimism and the impracticality of this group.[23]

Another, far more politically conscious group evolved in Belgrade, and was particularly active in Zagreb. It consisted of younger intellectuals whose politics lay to the left, but were not communist. They lamented the corruption as well as the centralisation of the aging Pašić's regime and of the military circle around King Aleksandar. In Belgrade they gravitated to several smaller political parties that had split off from the ruling Radical Party and its closest prewar rival, the Independent Radical Party. In Zagreb, where the political spectrum was dominated by the Radić's Croatian Peasant Party, the strongest voice of the young leftists was the journal *Nova Europa*. Its authors admitted the failings of the Kingdom of Serbs, Croats and Slovenes but believed they would be overcome by 'the dissolution of Serbs, Croats and Slovenes into a Yugoslav nation', with differences between the three reduced to a purely cultural dimension.[24] Their hopes for this new Yugoslav nationality rested with the general search for new entities and ideas that was one European reaction to the First World War and the failure of old ideas it represented.

The new Communist Party of Yugoslavia was founded in 1919 with precisely that name because the communists also believed that such a new single nationality would emerge, bearing them not incidentally to power. The industrial proletariat and also the peasant soldiers of the recent war were counted on to be the source of this new Yugoslav consciousness. It would displace not only Serbian and Croatian nationalism but also the conservative influence of the Orthodox and Catholic churches. At the conclusion of his insightful, new study of the long communist association with the Yugoslav national idea, Aleksa Djilas quotes the leading Croatian communist of the post-1918 period, August Cesarec: 'The task for us is to erect an insurmountable barrier, to dualize time and divide it into the black past and the white future'.[25] The ancient ethnographic distinctions and medieval state traditions of Serbian and Croatian nationalism would all fall into the black past; the future belonged to a *jednonacionalna*, a single-nation Yugoslav people.

The subsequent history of the first Yugoslavia did not bear out any of these expectations. The assassination of Stjepan Radić in October 1928 during his first appearance at the Yugoslav national assembly in Belgrade put an end to non-communist hopes that the capital city could become a non-nationalist cultural centre. King Aleksandar's new regime of January 1929 abolished the right of all parties to political power. The communists since 1921 had been declared illegal and had seen their membership shrink to a few thousand. No agreement could be reached between any Croatian representative and the Belgrade government until a few days before the outbreak of the Second World War in 1939. In order to hold the divided Kingdom of Yugoslavia together, the regent Prince Paul appointed a new prime minister to negotiate a *Sporazum*, or agreement, with Vladko Maček, the head of the Croatian Peasant Party. Its terms afforded Croatia internal autonomy on the order of the 1867 *Ausgleich* for Hungary, but left the rest of Yugoslavia under the unitary and undemocratic constitution of 1931, which had been pushed through by King Aleksandar three years before his assassination.[26] The *Sporazum* thus set no federal precedent for postwar Yugoslavia, it only created a confederal island in the middle of a centralised regime.

THE SECOND YUGOSLAVIA: CONSTITUTIONAL COMMUNISM TO CONSTITUTIONAL NATIONALISM

The victory of Tito's partisan forces during the Second World War followed not just from Italian surrender and German defeat but also from the communists' claim to represent all nationalities, rather than simply to defend one of them. The loosely led Chetniks of Draža Mihailović initially opposed the Nazi occupation, but fell victim to Serbian particularism as well as to poor military discipline. Maček's Croatian Peasant Party only passively opposed the racist regime of the radical *Ustaša* nationalists that had tried to expel or exterminate the Serb population of Croatia and Bosnia–Hercegovina. There would be no place in the second Yugoslavia for either of these two major representatives of the non-communist Serbs and Croats, nor for any of the several small democratic parties, mainly in Serbia, that tried to enter the 1945 elections. Only the communist-sponsored slate appeared on the ballot. Forty-five years would pass before non-communists would again have the chance to vote for their own political parties, let alone shape one of the constitutions that defined the Yugoslav national idea throughout the postwar period.

The first of four communist constitutions set down a federal framework, but filled it with the unitary substance of party power and the presumed fading of ethnic distinctions. The 1946 constitution did spell out the 'four equalities' that were to remain the basis of the presumed federal framework through the next two constitutions, those of 1953 and 1964. These were: (1) the equality of all individual citizens under the law regardless of ethnic or religious identity; (2) the equal rights and duties of all six republics (Bosnia–Hercegovina, Croatia, Macedonia, Montenegro, Serbia and Slovenia) such that no one (particularly Serbia) could dominate the others; (3) the equal standing of Croats, Macedonians, Montenegrins, Serbs and Slovenians as ethnic nations, with the Bosnian Moslems not included but otherwise identified as a separate group (unlike the Hungarians and Albanians who were excluded altogether); and (4) the presumption of equal contribution to the partisan war effort by all the ethnic nations plus the Bosnian Moslems (including Croats as much as Serbs and Montenegrins).

The federal institutions and interrelations needed to implement these equalities would have been complex. Yet little was done in 1946, Aleksa Djilas points out, because Tito and other communist leaders were confident that their Yugoslav national idea, *jugo-*

slovenstvo, would make such balancing arrangements unnecessary.[27] This was a Yugoslavism based not only on the long-standing Soviet principle of proletarian internationalism, here applied to a multi-ethnic state that Tito saw as the basis for a Balkan federation, but also on two other principles derived from the recent experience of the Second World War. One was the discrediting of narrow ethnic nationalism for which the *Ustaša* regime was most, if not exclusively, responsible; the other was the patriotic experience of a Yugoslav-wide effort fought against a Nazi-directed war machine that had been defeated, against all initial odds. The winning side in the civil war became Yugoslav 'workers and peasants' pitted against 'bourgeois nationalists' supported by 'reactionary religious elements'. The communist assumption that religious identity would cease to be significant in a socialist society fed the overconfidence of the immediate postwar period. Tito himself spoke of the borders between the new republics as symbols of their unity rather than their division, brushing aside the proposal of his leading ideologist, Moše Pijade, that the Serb Krajina area of Croatia be given regional autonomy.[28]

The Tito–Stalin split of 1948 made another constitution inevitable. The 1946 document had been closely based on Stalin's Soviet constitution of 1936, full of fine, federal words, but allowing arbitrary power from the centre to proceed unchecked. To make their 1946 constitution still more embarrassing for the Yugoslavs, the regime's post-1948 resistance to Soviet political and economic pressures, plus periodic military threats, had encouraged a still more centralised, security-driven state apparatus under direct party control. The popular support that had buoyed the regime and particularly its *jugoslovenstvo* in 1945–6 and 1948–9 was now fading. The constitutional revision of 1953 was designed by Eduard Kardelj and other communist ideologists to promise decentralisation for relief from domestic controls as well as to chart a non-Soviet course. Its provisions still paid lip service to the Yugoslav national idea, assuming that its spread would occasion 'the withering away of the republics'. The Council of Nations representing the six republics and the two autonomous Serbian provinces of Vojvodina and Kosovo was abolished, and a new, more powerful Federal Executive Council of republic representatives took its place. Other positive provisions confirmed the demise of any effective apparatus for a centrally planned economy and placed those economic powers, plus control of the media and the publication of school texts, in the hands of republic and local party leaders. The promise of workers' self-management, already put forward in 1950 legislation as a new non-Soviet approach, became instead a mechanism for political decentralisation under the 1953 constitution.[29]

The idea of *jugoslovenstvo* did not survive the 1964 constitution, mainly because of the substance that was finally given to workers' self-management from the early 1960s onward.[30] Its ideals of autonomous workers' councils cooperating in enterprise management with elected directors was already enshrined in the 1964 constitution, despite the fact that councils did not gain real authority to elect enterprise directors until 1969. Their autonomy created local political competition for enterprise control that made multi-ethnic management increasingly hard to maintain.

Kardelj's 1974 constitution ratified the right of *liberum veto* that local and republic party authorities used to oversee this competition for enterprise, and therefore financial control. The result was a confederal framework of six republics and the two autonomous provinces, each with the right to veto the unanimous vote required for any decision made at what was still called the federal level.[31] It was as though the rights of the 1939 *Sporazum* for Croatia had been extended to all the constituent parts of Yugoslavia, which also included Kosovo as an Albanian province. No semblance of ethnic convergence could have survived this delegation of authority from a civilian centre that could count only on the national bank and army as federal institutions.

What emerged instead after Tito's death in 1980 was a set of increasingly open struggles for political control of the formerly constituent parts. In 1986 the standard of Yugoslavia's federal unity passed unfortunately into the hands Slobodan Milošević and the new leadership of Serbia's Communist Party. Their subsequent efforts to eliminate the long-standing regional autonomy of Kosovo and the political power of its Albanian majority were so arbitrary as to discredit any prospect of federal reconciliation with other republics on terms to which Milošević would be party. Yet he won genuine approval among the majority of Serbs, particularly those who were rural or recently urbanised, by using a previously credible state-controlled television and press to blame the social problems created by a modern but faltering economy on ethnic adversaries, on the Albanians first of all.[32]

Then the collapse of communist regimes across Eastern Europe in 1989 removed even the rationales for a socialist economy or a single Yugoslavia unified against the Soviet bloc. Ethnic majorities in

Slovenia and Croatia responded to the nationalist call of newly created, non-communist parties and voted for complete independence from what was now widely seen as the fiction of Yugoslavia. The state might have survived the departure of small ethnically homogeneous Slovenia, but not Croatia with its central location and seacoast, its large population and resources. The new constitution of independent Croatia, as originally drafted, made its ethnic majority the sole repository of national sovereignty, with all others, Serbs included, described as minorities that would presumably assimilate or leave over time. This document combined with threatening television images and sound bites of what its provisions might mean for minorities to set the stage for the civil war that erupted in 1991. Robert Hayden has rightly called such 'constitutional nationalism' a biological concept that sees the 'nation' as a 'collective individual defined in part by shared physical substance'.[33]

The shared physical substance and the cultural heritage that goes with it are not elements that helped advance either the Yugoslav or Serbian national ideas since the nineteenth century. When initially successful, both were carried forward by modernising assumptions and realities of what a state united under a single constitution could accomplish internally and internationally. Both, however, failed to base these claims to legitimacy on the secular rights of individual citizens, rights recorded as early as the Serbian constitution of 1888, but rather on the capacity of the state itself to assimilate all inhabitants into a single nationality simply because it was successful.

When both were ultimately unsuccessful, they opened Croatia to a media-hyped amalgam of earlier ideas, ranging from the historic rights of Vitezović, to the cultural–religious supremacy of Starčević, to the natural rights of the Radić brothers. The Milošević media pushed the Serbian side to see this amalgam only as a revival of interwar Catholic hostility to the Orthodox monarchy, and especially of the wartime racism of the *Ustaša* regime. The Serbian response preserved the idea of a state only as a confused claim to rights over all Serb-inhabited territory in former Yugoslavia. Instead the Serbian national idea became its own amalgam of claims to historic, religious and natural rights, now a mirror image of Croatian claims that made the two more mutually exclusive than ever before. How such ideas can do more than feed the irrational sense of organic antagonism that now bloodies Bosnia–Hercegovina and its last Yugoslavs, the Bosnian Moslems, remains doubtful.

Notes and References

*This essay appeared in Studies in *East European Thought*, vol. 46, nos. 1–2 (1994), pp. 69–89. © 1994 Kluwer Academic Publishers. Printed in the Netherlands. Reprinted by permission of Kluwer Academic Publishers.

1. The readiness of these 'other Slavs' to accept the framework of postwar Yugoslavia and the singular potential of the Serb–Croat antagonism to break it apart emerge convincingly in Dennison Rusinow, *The Yugoslav Experiment, 1948–1974* (Berkeley: University of California Press, 1977). On the difficulties nonetheless posed for Tito's Yugoslavia by national ambitions other than those of Serbs and Croats both during and after the Second World War, see Paul Shoup, *Communism and the Yugoslav National Question* (New York: Columbia University Press, 1968).

2. For historical background on the limits to nationalism for the Slovenes, see Carole Rogele, *The Slovenes and Yugoslavism, 1890–1914* (New York: Columbia University Press, East European Monographs, 1977); for the Bosnian Moslems, Robert Donia, *Islam under the Double Eagle: The Muslims of Bosnia and Hercegovina, 1878–1914* (New York: Columbia University Press, East European Monographs, 1981); for the Macedonians, Stephen Palmer and Robert King, *Yugoslav Communism and the Macedonian Question* (Hamden: Archon Books, 1971); for the Montenegrins, Ivo Banac, *The National Question in Yugoslavia, Origins, History, Politics* (Ithaca: Cornell University Press, 1984), pp. 270–91. On the general course of interwar Yugoslav politics and the specific tendency of Slovene and Bosnian Moslem parties to align themselves with the Serbian side, see Joseph Rothschild, *East Central Europe Between the Two World Wars* (Seattle: University of Washington Press, 1974), pp. 201–80.

3. A brief summary of the struggle between the Albanian majority and the Serb minority in Kosovo may be found in Stevan K. Pawlowitch, *The Improbable Survivor, Yugoslavia and Its Problems, 1918–1988* (Columbus: Ohio State University Press, 1988), pp. 78–93. On the tragic fate of the Bosnian Moslems in 1992 and its immediate background, see Misha Glenny, *The Fall of Yugoslavia, The Third Balkan War* (New York: Penguin Books, 1992), pp. 138–76.

4. Eve Levin, 'The Slavic Orthodox Legacy and Other Religions' (paper delivered at the Woodrow Wilson Centre conference on 'Christianity and Islam in Southeastern Europe: Ethnic Antagonism or Religious Accommodation?' Washington, DC, 18 September 1992). Also see John Fine, *The Late Medieval Balkans: A Critical Survey from the Late Twelfth Century to the Ottoman Conquest* (Ann Arbor: University of Michigan Press, 1983), pp. 145–7, 279–81, 481–5.

5. Michael B. Petrovich, 'The Role of the Serbian Orthodox Church in the First Serbian Uprising, 1804–1813', in Wayne S. Vucinich (ed.), *The First Serbian Uprising, 1804–1813* (New York: Columbia University Press, East European Monographs, 1982), pp. 259–302.

6. See John R. Lampe, 'Balkan Historian, American Slavicist, and Religious Humanist: Michael Boro Petrovich, 1922–1989', *Modern Greek Studies*

Yearbook, vol. VI (Minneapolis: University of Minnesota Press, 1990), pp. 241–49.

7. Ivo Banac, *The National Question in Yugoslavia Origins History Politics*, (Ithaca: Cornell University Press, 1984), pp. 72–3.

8. Wayne S. Vucinich, 'Croatian Illyrianism: Its Background and Origins', in Stanley B. Winters and Joseph Held (eds), *Intellectual and Social Developments in the Habsburg Empire from Maria Theresa to World War I* (New York: Columbia University Press, East European Monographs, 1975), p. 61; Elinor Murray Despalatovic, 'The Illyrian Solution to the Problem of Modern National Identity for the Croats', *Balkanistica*, vol. I (1974), pp. 75–103.

9. Benedict Anderson, *Imagined Communities*, 2nd ed. (London: Verso Editions, 1991), pp. 191–5.

10. Vucinich, 'Croatian Illyrianism', pp. 55–113.

11. Paul N. Hehn, 'The Origins of Modern Pan-Serbianism: The 1844 Nacertanije of Ilija Garasanin', *East European Quarterly*, vol. IX (1975), 153–71; David Mackenzie, *Ilija Garasanin: Balkan Bismarck* (New York: Columbia University Press, 1985), pp. 42–61.

12. Mackenzie, *Balkan Bismarck*, pp. 279–96; Gale Stokes, 'Yugoslavism in the 1860's?', *Southeastern Europe*, vol. I (1974), pp. 126–35.

13. M. S. Spalatin, 'The Croatian Nationalism of Ante Starčević, 1845–1871', *Journal of Croatian Studies*, vol. 16 (1975), pp. 19–146.

14. Aleksa Djilas, *Contested Country: Yugoslav Unity and Communist Revolution, 1919–1953* (Cambridge: Harvard University Press, 1991), pp. 31–34. For a critical view of Hungarian relations with Croats and Serbs before the First World War, see Gabor P. Vermes, 'South Slav Aspirations and Magyar Nationalism in the Dual Monarchy', in Ivo Banac, John G. Ackerman and Roman Szporluk (eds), *Nations and Ideology* (New York: Columbia University Press, East European Monographs, 1981), pp. 177–200.

15. Banac, *National Question in Yugoslavia*, pp. 93–100; Mirjana Gross, 'Croatian National-Integrational Ideologies from the End of Illyrianism to the Creation of Yugoslavia', *Austrian History Yearbook*, vol. XV–XVI (1979–80), pp. 22–5.

16. Ernest Gellner, *Nations and Nationalism*, (London: Blackwell, 1983), p. 57; John R. Lampe, 'Modernization and Social Structure: The Case of the Pre-1914 Balkan Capitals', *Southeastern Europe*, vol. V (1978), pp. 11–32.

17. Charles Jelavich, *South Slav Nationalisms: Textbooks and Yugoslav Union Before 1914* (Columbus: Ohio State University Press, 1990).

18. Thomas A. Emmert, 'Kosovo: Development and Impact of a National Ethic', *Nations and Ideology*, pp. 70–77.

19. See Jelavich, *South Slav Nationalisms*, pp. 177–96.

20. Banac, *National Question in Yugoslavia*, p. 96; Gross, 'Croatian National-Integrational Ideologies', pp. 26–33.

21. Gale Stokes, 'The Yugoslav Committee and the Formation of Yugoslavia', in Dimitrije Djordjevic (ed.), *The Creation of Yugoslavia, 1914–1918* (Santa Barbara: ABC Clio Press, 1980), pp. 51–72.

22. John R. Lampe, 'Unifying the Yugoslav Economy, 1918–1921: Misery and Early Misunderstandings', in Djordjevic (ed.), *The Creation of Yugoslavia*, pp. 139–156.

23. For an introduction to this subject, see Vasa Čubrilović (ed.), *Istorija Beograda*, vol. III (Belgrade, 1974), passim.

24. Dušan Nečak, 'The Yugoslav Question Past and Future', in Uri Ra'anan *et al.*, *State and Nation in Multi-Ethnic Societies* (Manchester: Manchester University Press, 1991), p. 132.

25. Djilas, *Contested Country*, pp. 59, 183.

26. Srdjan Trifković, 'The First Yugoslavia and Origins of Croatian Separatism', *East European Quarterly*, vol. XXVI (September 1992), pp. 344–70; Jill A. Irvine, *The Croat Question: Partisan Politics in the Formation of the Yugoslav Socialist State* (Boulder: Westview Press, 1993), pp. 48–53.

27. Djilas, *Contested Country*, pp. 158–65.

28. Ibid., pp. 166, 172.

29. John R. Lampe, Russell O. Prickett and Ljubiša Adamović, *Yugoslav–American Economic Relations since World War II* (Durham: Duke University Press, 1990), pp. 43–6.

30. Steven L. Burg, *Conflict and Cohesion in Socialist Yugoslavia* (Princeton: Princeton University Press, 1983), pp. 25–6.

31. Ibid., pp. 242–300.

32. Whether the Serbian public's receptivity, at least among recently urbanised peasants, to this media campaign may be connected to an oral tradition that centres on the loss of Kosovo after 1389 and conflates past and present time deserves future investigation.

33. Robert M. Hayden, 'Constitutional Nationalism in the Former Yugoslav Republics', *Slavic Review*, forthcoming (December 1993).

10 What To Do About Nationalism? The Recurring Dilemma of Western Policy in East Central Europe

Paul Latawski

In the last seventy years East Central Europe has undergone funda-mental political reconstruction more frequently than any other part of Europe. From the birth of the 'successor states' in 1918 to the emergence of the post-Warsaw-pact states after 1989, East Central Europe has been a place where 'no peace settlement is ever final, no frontiers are secure and each generation must begin its work anew'.[1] For the nations of the region, finding a secure place in Europe has been the elusive ambition of the twentieth century. For the liberal Western powers – Britain, France and the United States – manoeuvering the small and middle-sized states into the European political puzzle has been a frustrating process.

In the search for East Central Europe's place in the twentieth-century European order the force of modern nationalism has been a central element in shaping the fortunes of the region. From the point of view of the peoples of East Central Europe, the realisation of nationalist aspirations against external, usually great-power, oppres-sion has been the common feature through repeated episodes of political reconstruction in the region. The role played by the great powers in the process of reconstruction has been either that of an oppressor or an unreliable partner. The western powers occupy the latter category. Hubert Ripka, a Czech journalist and politician, summarised East Central European misgivings about the great powers when he wrote:

> The disasterous 'Balkanisation' of East Central Europe cannot be blamed merely on excessive local nationalism; it was caused as well by the ambitions and rivalries of the Great Powers.

Only if we consider to what extent the Great Powers interfered in East Central Europe can we understand the complicated and dramatic history of this unquiet area of Europe.[2]

If great-power interference has been the bane of national aspirations of the peoples of East Central Europe, then 'excessive local nationalism' has been the *bête noire* of great-power politics in the region. 'Balkanisation' is East Central Europe's gift to the political lexicon.[3] The term nicely encapsulates all of what the liberal Western great powers perceive to be wrong with East Central Europe: fragmentation caused by petty, vociferous nationalism. Winston Churchill, no stranger to the world of great-power politics, expressed Western doubts about the fruits of nationalism in East Central Europe when commenting on the demise of Austria–Hungary: 'There is not one of the peoples or provinces that constituted the Empire of the Habsburgs to whom gaining their independence has not brought the tortures which ancient poets and theologians had reserved for the damned'.[4] US Secretary of State James Baker's Canute-like anouncement in June 1991 that he 'believed' Yugoslavia should remain intact is a modern echo of Churchill's preference for maintaining larger multinational units over 'Balkanisation'.[5] Such an approach, however, runs contrary to the realities of nationalism in the region.

Nations and nationalism in East Central Europe developed in a markedly different fashion from that in the western and southwestern reaches of the continent or in North America. The geographical boundaries of the state in Western Europe mostly conform to the boundaries of the nation. Ethnic diversity, where it exists, has been suppressed by the strength of the unitary state structure so that 'from an ethnical point of view, the West can be compared to an extinct volcano'.[6] In the western half of Europe and North America, the state forged the nation-state. Nation-building took place with an emphasis on liberty, the rule of law and economic development within a defined territorial sovereignty. It was achieved without exclusively promoting a particular language and culture. Individual rights prevailed rather than the collective rights of identifiable ethnic groups in the societies. Lord Acton, Victorian historian and critic of nineteenth-century nationalism, illustrated the democratic foundations of the political nation-state when he wrote: 'The nationality formed by the State . . . is the only one to which we owe political duties, and it is, therefore, the only one which has political rights'.[7]

In East Central Europe, however, political and economic conditions differed significantly from those in Western Europe or North America. In the nineteenth century the supranational empires that dominated the region – Austria–Hungary, Germany, Ottoman Turkey and Russia – precluded development of the nation on the West European model. These imperial states proved incapable of mimicking their more liberal Western counterparts in launching a process of political nation-building among their diverse peoples. Moreover, in each of the supranational empires, specific ethnic groups were the mainstay of the imperial political structures.

The mixture of political oppression, regional ethnic diversity and social and economic backwardness provided a potent cocktail for the emergence of nations that placed a premium on linguistic, cultural and religious factors in defining national identity. Unlike the liberal West where the state created the nation-state, in East Central Europe the impulse for the creation of the nation-state came from peoples languishing in supranational imperial states. The desire of the peoples of the region was not so much directed to self-determination within a supranational state, but for the right to national self-determination in a territorial homeland (*heimat*) often shared and claimed by a rival national group.[8] Therefore the nation-state was defined in terms of the ethnolinguistic nation.

The ethnic diversity of the region provided fertile ground for the proliferation of national movements reacting against the absolutist supranational powers. National self-determination came about only in a limited fashion in the Balkans, where Bulgaria, Greece, Romania and Serbia emerged at the expense of the crumbling Ottoman Empire. The 'Springtime of Nations' in 1848 and the Polish insurrections of 1830 and 1863 stand as notable failures to shake off the power of the supranational states. At first associated with the liberal risorgimento reformist or Romantic nationalism, the frustrated national movements by the end of the nineteenth century discarded the liberal–reformist model for a wounded, exclusive, integral nationalism that narrowly and intolerantly defined the nation.[9] Given the ethnic kaleidoscope of the region, the realisation of the nation-state could only be achieved at the expense of other nationalities and held out the prospect of fragmentation and ethnic strife.

What the markedly different historical experiences of the liberal West and East Central Europe reveal is that these two regions lack a common understanding and language with regard to the development of nation and nationalism. While the Western powers have searched for policies to deal with the seemingly intractable nationalism in East Central Europe, their efforts to find solutions have been blocked by the incompatibility of the differing views of nationalism. Thomas Masaryk, Czechoslovakia's first president, understood the nature of the problem when he wrote:

> Big peoples, like the British and the American, who are wont to apply continental standards of judgement and are not greatly troubled by questions of language, are wont to look upon the liberation of small peoples and the creation of small States as a bothersome process of political and linguistic 'Balkanisation'. Yet circumstances are what they are, determined by Nature and History. Turkey, Austria–Hungary, Germany and Russia simplified half Europe by methods of violence, mechanically and therefore, temporarily. As remedies for 'Balkanisation', freedom and democracy are preferable.[10]

THE FIRST RECONSTRUCTION: NATIONAL SELF-DETERMINATION

The First World War paved the way for the dissolution of the supranational empires dominating East Central Europe. By the end of the war Imperial Germany was suing for peace, Russia was gripped by revolution and civil war, while Austria–Hungary and the Ottoman Empire were disappearing from the political map. The ensuing power vacuum created the conditions necessary for the 'successor' states to emerge.

Britain, France and the United States played a prominent role in the building of the successor states. During the war they had championed the idea of self-determination, as can be seen in Prime Minister David Lloyd George's Caxton Hall speech and President Woodrow Wilson's 'Fourteen Points' speech.[11] These public pronouncements laid the ideological groundwork for what would become Allied policy by the conclusion of the war. The liberal Western powers convened and dominated the Peace Conference in Paris and subsequent inter-Allied conferences that shaped the peace settlement in East Central Europe. The involvement of Britain and the United States in establishing the Versailles settlement for East Central Europe was disproportionate to their real or perceived interests in the region. Only France saw concrete security interests in the establishment of the successor states.[12]

At the Paris Peace Conference and afterwards, the liberal Western powers found that applying the principle of self-determination consistently proved more difficult in practice than in theory. Only the French had a policy toward East Central Europe; the Americans and British had only reservations. The French endeavoured to construct an eastern alliance system against Germany, designed to replace the now ideologically contaminated Russia. French policy made little effort to apply consistently any doctrine of self-determination, preferring to build an eastern *cordon sanitaire* against Germany (and Bolshevik Russia) in partnership with states such as Czechoslovakia, Poland and Romania. The inclusion of substantial national minorities in the client successor states troubled the French little as they strove to erect a barrier of states on Germany's eastern flank.

American and British policy, however, favoured a stricter application of the principle of self-determination. This preference grew out the perception that the region was a cauldron of nationalism; replete with small wars, pogroms and the *petit* imperialism of successor states. Lloyd George accurately reflected the Anglo–American outlook toward the region's nationalism in a section of his Peace Conference memoires entitled 'anarchy in Middle Europe':

> The emancipated races of Southern Europe were at each other's throats in their avidity to secure choice bits of the carcases of dead empires'. . . . 'These areas were the mangrove swamps where the racial roots were so tangled and intermingled that no peacemakers could move inside them without stumbling. The resurrected nations rose from their graves hungry and ravening from their long fast in the vaults of oppression.[13]

The American and British delegations attempted to reduce the size of national minorities within the successor states and protect them with a structure of international treaty guarantees. The French supported the territorial aspirations of their East Central European clients while paying lip service to the minority treaty structure. At the Paris Peace Conference the representatives of the successor states were permitted to present their case, and they had varying degrees of influence on the territorial decisions taken by the great powers. In the end, however, conference decisions on territorial matters rested on what direct influence the great powers could exercise in the region or on which side the successor state had been during the war.

The countries that had sided with the central powers saw their boundaries considerably reduced by punitive settlements. The Allies forced Hungary to sign the Treaty of Trianon (4 June 1920), which made it one of the most homogeneous of the successor states by depositing three million Hungarians in neighbouring Czechoslovakia, Romania and Yugoslavia. Bulgaria received similarly tough treatment, ceding territory to Greece, Romania and Yugoslavia under the terms of the Treaty of Neuilly (27 November 1919). Subsequent population exchanges and migrations only reinforced the reality of a Bulgarian nation-state.

In contrast with the countries on the losing side of the war, the Allies allowed Romania a *carte blanche* with regard to its territorial claims. By annexing Bessarabia, Bukovina, southern Dobruja and Transylvania, Romania had gained its maximalist territorial designs and national minorities approaching 30 per cent. The rebirth of Poland led to a similar proportion of national minorities. While the French abetted the territorial aspirations of their most sizable client-state in the region, the Americans and the British endeavoured to reduce the new Poland to its narrowest ethnographic limits. In the end Polish *faits accomplis*, small wars and Allied-sponsored plebiscites shaped the country's frontiers. The Allied powers exercised great influence on the determination of Poland's western frontier, but in the east the Poles eventually received more territory than the American and British delegations favoured.

In the territorial settlements, Czechoslovakia and Yugoslavia were the two dedicated multinational states to emerge at the Peace Conference. Replete with minorities, the dominant group in each state (Czechs or Serbs) formed a plurality rather than a majority. Both states, however, had the virtue in the eyes of the Western powers of lending themselves to the application of the Western model of nation-building in the East Central European context. The state was in each case to ensure the harmony of their disparate nationalities by means of the extension of self-determination. Czechoslovakia to its credit enjoyed a reasonably successful democratic political system in the interwar years. Czechoslovakia's democracy and its undoubted economic prosperity, however, did nothing to assuage the nationalist impulses of the Sudeten German population and the Slovaks, as the events of the Munich crisis illustrated in 1938. In the case of the creation of Yugoslavia, it presented a tidy solution to some of the most complex ethnographic patterns of settlement on the Balkan peninsula. Moreover it appeared to the Serbs as something of a reward for Serbia's wartime sacrifices. The Allies, however, were more sanguine about the prospects for democracy in Yugoslavia. At the Peace Conference the Allied powers recognised the impossibility of creating nation-states in East Central Europe. The ethnographic distribution of peoples in the region mitigated against any neat solutions. With the reality that most states would harbour large national minorities, the Allied powers sought an international legal structure that would guarantee the rights of minorities. The Minorities Treaties were meant to protect national minorities by affording them fair treatment under law, religious freedom and facilities to preserve their language and culture. It was hoped that minority rights, enshrined in international law, would offset the imperfect application of national self-determination and make minorities 'loyal and contented citizens of their new state'.[14]

All of the successor states, either by specific treaties (Czechoslovakia, Greece, Poland, Romania and Yugoslavia) or in clauses included in other treaty instruments (Austria, Bulgaria, Hungary and Turkey), assumed international obligations to their minorities. The League of Nations became the guarantor of the Minorities Treaties with the Council of the League made responsible for monitoring and enforcing treaty provisions. Dealing with minority complaints became one of the Council's most frequent agenda items in the interwar years.[15]

The Minorities Treaties, however, represented an attempt by the Western powers to find a solution to the problems of nationalism in East Central Europe by drawing on the historical experience of nation-building in the West. By applying the idea of rule of law on an international scale, it was hoped to displace in East Central Europe ethnographic criteria of nationhood in order to protect minorities. Rule of law, however, which had been instrumental in creating the political nation in Britain, France and the United States, lacked the same resonance in East Central Europe. Law had been an instrument of oppression in the region: the supranational empires used it in their efforts to quash national identity. From the perspective of East Central Europe, the Minorities Treaties were an international legal mechanism designed to thwart the realisation of national aspirations.

The retreat from involvement in the affairs of East Central Europe in the interwar years by the liberal Western powers did nothing to buttress the international treaty structure intended to mitigate against the excesses of nationalism. With the American return to isolationism, the British unwillingness to undertake continental commitments (particularly those involving East Central Europe) and French unease over enforcing the terms of the Versailles settlement without British support, the interwar European political environment undermined the entire Minorities Treaty ediface constructed in Paris in 1919.

THE SECOND RECONSTRUCTION: TOTALITARIANISM

The Second World War allowed the Western powers to complete their retreat from the 'mangrove swamps' of East Central European nationalism. British and French misgivings about the success of the settlement of 1919 from the point of view of regional nationalisms reached full bloom between 1938 and 1939. During the Munich crisis of 1938, Britain and France were partners with Nazi Germany and fascist Italy at Munich in dismantling Czechoslovakia. Thus Britain and France abandoned the ediface they had so labouriously built up at Versailles. Ironically, by sanctioning at Munich the destruction of Czechoslovakia they were eliminating what in relative terms was something of a model for adherence to the minority treaty regime and the strength of its democratic institutions.

The decision to abandon appeasement of Nazi Germany in the spring of 1939 did not eliminate all misgivings about regional nationalism. The formal treaty of alliance with Poland, signed on 25 August 1939, avoided any commitment on the part of Britain and France to guarantee the territorial integrity of the Polish state. Moreover a secret protocol in the treaty limited implementation of the agreement to an attack by Germany. The framework of the treaty reflected British doubts about the legitimacy of the solutions found twenty years earlier to the problems of nationalism.

The British and French role in reversing the fruits of their earlier efforts ended with the outbreak of war in September 1939. These Western powers, whose role had been so prominent in the earlier reconstruction of the region, were now moved decisively to the political periphery. In their place Nazi Germany and the Soviet Union refashioned East Central Europe, and in doing so completed the job of burying the Versailles settlement.

East Central Europe was now in the grip of a totalitarian vice. Nazi Germany and the Soviet Union, first as partners (1939–41) and subsequently as enemies (1941–45), engaged in geopolitical remodelling on a massive scale. The Molotov–Ribbentropp agreement of 23 August 1939 led to the division of the region into spheres of influence. The agreement partitioned Poland as well as paved the way for Soviet annexation of the Baltic states and Bukovina/ Bessarabia. The rest of the region fell into the German orbit, with the remaining areas ending up either as client states (Bulgaria, Croatia, Hungary, Romania and Slovakia) or placed under direct control of Germany (Czech and Polish lands). After the German invasion of the Soviet Union in June 1941, the entire region fell into the Nazi 'new order', to be followed by Soviet 'liberation' after 1944.

The period of totalitarian cooperation and conflict between 1939 and 1945 had profound implications for the ethnographic map of the region. The Nazi and Soviet 'new orders' introduced policies that uprooted and murdered millions of people in an attempt to realise either a pernicious Nazi racial ideology or to eliminate Soviet 'class enemies'. Through mass deportations, terror campaigns and, most insidious of all, the Holocaust, the region underwent irreversible changes to the pattern of nationality settlement. Totalitarian 'ethnic cleansing' and 'ethnic homogenisation' took place on a massive scale and brutally simplified the ethnographic complexion of the region.

As a consequence of war, Poland emerged as an homogeneous nation-state moved westward and shorn of its national minorities; Czechoslovakia lost its German population and Carpathian Ruthenia to the Soviet Union; Hungary returned to its Trianon borders; Romania lost Bukovina and Bessarabia to the Soviet Union but kept its Hungarian minority; Bulgaria remained largely as it was, with few minorities; and Tito reconstructed a 'federal' Yugoslavia that retained its complicated ethnic–religious mozaic. Apart from lingering Hungarian diaspora and the restoration of the multinational constructs of Czechoslovakia and Yugoslavia, war had been a promoter of the ethnographic nation-state (see Chapter 3).

Wartime great-power politics worked in favour of the perpetuation of the ethnographic changes in East Central Europe. The elimination of France from wartime international politics (1940) and the construction of the 'grand alliance' of Britain, the Soviet Union and the United States (1941) marked a significant watershed in the policies of the liberal Western powers toward East Central Europe. Britain and the United States accepted a subordinate role to that of their Soviet ally in shaping the future of the region. The geopolitical reality of the inevitability of Soviet liberation of the region made it easy for American and British policy makers to accept the more rough and ready solutions to the problems of nationalism offered by their Soviet ally. The Western powers were able to accept the logic of creating more homogeneous states in East Central Europe, particularly as they were not asked to contribute directly to the dirty business of tidying the ethnographic map.

By the end of the war, however, they were moving toward becoming full partners in the totalitarian 'ethnic cleansing'. At the Teheran and Yalta Conferences America and Britain agreed to a reshaping of the Polish state that implicitly entailed major population movements. Britain and the United States crossed the political rubicon at Potsdam in June 1945, when they agreed to the expulsion of millions of Germans from East Central Europe.[16]

The complicity of the Western powers in accepting the ethnographic reconfiguration of East Central Europe could be seen in their reluctance to become bogged down in the nationalist minutiae of the region. At Teheran, Churchill was not prepared to make a 'big squawk' about Lwów when considering the Polish–Soviet frontier; at Yalta the Western powers seemed unable to distinguish between the eastern and western branches of the river Neisse when determining Poland's western frontier.[17] The nations of the region were only allowed to leave their fate to the indifferent geographical knowledge of the Western powers and the detailed brief of the Soviet leadership. Unlike the Versailles Peace Conference, the states of East Central Europe were not invited to discuss their future. The decisions taken by the big three – Churchill, Roosevelt and Stalin – at Teheran and Yalta were taken without reference to the people most directly affected.

The Americans covered the tracks of their abandonment of earlier principles with a mixture of idealistic statements underlining the right to 'self-determination' (universalism) married to inactivity, which has been appropriately described as a 'non-policy'.[18] The Atlantic Charter of August 1941 and, more notoriously, the Yalta Declaration on Liberated Europe of February 1945 are fine examples of this conscience salving.[19]

British policy saw no need for the fig leaf of high-sounding principle in order to accept Soviet totalitarian transformations of East Central Europe. Indeed the British government displayed a willingness to cut 'deals' with the Soviet Union to speed the political and demographic remodelling. Concerning Poland, Britain's *causus belli* in 1939, wartime British policy seemed intent on outdoing

Stalin in reducing the country to its narrowest ethnographic limits; it fully supported Soviet territorial aspirations in the east while attempting to limit Polish acquisition of German territory in the west. The most famous 'deal', however, was Churchill's 'Percentages Agreement' with Stalin in October 1944. It was an episode that offered a nostalgic return to old-fashioned great-power sphere-of-influence politics. The Percentages Agreement assigned Britain a majority stake in Greece (90 per cent) while giving the Soviet Union the dominant position in Bulgaria (75 per cent) and Romania (90 per cent). Both powers shared an equal stake in Hungary and Yugoslavia.[20] The weight of percentages in the Soviet favour made clear the British vision of the future East Central Europe.

Another casualty of the Second World War were the Minorities Treaties. With the postwar creation of the United Nations (UN) and such regional groupings as the Council of Europe, the international emphasis shifted toward universal and individual human rights.[21] This discarding of the collective-rights principle that underpinned the Minorities Treaty structure was the result of the perceived failure of the Minorities Treaties and the natural consequence of the replacement of the League of Nations with the UN. The Minorities Treaties had been under the supervision of the League of Nations, and with its demise they lost their *raison d'être*.

Despite wartime policies that effectively handed East Central Europe to the Soviet Union, Britain and the United States proved capable of a *volte face* toward Soviet policy in the region soon after the war. Ironically, communist takeovers in Czechoslovakia and Poland provided a convenient excuse for the shift of Anglo–American policy toward confrontation with the Soviet Union. It is therefore doubly ironic that during the Cold War the West maintained its wartime unholy alliance with the Soviet Union in smothering the nationalist impulses of the peoples of East Central Europe.

WESTERN POLICY TOWARD COMMUNIST EASTERN EUROPE

The beginning of the Cold War and the emergence of the Soviet Union and the United States as the dominant and competing powers in the new world order meant that Britain and France, which formerly had a large role in shaping the political reconstruction of the region, faded into the background. American power now set the agenda of the Western alliance toward the Soviet-dominated states of East Central Europe.

American foreign and security interests tacitly accepted Soviet domination of the region. The language of the Cold War illustrates this point. The countries of East Central Europe were referred to as the 'satellite states', the 'Soviet bloc' or the 'captive nations'. The expression 'Eastern Europe' became fashionable among politicians, journalists and academics, signifying the dragging eastward of a belt of states geographically but not politically near the centre of Europe. Such semantic changes stripped away the identity of individual nations and reflected a tendency in United States policy to define its position toward Eastern Europe in terms of its relations with the Soviet Union.

Such a position effectively made the United States a partner in the suppression of the aspirations of the nations of East Central Europe. George Kennan, that architect of American foreign policy during the Cold War and subsequently its fiercest critic, understood the effect that American bipolar tunnel vision toward the Soviet Union had on Eastern Europe:

> I was equally disinclined to settle for a European policy which left no room, even in concept, for the Eastern European peoples, which would have had no place for them even should they be able to liberate themselves, which offered them no alternatives to Soviet domination but an attempt at a reversal of alliances and association with a military grouping which the Soviet leaders regarded as directed against themselves. By holding out to them no other possibility than this, one was – it seemed to me – actually making oneself the ally of Moscow in the preservation of Soviet domination in that area.[22]

Kennan made this observation in his 1957 Reith Lectures as a outsider removed from the day-to-day running of American foreign policy. How close his remarks in 1957 were to actual policy was borne out by an embarrassing leak from the State Department in the mid-1970s of the so-called 'Sonnenfeldt Doctrine'. At a meeting in London of American ambassadors to Europe, Helmut Sonnenfeldt, a counselor at the State Department, suggested to his colleagues that the aim of American policy ought to be to transform the 'inorganic, unnatural relationship' between the Soviet and Eastern Europe to one that was 'organic' for the sake of peace and stability. When leaked, Sonnenfeldt's remarks sparked a public furore that led to Congressional hearings. In his testimony at a House of Representatives hearing, Sonnenfeldt confirmed the substance of his remarks as reported in the press (*New York Times*), but also stressed 'in the clearest possible terms that we [the State Department] support the independence, national sovereignty and identity, and the autonomy of all the peoples and countries of central and Eastern Europe'.[23]

Outside the world of official policy, the question of nationalism was not even a matter that seriously exercised the legions of area-studies specialists. Although a few scholars warned of the potential nationalist dangers lurking beneath the ideological mantel of communism, these voices were in a distinct minority.[24] Consideration of nationalism applied obliquely to the military calculations of NATO versus the Warsaw Pact. The issue of 'reliability' of the East Central European members of the Soviet alliance system spawned a body of academic literature more interested in exploiting a Soviet weakness than assessing the wider implications of nationalism in the region.[25]

The silent partnership with the Soviet Union in thwarting nationalism in East Central Europe did not stop the Western camp from occasionally using it as a means to cause Soviet discomfort. The cynical support for Nicolae Ceauşescu's 'national communism' in Romania and the encouragement of Solidarity in Poland were examples of the West's willingness to play the nationalism card if it made life more difficult for the 'evil empire'. The limits, however, of this toying with nationalism could be seen after Solidarity's demise in December 1981. President Reagan's encouragement of all Americans to place in their windows a lit candle for Poland was more an illumination of how far American policy makers were willing go in support of national aspirations in the region.

THE THIRD RECONSTRUCTION: BALKANISATION OR INTEGRATION?

The 'inorganic' relationship between East Central Europe and the Soviet Union ended in 1989. Two years later the Soviet Union was consigned to the dustbin of history. These watershed events have once again made nationalism a central factor in the post-communist reconstruction of the region. Western politicians have been slow to wake up to this fact. In the brave new world order, nationalism, particularly the East Central European variety, does not have a prominent place on the agenda.

In a 1989 article in *Foreign Affairs* entitled 'Post-Communist Nationalism', Zbigniew Brzezinski tried to raise the profile of this issue: 'The time has come for the West to confront as a policy issue a problem that for years most Western scholars have tended to ignore and that all Western policymakers still consider to be taboo: the rising tide of nationalism in Eastern Europe'.[26] The disintegration of Yugoslavia has only underscored the validity of Brzezinski's argument.

The breakup of the country began with the succession of Slovenia and Croatia from the Yugoslav federation in June 1991. At first member states of the European Community and the United States were reluctant to recognise the Yugoslav successor states. As one British political commentator remarked: 'Western leaders were more stubbornly wedded than the Yugoslavs to the principle of Yugoslav unity'.[27] By the end of 1992, however, virtually all the former Yugoslav republics had received international recognition, including the multinational Bosnia–Hercegovina and Macedonia. The West's tardiness in recognising accomplished facts was, at the core, the product of viewing Yugoslavia through the prism of the Western brand of nationalism. This can be semantically illustrated by the continued references to 'Yugoslavians' and the 'Yugoslav nation' among Western politicians. They had failed to grasp the essential reality that Yugoslavia existed without Yugoslavs by the 1990s.[28]

The conflict in former Yugoslavia, in keeping with the ethno-linguistic nature of nations and nationalism in the region, is about creating homogeneous nation-states. Given the ethnographic tangle within former Yugoslavia, such an aim could not be achieved without considerable human cost. The Serbs and Croats in particular are bent, either by means of violence or political stealth, on building an 'ethnically pure' greater Serbia and Croatia. The ruthlessness employed in pursuit of these aims has given rise to murder, rape and 'ethnic cleansing' as a matter of policy.[29]

In the face of such horrific circumstances Western policy, conducted through the auspices of the European Community (EC) or UN, has vacillated between intervention and inaction. At the root of the indecision has been an inability to tailor political solutions to the realities of Balkan nationalism. The war in Bosnia–Hercegovina underscores this western failure. The conflict in Bosnia, however much disguised by labels such as 'civil war', is essentially a struggle between two Balkan nations for control of a piece of territory. Caught in the middle are the last of the Yugoslavs, the Bosnian Muslims. For them the war has been the midwife of their emerging ethnic nationhood.

The West's solution to the Bosnian conflict has been an attempt to create a mini-Yugoslavia out of the rubble of its larger, failed predecessor. This has led to the Vance–Owen plan, devised under the joint stewardship of the UN and the EC. The Vance–Owen plan called for the division of prewar Bosnia into ten cantons, with boundaries of nine of the cantons drawn with a view to making them as ethnically homogeneous as possible. The Bosnian Muslims, Croats and Serbs would each receive three cantons, with the Sarajevo canton placed under the joint control of all three groups.

In May 1993 the plan was signed by all the warring parties. Lord Owen, commenting on what the plan was meant to achieve said: ' . . . for the people of Bosnia to live together, intermarry, share the same apartments and generally live together in the way they did before these horrors began'.[30] The substance of Lord Owen's remarks revealed that the Vance–Owen plan was grounded in a view of nation and nationalism alien to the region. It was a design for creating a Western nation-state; an idyll of self-determination, economic rationality, rule of law and multicultural tolerance in the Balkans. 'In reality', as Jonathan Eyal wrote, 'the West always had only two choices: either the dispatch of a massive force with the task of keeping Bosnia united, or the acceptance of the republic's irrevocable division'.[31] The former solution entailed the imposition of an alien concept of nationhood on Bosnia while the latter simply accepted the existing ethnic nationalism.

In confronting the crisis in former Yugoslavia, the Western powers (the principal members of the EC and the United States) have seemingly forgotten everything and learned nothing from the two previous reconstructions of the region. From the first reconstruction came the lesson that minority protection grounded in international treaties is not enough in states where one national group is intent on a dominant political position acquired by violence at the expense of other national groups. The Serbs are ascendant in Bosnia not by virtue of numbers but by their monopoly on firepower. Unless there is an opportunity or a desire by the international community (Western powers) for direct intervention, applying an international *rechtstaat* becomes a forlorn hope.[32]

The lack of will on the part of the international community does not mean that there is no place for international legal protection for national minorities. Global and regional organisations such as the UN or the Council of Europe need to adapt their universal and individual human-rights approaches to the reality of national minorities in Europe. Both these organisations are taking important steps in this direction by seeking to define what is a national minority and what are its rights. Provided definitions can be devised that have universal application rather than applying to specific countries, then one of the major pitfalls of the interwar minority treaties can be avoided.[33] The Conference on Security and Cooperation in Europe (CSCE) represents another avenue of development for national-minority protection and early intervention in budding ethnic conflict. Like the UN and Council of Europe, the CSCE needs to reshape an individual-rights focus toward group rights.[34]

More relevant for the situation in former Yugoslavia is an important lesson from the second reconstruction. The most effective solution to intractable nationality conflict is the separation of hostile groups into homogeneous states or regions. While the expulsion of the Germans from East Central Europe and the creation of an ethnographically homogeneous Poland were extreme measures, they nevertheless offered a definitive solution to dangerous national conflict. In the Balkans there is a precedent for population exchanges that predates the First World War. The Bulgarian–Turkish population exchanges in 1913 and the Greek–Turkish and Bulgarian–Greek population transfers after 1923 eradicated potential sources of minority ill-treatment and territorial irredenta.[35]

In Bosnia the original settlement patterns have been irrevocably destroyed and a large proportion of the population made into refugees as a consequence of war and 'ethnic cleansing'. Under such circumstances creating completely homogeneous regions in Bosnia may be the only long-term option left for the Western powers. The argument that such a policy would reward Serbian aggression and legitimate 'ethnic cleansing' loses a lot of its validity if the process of creating homogeneous regions requires the Serbs to yield territory and transfer out the Serbian population. Every group then shares the cost of mutual intolerance. The move to create 'safe areas', with the apparent demise of the Vance–Owen plan, could be used as the basis of such a solution to the Bosnian war.

The crisis in former Yugoslavia, however, represents the worse-case scenario regarding nationalism in East Central Europe. The ethnocentric nationalism of the region may contain qualities that may be latently dangerous, but the possibility of nationalist conflict in all parts of the region remains remote. Only the sizable Hungarian minorities in Romania and Slovakia offer a potential if unlikely reason for conflict between Hungary and two of its neighbours. The danger of further 'Balkanisation' can be greatly reduced by the extension of European integration.[36] The postwar experience with Western European economic and political integration offers new possibilities for insuring against the negative features of East Central European nationalism. Historically, German nationalism has had more in common with that of the eastern half of the European continent.[37] The combination of integration and democracy has been a resounding success in banking the fires of German nationalism. Extending European integration eastwards can offer a constructive framework for the nationalism of the peoples of East Central Europe and lay to rest Western fears of Balkanisation.

Notes and References

1. Jerzy Jedlicki, 'The Revolution of 1989: The Unbearable Burden of History', *Problems of Communism*, vol. xxxiv (July–August 1990), p. 40.

2. Hubert Ripka, *Eastern Europe in the Post-War World* (London: Methuen, 1961), p. 31.

3. The verb 'Balkanise' means to divide (a region) into a number of smaller and often mutually hostile units, as was done in the Balkan Peninsula in the late nineteenth and early twentieth century. See J. A. Simpson and E. S. C. Weiner (eds), *The Oxford English Dictionary*, 2nd. ed., vol. i (Oxford: Clarendon Press, 1989), p. 903.

4. Winston S. Churchill, *The Second World War: The Gathering Storm*, vol. i (London: Cassell 1948), p. 9.

5. Tony Barber, 'Wandering into a Balkan Blunderland', *The Independent on Sunday*, 30 May 1993.

6. Quoted from Walter Kolarz, *Myths and Realities in Eastern Europe* (London: Lindsay Drummond, 1946), p. 9. Regarding East Central European nationalism, see Hugh Seton-Watson, *Nations and States: An Enquiry into the Origins of Nations and the Politics of Nationalism* (London: Methuen, 1977), and Peter F. Sugar and Ivo J. Lederer (eds), *Nationalism in Eastern Europe* (Seattle: University of Washington Press, 1969).

7. Essay on 'Nationality' in J. Rufus Fears (ed.), *Essays in the History of Liberty: Selected Writings of Lord Acton*, vol. i (Indianapolis: Liberty, 1985), p. 429.

8. E. H. Carr makes an important distinction between the concept of self-determination that grew out of the French Revolution and the subsequent merger of this concept with doctrinaire nationalism producing the idea of

182   *What To Do About Nationalism?*

'national self determination'. See E. H. Carr, *Conditions of Peace* (London: Macmillan, 1942), pp. 37–50.

9. See Peter Alter, *Nationalism* (London: Edward Arnold, 1991).
10. Thomas Garrigue Masaryk, *The Making of A State: Memories and Observations 1914–1918* (New York: Frederick A. Stokes, 1927), p. 412.
11. David Stevenson, *The First World War and International Politics* (Oxford: Oxford University Press, 1988), pp. 192–8.
12. See Piotr S. Wandycz, *France and Her Eastern Allies 1919–1925* (Minneapolis: University of Minnesota Press, 1962).
13. David Lloyd George, *Memoirs of the Peace Conference* (New Haven: Yale University Press), p. 200.
14. C. A. Macartney and A. W. Palmer, *Independent Eastern Europe: A History* (London: Macmillan, 1966), p. 143. See also C. A. Macartney, *National States and National Minorities* (London: Oxford University Press, 1934) for a detailed study of the Minority Treaties.
15. Alfred Zimmern, *The League of Nations and the Rule of Law 1918–1935* (London: Macmillan, 1936), p. 450.
16. 'Protocol of the Proceedings of the Berlin Conference, Part XII – Orderly Transfer of German Populations', in Rohan Butler (ed.), *Documents on British Policy Overseas* (London: HMSO, 1984), p. 1275.
17. See Winston S. Churchill, *Closing the Ring* (New York: Bantam, 1974), p. 340; W. W. Kulski, *Germany and Poland: From War to Peaceful Relations* (Syracuse: Syracuse University Press, 1976).
18. See Geir Lundsted, *The American Non-Policy towards Eastern Europe* (Tromso: Universitetsforlaget, 1978).
19. The Yalta Declaration called for 'the right of all peoples to choose the form of government under which they will live'. See Gale Stokes (ed.), *From Stalinism to Pluralism: A Documentary History of Eastern Europe since 1945* (New York: Oxford University Press, 1991), p. 15.
20. Stokes, pp. 31–2.
21. Article 3 of the 'Statute of the Council of Europe' requires each member state to 'accept the principles of the rule of law and the enjoyment by all persons within its jurisdiction of human rights and fundamental freedoms'. See 'Statute of the Council of Europe', 5 May 1949, in J. A. S. Grenville, *The Major International Treaties 1914–1973: A History and Guide with Texts* (New York: Stein and Day, 1975), p. 402.
22. George F. Kennan, *Memoirs 1950–1963*, vol. II (Boston: Little, Brown and Company, 1972), p. 259.
23. 'United States National Security Policy vis-à-vis Eastern Europe', Hearings before the Subcommittee on International Security and Scientific Affairs of the Committee on International Relations House of Representatives, Ninety-Fourth Congress, Second Session, 12 April 1976, p. 2.
24. See for example Zbigniew Brzezinski, *The Soviet Bloc: Unity and Conflict*, 4th ed. (Cambridge: Harvard University Press, 1971), p. 440.
25. See for example Dale R. Herspring and Ivan Volgyes, 'Toward a Conceptualisation of Political Reliability in the East European Warsaw Pact Armies', *Armed Forces and Society*, vol. VI (winter 1980), pp. 270–96; Daniel N. Nelson, *Soviet Allies: The Warsaw Pact and the Issue of Reliability* (Boulder: Westview Press, 1984); Jeffrey Simon and Trond Gilberg (eds),

Security Implications of Nationalism in Eastern Europe (Carlisle Barracks: US Army War College, 1985).

26. Zbigniew Brzezinski, 'Post Communist Nationalism' *Foreign Affairs*, vol. LXVIII (winter 1989/90), p. 1.
27. Barber, 'Wandering into a Balkan Blunderland'.
28. See: Paul Lendvai, 'Yugoslavia without Yugoslavs: the roots of the Crisis', *International Affairs*, vol. LXVII (1992), pp. 251–61.
29. Robert Fisk, 'The Rapes Went on Day and Night', *The Independent*, 8 February 1993; Patrick Moore, 'Ethnic Cleansing in Bosnia: Outrage but Little Action', RFE/RL Research Report, 28 august 1992.
30. Quoted in Annika Savill, Davis Usborne, Anthony Bevins and Robert Block, 'Owen Begs US to Hold its Fire in Bosnia', *The Independent*, 3 May 1993.
31. Jonathan Eyal, 'Peace, or Myth Wrapped in Folly?', *The Independent*, 4 May 1993.
32. Jonathan Eyal offers a scathing critique of European policy toward the crisis in Yugoslavia in his *Europe and Yugoslavia: Lessons From a Failure*, Whitehall Paper Series 1993.
33. For the range of possible international approaches to the problem of protection of national minorities, see Stephen Kux, 'International Approaches to the National Minorities Problem', *The Polish Quarterly of International Affairs*, vol. I (summer/autumn 1992), pp. 7–26. For possible solutions tailored to East Central Europe, see Jonathan Eyal, 'Eastern Europe: What About the Minorities', *The World Today*, December 1984, pp. 205–8. The problems in devising a new system of protection for national minorities can be seen in the Council of Europe's attempts to adapt its statute to the problems in Eastern Europe. See Andrew Marshall, 'Britain Obstructs Action on Minority Rights', *The Independent*, 13 July 1993.
34. Kux, pp. 18–22. For a detailed review of CSCE and human rights, see Jerzy Menkes and Alina Prystrom, 'Institutionalisation of Human Rights Protection within the CSCE System', *The Polish Quarterly of International Affairs*, vol. I (summer/autumn 1992), pp. 27–46.
35. Joseph B. Schechtman, *Postwar Population Transfers in Europe 1945–1955* (Philadelphia: University of Pennsylvannia Press, 1962), pp. 22–3.
36. Brzezinski, 'Post-Communist Nationalism', p. 18.
37. Alter, pp. 50–4.

Further Reading

GENERAL NATIONALISM AND SELF-DETERMINATION

Alter, Peter, *Nationalism* (London: Edward Arnold, 1991).

Brown, Michael E. (ed.), *Ethnic Conflict and International Security* (Princeton: Princeton University Press, 1993).

Brzezinski, Zbigniew, 'Post Communist Nationalism', *Foreign Affairs*, vol. LXVIII (winter 1989–90), pp. 1–25.

Bugajski, Janusz, *Nations in Turmoil: Conflict and Cooperation in Eastern Europe* (Boulder: Westview Press, 1993).

Carr, Edward Hallett, *Nationalism and After* (London: Macmillan, 1945).

Chlebowczyk, Jozef, *On Small and Young Nations in Europe* (Wroclaw: Ossolineum, 1980).

Cobban, Alfred, *National Self-Determination* (Oxford: Oxford University Press, 1944).

_____ *The Nation-State and National Self-Determination* (London: Collins, 1969).

Griffiths, Stephen Iwan, *Nationalism and Ethnic Conflict: Threats to European Security*, SIPRI Research Report no. 5 (Oxford: Oxford University Press, 1993).

Halperin, Morton H. and David J. Scheffer, with Patricia L. Small, *Self-Determination in the New World Order* (Washington DC: Carnegie Endowment for International Peace, 1992).

Hayes, Carlton J. H., *Essays on Nationalism* (New York: Russell and Russell, 1926).

_____ *The Historical Evolution of Modern Nationalism* (New York: Macmillan, 1931).

Gellner, Ernest, *Nations and Nationalism* (Oxford: Basil Blackwell, 1983).

Hobsbawn, E. J., *Nations and Nationalism since 1870*, 2nd ed. (Cambridge: Cambridge University Press, 1992).

Kedourie, Elie, *Nationalism*, 3rd ed. (London: Hutchinson, 1969).

Kellas, James G., *The Politics of Nationalism and Ethnicity* (London: Macmillan, 1991).

Klein, George and Milan J. Reban (eds), *The Politics of Ethnicity in Eastern Europe* (Boulder: East European Monographs, 1981) [contains essays covering each country].

Kohn, Hans, *The Idea of Nationalism: A Study in its Origins and Background* (New York: Collier Books, 1944).

Lendvai, Paul, 'Eastern Europe I: Liberalism vs. Nationalism', *The World Today*, July 1990.

Moynihan, Daniel Patrick, *Pandaemonium: Ethnicity in International Politics* (Oxford: Oxford University Press, 1993).

Seton-Watson, Hugh, *Nations and States: An Inquiry into the Origins of Nations and the Politics of Nationalism* (London: Methuen, 1977).

Shafer, Boyd C., *Nationalism: Myth and Reality* (New York: Harcourt, Brace and World, 1955).

____ *Faces of Nationalism: New Realities and Old Myths* (New York: Harcourt, Brace and Jovanovich, 1972).

Smith, Anthony D., *Theories of Nationalism* (London: Duckworth, 1971).

____ *The Ethnic Origins of Nations* (Oxford: Blackwell, 1986).

Smith, P. (ed.), *Ethnic Groups in International Relations* (Aldershot: Dartmouth, 1991).

Snyder, Louis L., *Encyclopedia of Nationalism* (Chicago: St James Press, 1990).

Sugar, Peter F. and Ivo J. Lederer, (eds), *Nationalism in Eastern Europe* (Seattle: University of Washington Press, 1969. [contains essays covering each country].

Szlafer, H. (ed.), *Essays on Economic Nationalism in East-Central Europe and South America 1918–1939* (Geneve: Universite de Geneve, 1990).

GENERAL EAST CENTRAL EUROPE

Batt, Judy, *Economic Reform and Political Change in Eastern Europe* (London: Macmillan, 1988).

____ *East Central Europe from Reform to Transformation* (London: Royal Institute for International Affairs, 1991).

Brown, J. F., *Surge to Freedom: The End of Communist Rule in Eastern Europe* (Durham: Duke University Press, 1991).

____ *Nationalism, Democracy and Security in the Balkans* (Aldershot: Dartmouth, 1992).

Fine, John V. A., *History of the Early Medieval Balkans and History of the Later Medieval Balkans*, 2 vols (Ann Arbor: University of Michigan Press, 1983, 1987).

Glenny, Misha, *The Rebirth of History: Eastern Europe in the Age of Democracy* (London: Penguin, 1990).

Jelavich, Barbara, *History of the Balkans*, 2 vols (Cambridge: Cambridge University Press, 1983).

Kolarz, Walter, *Myths and Realities in Eastern Europe* (London: Lindsay Drummond, 1946).

Lampe, John R. and Marvin Jackson, *Balkan Economic History, 1550–1950* (Bloomington: Indiana University Press, 1983).

Macartney, C. A. and A. W. Palmer, *Independent Eastern Europe* (London: Macmillan, 1962).

Palmer, Alan, *The Lands Between: A History of East-Central Europe since the Congress of Vienna* (London: Weidenfeld and Nicolson, 1970).

Polonsky, Antony, *The Little Dictators: The History of Eastern Europe since 1918* (London: Routledge and Kegan Paul, 1975).

Rothschild, Joseph, *East Central Europe Between the Two World Wars* (Seattle: University of Washington Press, 1974).

____ *Return to Diversity: A Political History of East Central Europe since World War II* (New York: Oxford University Press, 1989).

Seton-Watson, Hugh, *Eastern Europe between the Wars, 1918–1941* (Cambridge: Cambridge University Press, 1946).

____ *The East European Revolution* (New York: Frederick A. Praeger, 1951).

Stavrianos, L. S., *The Balkans Since 1453* (New York: Holt, Rinehart and Winston, 1957).

Stokes, Gale (ed.), *From Stalinism to Pluralism: A Documentary History of Eastern Europe since 1945* (Oxford: Oxford University Press, 1991).

Zeman, Z. A. B., *Pursued by a Bear. The Making of Eastern Europe* (London: Chatto and Windus, 1989).

____ *The Making and Breaking of Communist Europe* (Oxford: Basil Blackwell, 1991).

NATIONAL MINORITIES AND POPULATION MIGRATION

Eyal, Jonathan, 'Eastern Europe: What About the Minorities', *The World Today*, December 1989.

Horek, Stephan (ed.), *Eastern European National Minorities, 1919/1980: A Handbook* (Littleton: Libraries Unlimited, 1985).

Jankowsky, Oscar I., *Nationalities and National Minorities* (New York: Macmillan, 1945).

Jungmann, Otto, *National Minorities in Europe* (New York: Covici, Friede, 1932).

Kamenetsky, Ihor, *Secret Nazi Plan for Eastern Europe: A Study of Lebensraum Policies* (New York: Bookman, 1961).

Kulischer, Eugene, M., *Europe on the Move: War and Population Changes, 1914–1947* (New York: Columbia University Press, 1948).

Liebrich, Andre, 'Minorities in Eastern Europe: Obstacles to a Reliable Count', RFE/RL Research Report, 15 May 1992.

Macartney, C. A., *National States and National Minorities* (Oxford: Oxford University Press, 1934).

Pearson, Raymond, *National Minorities in Eastern Europe, 1848–1945* (London: Macmillan, 1983).

Schechtman, Joseph B., *Postwar Population Transfers in Europe, 1945–1955* (Pittsburgh: Pennsylvania University Press, 1962).

____ *European Population Transfers, 1939–1945* (Cornell University Press, 1946; republished by Russell and Russell, New York, 1971).

Schopflin, George, 'National Minorities under Communism in Eastern Europe', in Kurt London, *Eastern Europe in Transition* (Baltimore: The Johns Hopkins Press, 1966).

____ 'National Minorities in Eastern Europe', in George Schopflin (ed.), *The Soviet Union and Eastern Europe* (London: Muller, Almond and White, 1970).

Schoplin, George, and Hugh Poulton, *Romania's Ethnic Hungarians* (London: The Minority Rights Group, 1990).

Stephans, J. S., *Danger Zones of Europe: A Study of National Minorities* (London: Hogarth, 1929).

Sword, Keith (ed.), *The Soviet Takeover of the Polish Eastern Provinces, 1939–41* (London: St Martin's Press, 1991).

BULGARIA

Bell, John D., *Peasants in Power: Alexander Stamboliski and the Bulgarian Agrarian National Union, 1899–1923* (Princeton: Princeton University Press, 1977).

_____ *The Bulgarian Communist Party from Blagoev to Zhivkov* (Stanford: Hoover Institution Press, 1986).

Brown, J. F., *Bulgaria Under Communist Rule* (New York: Praeger, 1970).

Constant, Stephen, *Foxy Ferdinand Tsar of Bulgaria* (New York: Franklin Wats, 1980).

Crampton, Richard J., *Bulgaria: 1878–1918, A History* (Boulder: East European Monographs, 1983).

_____ *A Short History of Modern Bulgaria* (Cambridge: Cambridge University Press, 1987).

Groueff, Stephane, *Crown of Thorns: The Reign of King Boris III of Bulgaria, 1918–1943* (Lanham, MD: Madison Books, 1987).

Jelavich, Charles, *Tsarist Russia and Balkan Nationalism: Russian Influence in the Internal Affairs of Bulgaria and Serbia, 1879–1886* (Berkeley: University of California Press, 1958).

Lampe, John R., *The Bulgarian Economy in the Twentieth Century* (New York: St Martin's Press, 1986).

Oren, Nissan, *Bulgarian Communism: The Road to Power, 1934–1944* (New York: Columbia University Press, 1971).

_____ *Revolution Administered: Agrarianism and Communism in Bulgaria* (Baltimore: Johns Hopkins University Press, 1973).

Perry, Duncan M., *Stefan Stambolov and the Emergence of Modern Bulgaria, 1870–1895* (Durham MC: Duke University Press, 1993).

Rothschild, Joseph, *The Communist Party of Bulgaria: Origins and Developments, 1883–1936* (New York: Columbia University Press, 1959).

CZECH REPUBLIC AND SLOVAKIA

Bradley, John F. N., *Czech Nationalism in the Nineteenth Century* (Boulder: East European Monographs, 1984).

Brock, Peter, *The Slovak National Awakening* (Toronto: University of Toronto Press, 1976).

_____ and H. Gordon Skilling (eds), *The Czech Renascence of the Nineteenth Century* (Toronto: University of Toronto Press, 1970).

Garver, Bruce M., *The Young Czech Party 1874–1901 and the Emergence of a Multi-Party System* (New Haven and London: Yale University Press, 1976).

Hroch, Miroslav, *Social Preconditions of National Revival in Europe* (Cambridge: Cambridge University Press, 1985).

Kirschbaum, Stanislav J. (ed.), *Reflections on Slovak History* (Toronto: Slovak World Congress, 1987).

Klima, Arnost, 'The Czechs', in Mikulas Teich and Roy Porter (eds), *The National Question in Europe in Historical Context* (Cambridge: Cambridge University Press, 1993), pp. 228–47.

Kusin, Vladimir V., *From Dubček to Charter 77* (Edinburgh: Q Press, 1978).

Mamatey, Victor S. and Radomír Luža (eds), *A History of the Czechoslovak Republic 1918–1948* (Princeton NJ: 1973).

Masaryk, Thomas G., *The Making of a State* (London: George Allen and Urwin, 1927).

Morison, John (ed.), *The Czech and Slovak Experience* (London: Macmillan, 1991).
Myant, Martin, *The Czechoslovak Economy 1948–1988* (Cambridge: Cambridge University Press, 1989).
Olivova, Věra, *The Doomed Democracy. Czechoslovakia in a Disrupted Europe, 1914–1938* (London: Sidgwick and Jackson, 1972).
Orton, Lawrence D., *The Prague Slav Congress of 1848* (Boulder: East European Monographs, 1978).
Pech, Stanley Z., *The Czech Revolution of 1848* (Chapel Hill: University of North Carolina Press, 1969).
Portal, Roger, *The Slavs* (London: Weidenfeld and Nicolson, 1969).
Skilling, H. Gordon, *Czechoslovakia's Interrupted Revolution* (Princeton NJ: Princeton University Press, 1976).
Szporlik, Roman, *The Political Thought of Thomas G. Masaryk* (Boulder: East European Monographs, 1981).
Tyrell, John, *Czech Opera* (Cambridge: Cambridge University Press, 1988).
Unterberger, Betty Miller, *The United States, Revolutionary Russia and the Rise of Czechoslovakia* (Chapel Hill and London: University of North Carolina Press, 1989).
Vyšný, Paul, *Neo-Slavism and the Czechs 1891–1914* (Cambridge: Cambridge University Press, 1977).
Weaton, Bernard and Kavan, Zdeněk, *The Velvet Revolution. Czechoslovakia 1988–1991* (Boulder, San Francisco and London: Westview Press, 1992).
Whipple, Tim D. (ed.), *After the Velvet Revolution* (London: Freedom House, 1991).
Wolchik, Sharon, *Czechoslovakia in Transition* (London, Pinter, 1991).
Zacek, Joseph F., *Palacký. The Historian as Scholar and Nationalist* (The Hague and Paris: Mouton, 1970).

HUNGARY

Borbándi, G., *Der Ungarische Populismus* (Mainz: v. Hase and Koehler, 1976).
Deák, I., 'Hungary', in H. Rogger and E. Weber (eds), *The European Right. A Historical Profile* (London: Weidenfeld and Nicolson, 1965), pp. 364–407.
Hoensch, J., *History of Modern Hungary 1867–1986* (London: Longman, 1988).
Janos, A., *The Politics of Backwardness in Hungary 1825–1945* (Princeton: Princeton University Press, 1982).
Kovrig, B., *Communism in Hungary. From Kun to Kadar* (Stanford: Hoover Institution Press, 1979).
Lackó, M., *Arrow Cross Men. National Socialists 1934–1944* (Budapest, 1969).
Macartney, C. A. *Hungary* (Edinburgh: Edinburgh University Press, 1934).
____ *October the Fifteenth, A History of Hungary 1929–45*, 2 vols (Edinburgh: Edinburgh University Press, 1956–7).
Niederhauser, Emil, 'The National Question in Hungary', in Mikulas Teich and Roy Porter (eds), *The National question in Europe in Historical Context* (Cambridge: Cambridge University Press, 1993), pp. 248–69.
Rady, Martyn, 'Hungary', in *Eastern Europe and the Commonwealth of Independent States 1992* (London: Europa Publications, 1992), pp. 176–81.

190   *Further Reading*

Schopflin, G., 'From Communism to Democracy in Hungary', in A. Bozóki, A. Kőrösényi, and G. Schöpflin (eds), *Post-Communist Transition. Emerging Pluralism in Hungary* (London: Pinter Publishers, 1992), pp. 96–110.

Weber, E., *Varieties of Fascism. Doctrines of Revolution in the Twentieth Century* (Princeton: Robert E. Krieger, 1982), pp. 88–96.

POLAND

Davies, Norman, *God's Playground: A History of Poland*, 2 vols (Oxford: Clarenden Press, 1981).

____ 'Ethnic Diversity in Twentieth Century Poland', *Polin*, vol. IV (1989), pp. 143–58.

____ *Heart of Europe: A Short History of Poland* (Oxford: Clarendon Press, 1984).

Gella, Aleksander, 'The Life and Death of the Old Polish Intelligentsia', *Slavic Review*, vol. XXX (1971), pp. 1–20.

Jelenski, K. A., 'Paradoxes of Polish Nationalism', *Survey*, vol. XXVI (1982), pp. 176–83.

Kieniewicz, S., *The Emancipation of the Polish Peasantry* (Chicago: University of Chicago Press, 1969).

Latawski, Paul (ed.), *The Reconstruction of Poland, 1914–23* (London: Macmillan, 1992).

Leslie, R. F., *Polish Politics and the Revolution of November 1830* (London: the Athlone Press, 1956).

____ *Reform and Insurrection in Russian Poland 1856–1865* (Westport: Greenwood Press, 1969).

Lukowski, Jerzy, *Liberty's Folly: The Polish–Lithuanian Commonwealth in the Eighteenth Century, 1697–1795* (London: Routledge, 1991).

Polonsky, Antony, *Politics in Independent Poland 1921–1939* (Oxford: Oxford University Press, 1972).

Rothschild, Joseph, *Pilsudski's Coup d'Etat* (New York: Columbia University Press, 1966).

Tomaszewski, Jerzy, 'The National Question in Poland in the Twentieth Century', in Mikulas Teich and Roy Porter (eds), *The National Question in Europe in Historical Context* (Cambridge: Cambridge University Press, 1993), pp. 293–316.

Walicki, Andrzej, *Philosophy and Romantic Nationalism* (Oxford: Clarendon Press, 1982).

____ 'The Three Traditions in Polish Patriotism', in Stanislaw Gomulka and Antony Polonsky, *Polish Paradoxes* (London: Routledge, 1990).

Wandycz, Piotr, *The Lands of Partitioned Poland 1795–1918* (Seattle: University of Washington Press, 1974).

ROMANIA

Almond, Mark, *Decline Without Fall: Romania Under Ceauşescu* (London: Institute for European Defence and Strategic Studies, 1988).

_____ *The Rise and Fall of the Ceauşescu's* (London: Hamish Hamilton, 1991).

Chirot, Daniel, *Social Change in a Peripheral Society: The Making of a Balkan Colony* (New York: Academic Press, 1976).

Deletant, Dennis, 'The Past in Contemporary Romania: Some Reflections on Current Romanian Historiography', *Slovo*, vol. I (1988), pp. 77–91.

Fischer, Mary Ellen, *Nicolae Ceauşescu: A Study in Political Leadership* (Boulder: Lynn Rienner, 1989).

Gilberg, Trond, *Nationalism and Communism in Romania: The Rise and Fall of Ceauşescu's Personal Dictatorship* (Boulder: Westview Press, 1990).

Hitchens, Keith, *The Romanian National Movement in Transylvania 1780–1849* (Cambridge: Harvard University Press, 1969).

Jowitt, Kenneth, *Revolutionary Breakthroughs and National Development: The Case of Romania* (Berkeley: University of California Press, 1971).

King, Robert R., *History of the Romanian Communist Party* (Stanford: Hoover Institution Press, 1980).

Macartney, C. A., *Hungary and Her Successors 1919–37* (London: Oxford University Press, 1937).

Rady, Martyn, *Romania in Turmoil: A Contemporary History* (London: IB Tauris, 1992).

Roberts, Henry, *Rumania: Political Problems of an Agrarian State* (New Haven: Yale University Press, 1951).

Schopflin, George, 'Romanian Nationalism', *Survey*, vol. XX (1974), pp. 77–104.

Shafir, Michael, 'Men of Archangel Revisted: Anti-Semetic Formations Among Romania's Intellectuals', *Studies in Comparative Communism*, vol. XVI (1983), pp. 223–43.

_____ *Romania: Politics, Economics and Society* (London: Frances Pinter, 1985).

Verdery, Katherine, 'Nationalism and National Sentiment in Post-Socialist Romania', *Slavic Review*, vol. LII (1993), pp. 179–203.

YUGOSLAVIA

Banac, Ivo, *The National Question in Yugoslavia: Origin, History, Politics* (Ithaca: Cornell University Press, 1984).

Behschmidt, Wolf Dietrich, *Nationalismus bei Serben und Kroaten, 1830–1914* (Munich: Oldenburg Verlag, 1980).

Burg, Steven, *Conflict and Cohesion in Socialist Yugoslavia* (Princeton: Princeton University Press, 1983).

Cohen, Lenard, *Broken Bonds, The Rise and Fall of Yugoslavia* (Boulder, Co: Westview Press, 1993).

_____ and Paul Warrick, *Political Cohesion in a Fragile Mosaic: The Yugoslav Experience* (Boulder, Co: Westview Press, 1983).

Despalatović, Elinor Murray, *Ljudevit Gaj and the Illyrian Movement* (New York: East European Quarterly, 1975).

Djilas, Aleksa, *The Contested Country: Yugoslav Unity and Communist Revolution, 1919–1953* (Cambridge, Mass: Harvard University Press, 1991).

Djordjević, Dimitrije (ed.), *The Creation of Yugoslavia, 1914–1918* (Santa Barbara, Ca: ABC Clio Press, 1980).

Donia, Robert, *Islam under the Double Eagle: The Muslims of Bosnia–Hercegovina, 1878–1914* (New York: Columbia University Press, East European Monographs, 1981).

Glenny, Misha, *The Fall of Yugoslavia, The Third Balkan War* (New York: Penguin Books, 1992).

Irvine, Jill A., *The Croat Question: Partisan Politics in the Formation of the Yugoslav State* (Boulder, Co: Westview Press, 1993).

Jelavich, Charles, *South Slav Nationalism-Textbooks and Yugoslav Union before 1914* (Columbus, Ohio: Ohio State University Press, 1990).

Palmer, Steven E. Jr Robert R. and King, *Yugoslav Communism and the Macedonian Question* (Hamden, Conn: Archon Books, 1971).

Pawlowitch, Stevan K., *The Improbable Survivor: Yugoslavia and Its Problems, 1918–1988* (Columbus, Ohio: Ohio State University Press, 1988).

Petrovich, Michael Boro, *A History of Modern Serbia, 1804–1918*, 2 vols (New York: Harcourt, Brace and Jovanovich, 1976).

Pipa, Arshi and Sami Repish (eds), *Studies on Kosova* (New York: Columbia University Press, East European Monographs, 1984).

Polton, Hugh, *The Balkans, Minorities and States in Conflict* (London: Minority Rights Publications, 1991).

Ramet, Sabrina P., *Nationalism and Federalism in Yugoslavia, 1962–1991*, 2nd ed. (Bloomington: Indiana University Press, 1992).

Roberts, Walter R., *Tito, Mihailović and the Allies, 1941–1945* (Durham, NC: Duke University Press, 1987).

Rogele, Carole, *The Slovenes and Yugoslavism, 1890–1914* (New York: Columbia University Press, East European Quarterly, 1977).

Rusinow, Dennison, *The Yugoslav Experiment, 1948–1974* (Berkeley: University of California Press, 1977).

Rusinow, Dennison (ed.), *Yugoslavia, A Fractured Federalism* (Washington, DC: Wilson Center Press, 1988).

Shoup, Paul, *Communism and the Yugoslav National Question* (New York: Columbia University Press, 1968).

Stokes, Gale (ed.), *Nationalism in the Balkans* (New York: Garland, 1984).

Sundhausen, Holm, *Geschichte Jugoslawiens, 1918–1980* (Stuttgart: Verlag W. Kohlhammer, 1982).

Vucinich, Wayne *et al.*, 'The Nationality Problem in the Habsburg Monarchy in the Nineteenth Century: A Critical Appraisal, The South Slavs', *Austrian History Yearbook*, vol. III, no. 2 (1967).

Index

Note: 'n.' after a page reference indicates the number of a note on that page.

193

194   *Index*